THE EARLY YEARS

Laurie Driver

authorHOUSE®

AuthorHouse™ UK Ltd.
500 Avebury Boulevard
Central Milton Keynes, MK9 2BE
www.authorhouse.co.uk
Phone: 08001974150

First published by AuthorHouse   04/12/2011

ISBN: 978-1-4490-9043-2

A Manchester Childhood
1946 - 1962

Foreword

I have, since publishing my two earlier volumes, This Truckin' Life and The Railway Years, been approached, oft and many times, by numerous people who have read those earlier memoirs, to write a third volume of the adventures of Laurie Driver and thereby create a trilogy. For those fans that requested a third volume and caused me to dig ever deeper into my past, this volume is the result. The Early Years is written in the same style as the previous two volumes and contains numerous anecdotes both humorous and serious. This book, like the two before it, are about a fictitious truck driver who, in actuality, is myself, Dennis Burnier-Smith. The books, therefore, are of an autobiographical nature and all the incidents and situations within these pages and those that went before actually happened. It is intended as a humorous outing and though true it is written with my tongue firmly in my cheek. There may be time lapses and some of the events may have happened somewhat earlier or later than where the text sets them. This is, of course, author's licence and is used to keep a certain fluidity, continuity and momentum to the occurrences.

The two earlier volumes dealt specifically with Laurie Driver's working life in the haulage industry, whereas this latest offering deals with Laurie's life from his birth to leaving school; sixteen years in all. It attempts to explain what events in his young life turned him towards the life of a LGV driver. Like the previous books I have attempted to keep the humorous events to the fore, backed up with informative, serious and factual historical pieces and pieces that people of my own age, unless some form of dementia has kicked in, will remember well. There are numerous anecdotes, some serious but most humorous and I hope that the humour contained within these pages is to all my reader's tastes and that the informative pieces serve to do just that, inform. It is very much a nostalgia trip, going back to the late 40's through to the early 60's and as such I hope that it will evoke a lot of pleasant memories for a lot of people. I have included three small pieces documenting the notable and interesting achievements from dates in the late 40's, from 1946 to 1949, each year through the 50's and from 1960 to 1962, which are the years that this book covers.

Certain names within these pages have been changed to save any embarrassment to the persons involved and to save any embarrassment to me. Others in this memoir are known by their true names and will recognise themselves and the situations referred to, yet others, who are mentioned within this book, are no longer with us, some were friends and some relatives and some were even enemies. Although names have been changed all the incidents and anecdotes are true and actually happened. Certain parts of the chronology may be a little out of time but they are as I remember them and I apologise for any parts that may seem a bit out of place.

After all, when all is said and done, 'Nostalgia is just a thing of the past,' and if people were to ask me what this book is about I would respond in my usual short, terse and pithy style thus: 'Mine is a labyrinthine, historical adventure, it is a convoluted and colourful journey of great magnitude and breadth, a tale of woe and of joy, a story of optimism and failure, a narrative from birth to adolescence, a task of phenomenal recall and one that may have remained untold and lying dormant within the darkest recesses of my psyche but for the begging, cajoling, wheedling and the requests that I have received to put pen to paper or rather fingers to keyboard.'

Other than that it is a tale of growing up in the suburbs of Manchester, long ago.

Chapter One

My Antecedents

I first blinked my eyes and saw the light of day on the 29th day of January, in the bleak midwinter of 1946 when, after being expelled from my mother's womb, after a lengthy and painful term of labour and after the umbilical cord was severed and tied off, I was held aloft by the midwife and soundly slapped upon my derriere. That slap had the determined effects of causing me to cough up any half swallowed fluid, mucus and blood from the embryonic sac and to bellow loudly and set in progress the pattern of regular breathing so desired for life.

It was not, nor could it have been, my choice to be the second born child of Elizabeth Alice Driver (nee Hampson) and Auguste Burnier Driver, their desire was for one child of each sex and that's what they got. In which order they came was immaterial. Gus and Betty had met whilst she was a land army, northern, working class girl sent to work in the county of Kent and he, a Londoner by birth, was stationed in the R.A.F down there; they had met and each had become the recipients of Cupid's love tipped arrows and were thus smitten. They married on 3rd April 1943 at St Jude's Church, Southwark in South London. Their first born child was my elder sister who was born on the 10th day of August 1944, prior to the end of the hostilities of WWII; and eighteen months prior to my arrival into a world of bomb sites and ruins and which was still beset by the ravages and after affects of the second great conflict of the twentieth century.

Elizabeth (Betty) Alice Hampson, my mother to be, was one of nine children born to Annie Hampson (nee Cookson) and George Hampson. There must have been something in the water in those days, or was it just that television, as such, was out of the reach of working class families? That was probably due to the somewhat prohibitive price of the sets and so other recreational pastimes had to be pursued. Television came along in 1926 when John Logie Baird, (1888-1946), a Scottish engineer from Helensburgh moved to Hastings for convalescence reasons. Whilst there he carried on his experiments until he succeeded to transmit television pictures. He first demonstrated his invention in an attic laboratory above a Soho restaurant in London. Baird's system was superseded by Marconi's system in 1937. Whatever, it seems that Protestant families were just as prolific as those of a Catholic persuasion and large families were the norm. It seems that Catholics could not use contraception and Protestants would not. There were six girls and three boys in the Hampson family. Harriet, known as Hetty was the eldest, followed by George and Walter then Elsie and John, Beatrice, known as Beatty, then Elizabeth Alice known as Betty, Joan and lastly Annie.

My mother was born on 19th February 1922, in Hulme in a slum on Leinster Street not far from Great Jackson Street, the Gaythorn Gasworks and Dunlop's Rubber factory. She was older only than two of her sisters, Annie and Joan, her six other siblings sisters and brothers, being older than her. She grew up amongst the slums of Hulme and moved to Newton Heath prior to the outbreak of WWII and during the war was assigned as a land army girl and sent to work in Kent. In 1944 she returned from her stint on the land as a pregnant married woman to her home in Newton Heath. She lived with her mother and father and a couple of her unmarried sisters and shortly after her return she gave birth to her daughter, Valerie. I, as a child, remember my mother as being a beautiful, slim woman who cared for her offspring with the same tenderness and devotion that she showed her husband. I certainly do not remember being suckled at the breast but I do remember the love and care she showed to both me and my sister when we fell or bumped our heads or received other such minor injuries. She was there for us through thick and thin and did not take sides when my sister and I fought. She was always there with the antiseptic cream, sticking plaster and a kiss and a cuddle. My mother died aged 84 on January 29th 2006, my Sixtieth Birthday.

My father to be, Auguste (Gus) Burnier and his younger brother Charles were the illegitimate offspring of an illicit and intermittent affair between my Grandmother, Nellie Driver (nee Pepper) and a French speaking, Swiss waiter whom she met whilst working as a waitress in her husband's public house in the borough of Southwark in South London where the Swiss waiter was also working. The first born, illegitimate child who was destined to be my father was named after his putative father and was christened Auguste Burnier. Nellie embarked on that clandestine affair during the closing years of the 1st World War, while she looked after the pub whilst her husband, Ernest Driver, was far away in France, doing his bit for his King and his country. She was left at home to service the pub and also, unfortunately, depending on one's point of view, to service the Swiss waiter. Nellie also had one legitimate child to her husband; this child was a daughter named Louise Maud Juliet, my father's older half sister who was conceived when Ernest had a short spell of leave before shipping out to France. Besides Auguste and Charles, there was another pregnancy and birth to the Swiss waiter in which the child, a boy who was named Philip Burnier, died in infancy.

My father was born on Guy Fawkes Day, the 5th of November 1919 and like the fireworks ignited and set off on that day he had a rather colourful, fiery and explosive childhood. He was treated like an unwanted puppy and most of the time he was left to fend for himself, by his parents who neither loved him nor wanted him. He was ignored and rejected; he, his brother and his half-sister Louise were beaten, cruelly treated and blamed for all the woes that befell the family. Gus and his siblings were little more than an encumbrance to their guardians. They were a hindrance, an impediment on the lives of those that were supposed to care for them. Ernest Driver, after his demobilisation in 1921 and upon returning home from his tour of duty, had discovered his wife's infidelities and certainly wanted nothing to do with her or the bastard children. There was a stigma attached to illegitimacy in those days and he and Nellie divorced in1921. The Swiss waiter moved in with Nellie who, after the divorce, had moved in with her mother, taking the kids with her.

The Helvetian turned out to be a violent and heavy drinking man who beat his lover and children regularly and he was eventually given his marching orders by Nellie's mother who could not stand to see her daughter and her daughter's offspring ill treated in such a way, even though Nellie was directly implicated in and guilty of the neglect and maltreatment of her own children. It seems that my father, at times, was cared for and lived with a couple who were friends of Nellie's who he affectionately called Aunty Mary and Uncle Joe, although they were not blood relatives. The couple lived in Bermondsey and later at the Elephant and Castle and they cared for Gus more than Nellie ever did and when he wasn't living at home he stayed with the caring couple. My father, as a small child, was unkempt, unclean, unloved, malnourished, and woefully abused and Nellie, once the Swiss waiter had abrogated his responsibilities, certainly could not afford to keep him and his siblings in the atrocious way to which they had become accustomed and so along with his half sister he was placed into the care of Dr Barnardo's Charitable Homes and Orphanages.

Nellie applied to Barnardo's to take in the children but while she was awaiting a decision from Barnardo's she withdrew the application hoping to get the boys into the Hanwell Schools for orphans and destitute children and keep Louise at home, but as the Local Authority refused, for whatever reason, to take them, the application to Barnardo's was renewed. On the 28th of August 1930, Gus was placed into the care of the Boy's Garden City at Woodford and Louise at the Girl's Village Home at Barkingside, both in North London. Nothing is known, through this period of the whereabouts of Gus's Brother Charles, there is no record of him being put into the care of Barnardo's.

The Hanwell Schools, which also became known as the 'Cuckoo' Schools, after an old name for the area where they were situated which, was in Hanwell near Ealing in North West London. They were orphanage schools where destitute and homeless children boarded and were given an education and taught a trade. The schools, one for girls and one for boys, were next to each other but segregated. They were run by the local authority and did much the same work as Barnardo's orphanages and homes. The most famous inmate to reside at the Hanwell Schools was Charlie Chaplin who was admitted in June 1896 and stayed until January 1898. The Hanwell Schools closed in 1933 but re-opened briefly in 1934 to accommodate the boys from the naval training ship 'Exmouth,' where there was an outbreak of ringworm. The buildings, of which the Hanwell Schools were comprised, became, in 1945, the Hanwell Community Centre and the buildings that survive still serve the community to this day.

My father seemed to enjoy his time in the care of Dr Barnardo's and at one time he told me that it was there that he enjoyed the best times of his young life. Even though he was slightly myopic, Gus, whilst in the care of Barnardo's, took up the noble art of pugilism and later in life he boxed for the RAF, fighting under the name of 'Boy' Pepper, Pepper being his mother's maiden name. He took up the pugilistic art of self defence in order to protect himself from the bullying that went on at Barnardo's. Bullying was endemic in such institutions and was bound to happen in a home where poor and orphaned lads had to fight to be the best and even to exist normally. After the passage of five years, at fifteen years of age, Gus was removed from the care of Barnardo's by his mother. It so happened that on the 23rd of January 1935, Barnardo's had found Gus a placement in the West End Home of a Miss Fleming of Park Lane Court, 143 Park Lane, W1, where he was to work in service as a kitchen hand; the terms of engagement were twelve shillings and sixpence (62 ½p) per week wages plus board and lodgings. His mother withdrew him from the care of Barnardo's, against the charities wishes that she should not unsettle the boy. Nevertheless and against Barnardo's wishes she withdrew Gus from the care of the institution and away from Miss Fleming's home so that she could benefit from his meagre earnings. Upon reaching eighteen years of age Gus decided to leave the hostility and enmity of the family home and so he severed his connection to his mater and joined the RAF. As for the Swiss waiter, his bloated body was found washed up on the southern bank of the River Thames on the 30th March 1944, close to the Wandsworth Gas Works and the Battersea power station. Apparently he had taken his own life whilst suffering from a bout of depression and while the balance of his mind was disturbed. Nellie, by then, had remarried. She wed, in 1932, a small, bespectacled, insignificant chap called Benjamin Mills, like her first husband he too was a publican by trade, and that marriage lasted until Benny died in 1949. My father died, age seventy one, on 29th January 1991, my forty fifth birthday.

After Elizabeth had returned to Manchester, her husband Gus was still stationed down South with the RAF until his demobilisation. After the cessation of world wide hostilities, Gus followed Elizabeth North to her mother's house where they were to lodge until an abode of their own became available. He wasted no time in filling out an application to be placed on the housing list. The move up North was something of a culture shock to Gus who had never been North before and believed anywhere above Watford Gap was a foreign domain where it rained incessantly and where every man wore a cloth cap, moleskin trousers, hobnail boots or maybe wooden clogs and kept ferrets and raced whippets and where all the women, except his beloved Elizabeth, were like fishwives; coarse, foul mouthed and common. Upon arriving in Manchester he found the northerners to be a warm hearted, gregarious and friendly people and he was welcomed, kindly and unreservedly, into the fold.

Prior to my birth, Auguste Burnier had managed to secure a job at West's Gas Works in the Manchester borough of Bradford, now swallowed up by the districts of Beswick and Eastlands. He had taken an intensive course to become a plumber and gas fitter prior to leaving the R.A.F. and this was the job he undertook for West's. During his working life, I never once knew him out of work. His sister Louise married a wealthy builder named William Bellini and they moved to the relatively affluent area of Stoke Newington in North London which wasn't that far away from the slums of the East End. Sadly, his brother Charlie, whose earlier life seems shrouded in mystery, sometime prior to the outbreak of WWII, sailed away to Australia and joined the ANZAC'S and was unfortunately killed on active service in Singapore and is buried out there. Whether he went on some kind of assisted passage I do not know, but assisted passage to the antipodes has been going on since the mid 19th century in one form or another. It is also believed that Charles lied about his age when he joined up and was actually, for the first year of service, too young to serve.

The acronym ANZAC, which stands for the Australian and New Zealand Army Corps, was originally used for those soldiers who were in the armies of Australia and New Zealand during the First World War but has now come to mean Australian and New Zealand troops in theatres of war generally.

When I had the effrontery to pop into a stark, harsh, post war society, during a winter when snow fell thickly and winds blew harshly and where money and housing were in short supply, it was deemed that Grandma Annie's house, where we were living and which belonged to and was rented from the Catholic Church, was too small to house us all. Granddad George and Granny Annie and their remaining children had left Leinster Street in the Hulme area of Manchester where they lived in a small back to back terraced house in slum conditions in a notorious slum area where the living area of the house doubled as a bedroom and where the kids slept two and three to a bed. The family were evacuated to Newton Heath just prior to the outbreak of WWII, after a massive slum clearance in Hulme and the surrounding area. The two eldest daughters, Hetty and Elsie and the three sons George, Walter and John had married whilst still living in Hulme or whilst they were in the army and they had moved out of the family home leaving a little more room for the remaining kids. Fortunately for our family and many more like us, after the war, the government of the day had embarked upon an innovative and cheap, national housing program to accommodate the disenfranchised families and those that were homeless due to the actions of Hitler's Luftwaffe.

Hermann Goering, under Adolf Hitler, established the Luftwaffe in 1935. He was a fighter pilot in the First World War and became a powerful figure in the Nazi movement and head of Hitler's armed forces during WWII. He was also, with others, instrumental in setting up the concentration camps. After the war Goering was tried as a war criminal at the Nuremburg War Trials, for crimes against humanity, found guilty and sentenced to hang. He asked to be executed by firing squad as befits a soldier. That was not permitted but Goering evaded the sentence of hanging by taking his own life. He committed suicide by ingesting potassium cyanide just hours before he was due to be executed. He died on 15th January 1946. It is surmised, a person whose job it was to guard him gave him the poison.

The late 40's

The decade that I was born into was the 1940's and I believe that the most important date in the year of 1946 was the 29th of January, which was my birthday. Other notable dates of the second half of the decade were the 5th of March, 1946 when Winston Churchill made his inspirational *'Iron Curtain'* speech. On the 22nd of March 1946, Britain recognised the Independence of Jordan as the Kingdom of Jordan, under King Abdullah I. On May 20th 1946, Cherilyn Sarkisian was born; she shortened her name to Cher and became one of the biggest recording stars of the 20th century. Also in May bread rationing began in Britain and in June, the USA started tests of nuclear bombs in the Bikini Atoll. On June 14th in New York City, Donald Trump, the American business magnate, was born. On the 22nd of July, the British Headquarters in Jerusalem was bombed by Jewish militants; ninety one people lost their lives. In August, more than 5,000 died during outbreaks of Muslim–Hindu violence in Calcutta and in September, Nehru was elected Prime Minister of India. On November 4th 1946 Laura Welch was born; she later married George W. Bush and became America's first lady. The 6th of November 1946 saw the passing of the Bill that brought the National Health Service into being. During 1946, Terence Rattigan's play *The Winslow Boy* was published. On January 1st 1947, the National Coal Board took charge of the newly nationalised coal mines and between January and March the country suffered a severe cold spell and a fuel crisis. The 1st of August brought anti-Jewish protests in Lancashire following the discovery of two British servicemen killed by Jewish militants near Haifa, Palestine. India and Pakistan gained their independence on the 15th August 1947 and nine days later on the 24th August the Edinburgh Festival opened for the first time. October 14th 1947 was the day Major General Charles 'Chuck' Yeager, flying a Bell, X-1 rocket plane became the first man to break the sound barrier. Just before my second birthday on the 20th January 1948 Gandhi was assassinated in Delhi. The 21st of June saw the docking of the SS Empire Windrush at Tilbury. It brought to England the first cargo of five hundred people from Jamaica and Trinidad who came on an open door policy on an assisted passage, the cheapest fare was £28.10s. They came to fill the many jobs that could not be filled by British people. Many of the passengers from Windrush had served in the British forces during the war and a significant number found jobs in the NHS and British Railways which were established a few days after their arrival. Others found work on London transport as bus drivers and conductors. The 1st of July that year was the first official day of the newly nationalised British Railways and the 5th of July was the first official day of the National Health Service. The 30th of July was when the British Nationality Act became effective; giving all Commonwealth subjects British Citizenship. November saw Harry S. Truman win the US presidential elections. Towards the end of the year on the 10th of December, T.S. Eliot was awarded the Nobel Prize for literature. August 16th 1948 saw the death of the legendary baseball player, George Herman 'Babe' Ruth. On my third birthday 29th of January 1949, Britain recognised the independent state of Israel and on April Fools Day, 1st April, the National Parks Bill was passed. The Republic of Eire officially came into being on the 18th of April 1949. August 10th 1949 saw the death of 'Acid Bath' murderer John Haigh when he was executed at Wandsworth prison. October 1st 1949, communist Mao Zedong, (Mao Tse Tung, 1893-1976), took control of China and established The People's Republic of China.

Prefabs -v- Slums

The site allocated for the innovative new homes that were in the process of being constructed in Newton Heath was less than ½ of a mile from Annie Hampson's abode and covered an area of approximately fifty acres. I do not know what was there before the prefabs were built, but I assume there were streets of back to back terraced houses that had out seen their usefulness and had been pulled down during the slum clearances, or they may have been bombed out during the war, for Manchester was and is an industrial town and close by was the massive engineering plant of Mather and Platt. The new residential cottages that were under construction were of the pre-fabricated type and were known colloquially and locally as prefabs. The external walls were made from pebble dashed, pre-cast concrete panels; the roofs were of corrugated, asbestos sheets. The footings and chimney stacks were the only parts of those buildings where brickwork was used and the new homes which came in sections on the backs of lorries, were unloaded and erected in record time, in the manner of giant, three dimensional, jig-saw puzzles where everything was slotted together and then bolted and sealed. Insulation was installed and the internal walls were plastered and then finally the interior fitments were installed to make snug, comfortable, and quite desirable off the peg residences.

When they were finished with everything in place and basic painting and decorating completed, those prefabs were warm and cosy detached homes. Although they were not exactly capacious they were spacious enough for a family like ours. They had two bedrooms, a fitted kitchen, living room and a hallway and bathroom with fitted suite and low level flushing toilet. They were fitted with gas operated refrigerators, gas or coal fire and hot and cold running water. Some prefab kitchens were fitted with gas stoves whilst others had electric cooking facilities. There was a large cupboard next to the bathroom which, in its upper compartment, contained the hot water cistern with an immersion heater, which, when in use, helped to warm the single storey dwelling as it heated the domestic water supply. The bottom part of the cupboard served as a storage or airing cupboard. Each prefab in a row of five or six was equipped with different fitments and had slightly different lay outs to give them a little individuality, then the next row would start the process again. Prefabs in other areas did not have pebble dashed panels but rather, had textured painted panels and yet others were clad with aluminium sheeting; again, to give them some individuality.

Prefab living was luxurious when compared to the lives of those still living in two up, two down, back to back, 19th century terraced houses with flagged floors and outside toilets, where the bath was a galvanised tub hung on a six inch nail hammered into the back yard, brick wall, which, on bath night, had to be dragged into the home by the lady of the house and placed on newspapers in front of the coal fire where it was filled manually with kettles and sauce pans which had been filled with water and heated on the gas stove, again by the woman of the house. In those days the man was the breadwinner, the man who brought home the bacon, the latter day hunter gatherer and suffice it to say that his job was to work long hours in some underpaid, thankless, manual job in order to bring home the wages, whereas anything home based was deemed to be the job of the housewife. Working class men either served an apprenticeship to become a time served artisan in a manual trade or they became labourers. The more educated within the workforce took on clerical and office based work. The lady of the house might have had a part time job, but mainly she was the homemaker who looked after the household chores such as the washing, ironing, shopping, cooking, cleaning and, of course, the arrangements for the bath night etc. The galvanised bath tubs could be purchased in various sizes and the size of bath one owned reflected upon the comparative wealth of the family. Some tubs were as long as a fitted bath and others were only big enough for a man to sit in. If a home did not have a galvanised bath tub the dwellers of that abode would avail themselves of the local baths and wash house to retain their standards of personal hygiene.

The weekly bath night in the winter months offered different and harsher challenges from those in the warmer months. The bathtub may have been covered in frost, ice or even snow and in some really cold spells could be frozen to the back yard wall from where it hung. Forward thinking individuals would have built a wooden, lean-to shed with a corrugated tin roof, against the yard wall, to keep out the ravages of the cold, British winter months and to protect the bathtub and, perhaps, store the family's bicycles etc. The female householder of homes that didn't have such a protective shelter would don their wellies, top coats and gloves before venturing forth to pour hot water over the tub before attempting to bring it into the house. When the hot water was poured onto the frozen tub there would be loud, eerie, tinny and melodic cracking noises as the ice split asunder as the metal expanded.

Even though the bath tubs were made of electro-plated, galvanized steel, those tin reservoirs eventually suffered the blight of oxidization due to being left outside in the inclement, British, winter weather. Over a period of time they developed patches of rust, especially along the seams which, if left untended, would corrode through the metal and lead to leaks and eventually the need for a new bathtub which was an expense that few working class people could afford in those desperate post war days of hardship and adversity, when every farthing counted and when the pawn shop did a brisker trade than the butcher's, baker's, grocer's and greengrocer's.

After clearing any creepy crawlies and bits of debris from the bath tub the man of the house, being the head of the household, would bathe first, then his wife and lastly, the kids; it was a moot point whether the kids were cleaner before or after bathing. There is a possibility that this arrangement for bathing was the origin of the saying 'Throwing out the baby with the bath water,' because the water would be too dirty to allow the baby to be seen. Singing in the bath was not just for pleasure, it was an audible warning that the weekly hygiene ritual was under way and that a little privacy was required.

Some families bathed in the kitchen in case visitors called and indeed some of those old terraced houses had a fireplace in the kitchen, especially those that had a central chimney breast with a fireplace on either side both upstairs and downstairs. This, of course, made bathing a safer and more private affair in those days when everybody left their front doors off the latch. Imagine the scene if the man of the house was stood up in the bath, in the front room, in front of the fire, reaching for his towel, steam rising from his naked flesh, coloured to a reddish hue from the hot water, when a friend of the lady of the house lifts the latch and walks in, hoping to see the lady and instead sees the man of the house in all his naked glory; in the buff; starkers, bending forward for his terry towelling, absorbent, drying cloth; his rosy red buttocks shining back at her like a blazing sun in a midsummer sky. The visiting lady would shriek in horror and take a step backwards and, one would hope, avert her gaze as the naked man hurriedly grabbed his towel to hide his nudity and his embarrassment, and other things of a private nature. There were crimson blushes on both sides, I'm sure.

When the weekly ablutions were completed and the family had achieved a ruddy, healthy glow, the bathtub would be pulled and manhandled through the house, the water sloshing from one end of the tub to the other in wavelets, causing some of the dirty, soapy water to splash over the sides and spill onto the newspapers placed there in a futile attempt to hopefully protect the rug and it would also spill onto the kitchen floor as the heavy, tin tub was manoeuvred through the house. Finally, upon reaching the back door which led into the yard, the bathtub was unceremoniously upended. The man of the house was responsible for the emptying of the bathtub, solely because it was deemed too heavy for the lady of the house to move and lift. Once the bathtub was upended the dirty bathwater would course down the yard in a frothy torrent, splashing against the yard walls and the outhouse, some finding the drain and the rest pouring, stream like, under the back-yard gate to tumble in a tiny waterfall over the step to cascade into the alleyway to form smaller tributaries as it wound its way the through cobblestones, watering the dandelions and sparse blades of grass that grew in the cracks between the cobbles until the flow of water finally diminished and petered out.

A lot of those old terraced houses only had cold running water from a single tap over the kitchen sink and those householders that could afford one would have an Ascot Electric or Gas Water Heater fitted above the porcelain basin. There were other types of instantaneous water heaters, of course, but it seemed, at the time that the Ascot's were most prominent and popular. The Ascot was only any good for heating small amounts of water for washing pots and hands etc, the bathtub still had to be filled manually. Electric lighting was a recent innovation in some of those old terraces and they were originally fitted with small bore, gas piping which ran up the walls and terminated at wall brackets that held the gas lamps which were fitted, with gas mantles, to provide incandescent lighting. The brackets that held the light fixture and mantle which emitted a naked flame, albeit behind a glass shade, were usually sited close to the windows of a room where the drapes hung and which could and probably did, on occasions, catch alight. There was the danger of a major conflagration that was ever present in those gas lit days.

In the backyard there stood an unlit, brick, outbuilding with a slate or stone roof and an uneven, cold, flagstone floor and those outhouses could either be adjoined to the main building or be a stand alone building at the far end of the yard. They were the homes of big, hairy, long legged spiders and other creepy crawlies and they also housed the toilet where, in the winter, the water in the cistern and the bowl would freeze over and where the winter winds blew dead leaves and other debris under the door and chilled the bare legs of the occupant. Some householders took to leaving a small, portable paraffin heater inside the toilet outhouse to offset the freezing conditions and offer a modicum of warmth whilst they performed their bodily functions. The poorer individuals left a candle or two placed on a saucer, burning on top of the cistern. The candles stood in a pool of solidified wax to hold them upright and were surrounded by spent matches. Because candles have unprotected naked flames they would often be blown out by night-time breezes and were thereby rendered useless. Those few that could afford it would have had an electrical cable run through a length of conduit pipe into the toilet terminating in a light fitment, fixed to the ceiling, often fitted by the amateur do-it-yourself resident. Those that could not afford such a fitment or who hadn't the wherewithal to do it themselves either took a torch or went in the dark. Heat and light made things so much more cosy and comfortable when performing one's bodily functions. Those that had no form of lighting or heating in the outside lavvy sat in discomfort and faced the prospect of burst lead pipes and leaks when the warmer weather finally brought the thaw.

The toilet paper used in the privy was the newspaper of two days previous which, after being used as a tablecloth for a day; that which was usable, was then cut into manageable squares and hung, by a piece of string, threaded through each square, onto a nail hammered into the door or the wall of the outhouse. Note: one did not use the pages from glossy magazines for obvious reasons. The alternative to newsprint was to use San-Izal toilet tissue which was cheap and rather coarser than the newspaper but it did not leave the buttocks covered in the headline news or the sports fixtures from a couple of days previous. San-Izal came in two forms, either on a roll or in pre cut squares in a box and strangely, both types of San-Izal had a smooth side and a rough side. The outhouse toilet in the backyard, although primitive and not quite as sanitary as one would wish, was an improvement on the communal toilets and earth closets of slum areas a few years earlier.

A lot of those slum houses were built before the advent of the 20th century and in the early days had no running water piped into them. There would have been a single stand pipe for each street from which to draw water. The stand pipe would have originally been fitted with a steel cup attached to a chain, which could and would become detached and lost over time. Children and maybe adults would drink directly from the end of the taps. It was those conditions and the lack of a decent sewage system that led to and caused the typhus, cholera and dysentery outbreaks in the East End slums of London and other major cities, in the late 19th century, which killed untold thousands of citizens. Working class areas were the last to receive proper sewage disposal facilities and piped water. Consequently and as was and is the norm, it was the expendable, working class families who mostly suffered and died.

Because those early back to back terraced houses had flagged floors, (Rough cut granite slabs instead of floorboards), and because the flagstones were laid directly on top of bare earth there was no airflow beneath them. The floors were uneven and rough and no matter how many layers of cheap carpet or rugs were put down, there was no disguising that fact. Due to the lack of airflow the houses were damp but warm, precisely the environment that cockroaches thrived upon. Consequently those old houses were overrun with roaches and other insects. Cockroaches lived behind open fireplaces and behind cooking stoves or any dark, warm hidey hole that they could find; they came out at night when the house was in darkness and the inhabitants had gone to their beds to be bitten by a different infestation; bed bugs.

When the terraced house dweller arose early the next morning and turned the downstairs light on the floor or rug looked alive as numerous black or red-brown beetles scurried to their daylight hiding places in the warm, dark, cosy nooks and niches. The householder would grab hold of the coal shovel and try to kill as many of the fast moving, scuttling vermin as he could. As they scattered for refuge, scrambling over one and other, he would bring the shovel down, like a giant fly swatter, numerous times on the scurrying insects, but he would not make a noticeable dent in their numbers. When the beetles had all disappeared into their nooks and crannies it was left to the householder to sweep up the carcases of the dead bugs and dispose of them. Later, as night time fell and darkness descended and the residents had retired to the dubious comfort and warmth of their beds the noxious creatures would, once again, scuttle from their hidey holes to eat and frolic and do whatever it is that cockroaches do after dark.

Cockroaches like all insects have no internal skeleton but have a hard external casing known as an exo-skeleton. They have wings and some varieties actually fly. They are notoriously difficult to kill and have inhabited the Earth since before the dinosaurs. It is supposed that if there was a nuclear conflagration only cockroaches would survive the holocaust. They can run around for hours after having their heads chopped off. A lot of the proprietary insecticides, such as FLIT, were petroleum based. It seems that petroleum based mixtures broke down the exo-skeleton and thus destroyed those horrible six legged creatures. FLIT was poured, from a can, into a spray pump that atomised the liquid as it was sprayed, under pressure, into the nooks and crannies that hid those nasty, crawling, winged insects.

Tenants of infested and overrun properties would, in desperation, call in the local council's pest control operatives to fumigate their little palaces. People who lived in those slum conditions did not consider themselves slum dwellers and to them their humble abodes were indeed palaces. The fact that those dwellings were overrun with insects was no reflection on the cleanliness of the householders; rather it was the house design that was at fault. While the fumigation was being undertaken the tenants would move in with friends or relatives and after a couple of days they would move back into their property. I believe that there was a statutory forty eight hour period that had to elapse before the property could be re-inhabited. The said property would be clear of the pestilence for a few weeks and then it would, once again, become overrun with the creepy crawlies. It was a case of if one house was infested, then so were the rest. Most modern estates that are built today are built on concrete bases with no airflow beneath them and with central heating being a normal fixture I foresee, when they are older, that they will suffer the same type of infestation as those old stone floored, terraced houses.

The cheap, modular built, prefabs, were the height of luxurious, modern, bijou accommodation in those bleak, austere, post war days and my father had applied to the Manchester City Council Housing Department to be placed on the housing list. Because of our family circumstances and the plight in which we found ourselves it was into one of those newly erected pre fabricated homes that we were soon comfortably ensconced. Although the prefabs in which my family lived were built on flat concrete bases and because they were new, utilitarian and temporary accommodations; they were only supposed to have a lifespan of ten years, they were not overrun with cockroaches and other pestilence, although I do remember seeing field mice within our property. The ten years lifespan of the prefabs was most certainly not adhered to. The prefabs where my family lived were standing and inhabited for at least twenty years and this was the case up and down the country.

I do not recall the move from Rosebank Road to the prefab at Elbain Avenue because I was still a toddler, but it was affected, so I was told, by way of numerous trips with a home made, flimsy, two wheeled, hand cart constructed by my father from old timber and the larger wheels off an old Silver Cross perambulator. It was not a moonlight flit, whereby people moved in the dead of night to escape debts etc; it was a legitimate move into a home of our own. The removal took place on a Saturday morning and in that endeavour my parents were ably assisted by my Uncle John; my mum's brother. The story that I was told was that on the last journey as my father and John struggled up the incline of the rough, unpaved track that was Taylor's Lane, while my mother awaited their arrival in the prefab, the laden cart started to veer from side to side and like a modern day supermarket trolley took its own course. One of the wheels was wobbling as it slowly crept, unnoticed by those doing the shoving and pulling, ever nearer to the edge of the axle. The split pin that held the wheel onto the axle had broken and as Gus and John pushed and pulled in an effort to keep the cart on an even keel it suddenly lurched to one side, as the wheel fell off, spilling our worldly goods over and about Taylor's Lane. Flimsy suit cases, made from compressed cardboard, burst open upon impact with *terra firma,* scattering habiliments, including male and female under garments, along the stony trail. Tea chests, given by the local shopkeepers and packed with smaller items and ornamentation, crashed to earth, decanting their cargo upon the rocky, rutted ground. A bedside cabinet was rendered asunder and amongst other things such as glasses, cups, saucers, plates and dishes, a glass fronted cabinet was shattered, distributing sharp shards and slivers of glass and pottery about the path. Upon seeing the danger that those shards would present to animals and children, my father and John cleared them up as best they could and disposed of them in the dustbin back at the prefab.

A temporary repair was affected on the stricken cart. The wheel, which had become buckled and detached, was, by the action of John standing upon it and applying pressure returned to a more amenable shape. It was then manhandled back onto the axle stub by Uncle John as my father held the cart up. A rusty nail, found on the track, was hammered home through the axle with a half of a house brick which was lying close by and the cart was then reloaded with only fifty yards to go. Knickers, brassieres, vests, underpants and other items of raiment were repacked into their cases and stowed on the cart. The tea chests were refilled and loaded on the cart which was then pushed with some difficulty, due to the wheel not being perfectly aligned, the remaining few yards to our new abode. Once at the prefab a snack and cups of tea were provided by my mother who had brewed a pot in anticipation of the arrival of her husband and her brother and their cargo. The goods were then sorted into what was reparable and what was beyond repair. Those things which were irreparable were put to one side, along with the cart, which was then itself in a state of ill repair and was no longer fit for purpose and had been condemned as surplus to requirements. Those household effects, chattels and accoutrements which could be repaired were put into the storage shed until such times as they could be given some tender, loving care and be restored to a state of usefulness. The furniture and various paraphernalia that were not damaged in the catastrophe were taken indoors and placed in their allocated rooms. The cart had one more duty to perform before being sent to its doom and so the broken, ruined and discarded goods were loaded back onto the rickety wain and pushed to the local tip on Grimshaw Lane where all and sundry, including the then defunct, stricken and doomed cart, were finally disposed of.

Two, black, cast iron, single, army surplus cots with sprung bases were bought for my sister and me to sleep on. The pillows and mattresses were the typical pattern of white with black stripes which were used in all the government run establishments from prisons to the armed forces and they were very lumpy but strangely comfortable. Even so, we received more joy from bouncing up and down on them than we did sleeping in them. Other furniture was either bought second hand or donated to us by well wishers. Even though both my mother and father were working, father full time and mother part time, pay was low and times were still hard in those uncertain days. Household furniture, due to a lack of raw materials and finished goods, was expensive and hard to come by, although it appeared that the better off in society could get all that they needed and did not suffer unduly.

Our new abode had its own front and rear plots of land which at the time were uncultivated and barren and which in time would be turned into gardens. There was a shed constructed from corrugated asbestos sheets bolted to a steel framework and anchored to a concrete base which served as a storage shed and as the coal hole. The shed took up a corner of the back garden opposite to the rear entrance of the living accommodation. We were the envy of a lot of post war, desperate and destitute families because of the fact that we had access to all the modern conveniences and were living in a brand new structure on one level and as such we appeared to those in older properties to be the *nouveau riche,* bungalow dwellers.

Although the prefab contained a proper bathroom with a fitted suite comprising a wash hand basin, a toilet and a full size bath, I still vaguely remember, from an early age, both my sister and I, occasionally and mainly in the spring and summer months, sitting, quite naked, on the wooden draining board in the kitchen, waiting to be washed down in the white glazed, Belfast sink. My sister would be washed and scrubbed first and then I with my feet resting in the sink, half full of warm water, would be sluiced off by my mother as she washed my hair and scalp with Derbac Shampoo. The Derbac had to be left on for five minutes before my mother rinsed it off and then lathered my body and limbs with Lifebuoy Carbolic Soap or Wright's Coal Tar soap and gave me a wash down. Derbac was a proprietary brand of soap and shampoo for the treatment of head lice and nits. It was both effective and remedial and I believe that it is still available to this day as is Wright's and Lifebuoy but without the carbolic acid. I remember being dried roughly with a towel and sprinkled with fragranced talcum powder and on cooler days, after being dried off we would be dressed in liberty bodices with rubber buttons.

Liberty bodices were made of a quilted, fleecy fabric and were worn over the top of a vest to keep an individual warm. They were a practical piece of clothing worn mainly in the winter. The name liberty bodice was a contradiction in terms as the garment, as I remember it, was quite restrictive and served more as a child's, padded straitjacket. Both my sister and I were dressed in the liberty bodices, although I am now pretty sure they were designed strictly as a female garment.The liberty bodice had extra rubber buttons at the bottom, back and front which, I believe, were a throwback to the days when hosiery and stockings were connected to the bodice which, I suppose, served as a suspender belt for girl guides and brownies, although when my sister and I wore the bodice it was a shorter version that served solely as winter underwear.

The reason for the wash down in the sink was because it was far too expensive, in those somewhat poverty stricken and straitened times, to heat a full cylinder of hot water, for a bath, with the immersion heater. When my sister and I were dried and clothed in the rudiments of underwear and the liberty bodices, we would walk, barefooted, through the kitchen into the living room to sit by the fire on father's knees. Behind us we left little, white, talcum powder footprints on the kitchen linoleum and the living room carpet, to register our passage.

The living room in the prefab was a long room and a quarter of it, closest to the kitchen was dedicated to dining, so the living quarters doubled as a dining area. The floor was covered in patterned linoleum with a rug in front of the hearth over a large square of carpet. The dining table was of the extendable leaf type which could be enlarged by pulling the lower leaves from under the upper which would then drop into place to give a larger, flat dining table. In its shortened position, as we generally used it as a family, it would be draped with an easy clean, wipe over table covering made from oilcloth and if we had guests, and the table was lengthened, mother would get out her best lace tablecloth and cork place mats would be placed on top of the lace to ensure that the polished finish of the table was protected from spills and from heat.

The Bogeyman & the Laundry

Granny Annie's Church owned house on Rosebank Road, Newton Heath was what, today, would be described as a quasi-semi with four houses in a row with a central, covered ginnel between the middle two. A ginnel is a narrow passageway between two houses that gives access to the rear of the buildings. It is usually built into the houses and is therefore covered rather than being an open passageway. They were well built, red brick accommodations, having two bedrooms and a box room, and an upstairs bathroom with a cast iron bath stood on eagle claw feet, downstairs was a main living room and a kitchen with a pantry. There was also a downstairs inside toilet with a high level flushing system and there was a large storage room. Each house had a large back garden and a smaller front garden.

Beneath the stairs, inside the house, was a little storage cupboard known to us kids as the Bogeyhole. We were told by our Grandmother that this was the place where the Bogeyman lived and so we never entered the home of the unseen ghoul for fear of meeting that dreaded, mysterious phantom. No one had ever seen the Bogeyman; he or it was a supernatural being with which naughty children were threatened by their elders. If a child sucked his thumb, bit his nails, picked his nose or told fibs, the cure was to tell that child that 'The Bogeyman will get you.' Any misbehaviour, misdemeanour or childish transgression was curtailed by the threat of the Bogeyman. The Bogeyman was and is universal and covers all continents, religions, creeds and colours. He may go by different names in different places but all children fear the unseen, terrible spectre.

The large storage room at fourteen Rosebank Road, which was situated between the kitchen and downstairs toilet, was home to a barrel shaped, galvanised, steel dolly tub and plunger, with a washboard attached, also in the storage room were kept two, hand turned mangles, one with wooden rollers and a damper on top which could be screwed down to exert extra pressure and a smaller one with rubber rollers for more delicate items. Washing the family laundry was no easy task in those days and took a lot of strength, energy and stamina. The dolly tub would be filled with hot water and the clothes and detergent would be placed within. The detergents or washing powders of the day were Tide, Rinso, Persil and Lux flakes. The three legged plunger (dolly or posser) would be pushed up and down and rotated, by way of two wooden handles situated close to the top of the plunger, onto the clothes to squash and agitate them in order to remove the ingrained grime. Stubborn stains would be removed by rubbing and scrubbing the item of clothing against the serrated profile of the washboard. There was a second dolly that did not have three legs but had a copper, half round, plunger at its business end; they both served the same purpose.

Really dirty clothes such as work wear, hankies and underwear would be put into the gas boiler which was situated under the draining board, in the kitchen. The boiler was a vitreous enamel coated, steel appliance with a hinged lid and it stood on four legs, the back two of which had castors attached to assist in the movement of the boiler for emptying. The boiler would be pulled from under the draining board and connected to the gas supply. It was then filled with water and the gas ring beneath it would be lit, bleach and detergent was added and the dirty clothing would be boiled to a germ destroying, high standard of cleanliness. The boiler was filled by way of a short piece of hose pipe connected to the tap over the sink and was emptied by way of a small outlet tap at the base of the boiler. The boiler had to be manhandled and pushed outside to facilitate the emptying process.

When the clothing etc; was thoroughly cleaned it would be rinsed manually in the big, white glazed, Belfast sink. For the final rinse a block of Reckitt's Dolly Blue and the requisite amount of Reckitt's Robin starch would be placed in the cold water. The Dolly Blue was a whitening agent and was used on all the white laundry including shirts, blouses and sheets. As well as in blocks it came in a muslin bag attached to a dolly peg which was thrown into the rinsing water. The starch was used on shirts and blouses to give them that stiff smooth look when ironed with the heavy flat iron, heated on the stove and stood on its own cast iron trivet. The clean and rinsed washing would be wrapped in the largest item of laundry, usually a sheet, put into a large basket and transported back to the storage room. Once there, it would be put through the mangle to remove any excess water before being hung out to dry on the washing line in the back garden which would then be hoisted up high, to catch the breeze, by means of a wooden prop with a notch cut into it to accommodate the washing line. If it was not a drying day outside, the washing would be hung up to dry inside the house, on the clothes rack which was suspended from the ceiling in the kitchen and was lowered by a pulley mechanism. When it was full of damp clothing and sheets it would be hoisted upwards to allow the clothes to dry. When the rack was full and there was more washing to be dried, the clothes horse was brought out and placed in front of the fire and loaded with the damp washing. When used in the storage room, the mangle had to have, placed beneath it, a bucket to catch the water that was squeezed from the laundry by the wooden rollers. During the summer the mangle was pulled out of the storage room and into the paved area of the back garden and against the drainage grid. It was easier to dispose of the excess water that way.

When we were a little older, cousin Bobby and I would often play in the back garden at Grandma's and we would make use of the wooden clothes prop as a plaything. We would throw it up and down the garden like a spear or use it like a pole vaulter's implement to see who could jump highest and furthest. We would straddle it as it leant on the clothes line. Invariably, due to the rough treatment and abuse that it received or because of the weight imposed upon it by two young lads, the prop would be broken and the line snapped. If Aunty Annie, who did most of the laundry at Grandma's house, saw us playing with, or indeed, breaking her prop she would run out of the house into the garden to chastise us. Bobby and I would run in different directions to dodge Annie. As she made futile lunges at either one of us we would make a dash for the back gate and make our escape through the ginnel and into the road. Aunty Annie would pursue us carrying and brandishing a remnant of the broken prop. She would shout after us, 'Come here, you jumped up little villains! I'll teach you to break my prop.' It was a funny thing to say, really, because Bobby and I were quite adept at breaking props and therefore did not need any teaching.

Gran's house, it seemed, did not need a fridge; it had a pantry or larder. The pantry was in the corner of the kitchen and was a small, white tiled room that stayed very cool. There was no window in the pantry, just a brick sized aperture, lined with the white tiles and covered with wire mesh to keep out flies and crawling insects.All perishable foodstuffs were kept in the pantry and they never seemed to go off. That was probably due to the fact that my Grandmother had a constant stream of hungry visitors and family and the food was never in the pantry long enough to go off. Except for smoked hams and the like which, were a rarity, and were left in there until the outer coating had turned almost black and when it was required the black bits would be cut away to reveal the tender ham beneath. When she could afford it my Gran would buy a large block of ice from the ice delivery cart. She would stand the block in an enamel bowl in the pantry to keep the temperature low and thus elongate the time that things would keep in the larder.

When my mum and dad, my sister and myself moved out of the house on Rosebank Road and into the prefab it left, living at Gran's house, my grandmother and grandfather, my mother's unmarried sister, Annie and her married sister Joan and her young son Bobby and, of course, the Bogeyman beneath the stairs. Joan's husband Robert Durber was still serving in the army, in Germany, as a military policeman and a few years later, after his army service was over, he, his wife and his son would live at Granny's house until they could find a place of their own. That, of course, was still more residents than the house was built for and I am sure that the landlords did not know that their property was being sub-let to my Auntie Joan, Uncle Bob and Cousin Bobby.

The Death of Granddad

All the above are statements of fact that I have gleaned from family members. I can only, actually recall incidents from being 3½ years old. One of those earlier recollections was going, with my sister and parents, to Granny Annie's house and going upstairs to visit Granddad George. I can only ever recall my granddad being in bed, although I did not realise, at the time, that it was, very shortly, to be his death bed. Granddad was sixty five years old when he died in 1949; Granny Annie Hampson lived until 1966 and was seventy nine years old when she passed away.

As we entered his bedroom all that could be seen of granddad George was the shiny, pink dome of his prematurely bald head which would be peeping over the top of the blankets. Upon our entrance to his bed chamber he would struggle to sit up which would cause him to go into a rasping coughing fit that turned his face purple; he looked as if he was about to burst a blood vessel as his colour deepened from red to scarlet to purple, starting from his neck and finally reaching the top of his head. We would stand tentatively at the bedroom door until his body had stopped racking and convulsing and his colour had returned to what was normal for a sick aging gentleman and he had rid himself of his expectoration into a large handkerchief. We would then walk to his bedside; he would sit up showing a mass of white chest hair protruding through the open top of his pyjamas. He would reach for his spectacles and greet us all with a cheery 'Hello young uns.' He was always glad to see his many grandchildren, although he was terrible at remembering names. He always had grapes, oranges or apples, which were kept in a fruit bowl by his bed, for each child that visited and considering that he had nine children of his own, eight of whom were married and had varying amounts of children of their own, that turned out to be a substantial amount of grandchildren. He must have single-handedly kept the local greengrocer in business. The fruit in the bowl by Grandfather's bed was actually part of his healthy diet during his illness but that did not stop us innocents devouring it when it was offered. We knew no better.

I remember Granddad George dying; he passed away on 18th June 1949, when I was 3½ years old and the funeral was held a few days later. I am sure that Granny Annie used the Co-operative Funeral Service so that she would get her dividend from the Co-op. She had paid into a funeral plan for years and now she would even make money out of the death of her husband. The hearse was a horse drawn carriage and the two extra cars were black, Humber Pullmans. I wondered whether the horse used to draw the hearse was one that also pulled a co-op milk cart. I, being of such a tender age, along with some of my cousins of around the same age, did not appreciate or understand the gravity of the occasion. The hearse and two funeral cars came around to Grandma's house to pick up granddad's body and to take it and the mourners to the burial ground. The coffin bearing the corpse, which was laid out in the front room, with just Granddad's head showing above the silk shroud stood on a bier made from two folding trellises. The pale face of my late Grandfather, which was smooth and shiny and almost white looked like a waxwork dummy and had, placed over its eyes, the traditional copper pennies. The pall bearers, after placing the lid on the casket and screwing it down, carried the coffin and the trellises to the Hearse. I don't know which of the funeral attendants pocketed the two pennies.

There is, in my mind, a distinct memory of Cousin Bobby, Cousin George, Cousins John and Kevin and myself playing and running around the long, black funeral cars. We were each duly chastised by our respective parents and had our ears boxed. The rest of the mourners, all dressed in black or wearing a black armband or black tie, were crying in grief, Bobby, George, John and Kevin and I were crying because our ears had suddenly turned bright red and had started to throb.

None of the family owned a car in those days and so those of the distaff side that could get into the funeral cars did so. Female family members were crammed in as closely as sardines in a can, black hats and veils sat askew on the heads of the ladies. They were squashed up against the doors, their arms trapped by their sides by the sheer weight and volume of human flesh; faces were pressed and distorted against the glass of the windows in the doors as the cars followed the hearse which carried the deceased to his final resting place in Philip's Park Cemetery. When those ladies clambered out of the funeral cars their faces were criss-crossed with diamond shaped patterns where the black veils that they wore had been pressed firmly against the facial skin. Those friends and relatives who could not secure a place in the funeral cars either walked or rode their bikes to the cemetery to witness the funeral service and interment of Grandfather George. Luckily, the graveyard was less than ½ a mile away and most of the family had started to make their way there before the cortege left Rosebank Road with the plodding nag walking slower than any human. Leading the procession was a mute clothed all in black with a frock coat and with a top hat perched upon his head. The top hat had, in place of a hat band, a long black ribbon attached. After the service and the interment, in the family plot, and when everybody had paid their last respects and threw their clods of earth onto the coffin, all of the family members and a few friends returned to Gran's house for tea and ham and cucumber sandwiches but soon bottles of beer, Guinness and Mackeson and a bottle each of whisky and rum appeared on the parlour table and by the time we departed for home, most of the mourners were singing merrily and laughing and joking.

The tradition of placing pennies over the eyes of the dead has two roots. One suggestion is that the weight of the pennies would keep the eyelids of the cadaver firmly closed as muscle spasms during rigor mortis may cause them to open. The sight of a corpse gazing back up at the mourners from the silk lined cosiness of a made to measure coffin could have a rather disturbing affect. Secondly, it was thought that the tradition came from Greek mythology whereby the pennies were to pay the ferryman, Charon, for passage across the River Styx to eternity. No Payment, no passage and the soul would be left to wander the banks of the river in limbo. The second explanation fails insomuch as in the Greek mythology that I have read, the coins were placed in the mouth of the deceased and were removed by Charon before the final journey. I will, therefore, go with the first explanation.

After the death of my Grandfather, my father bought a family pet, probably to alleviate the grieving of my sister and me for the recently deceased Granddad George. I remember that the family pet was a little, brown and white, cross Jack Russell puppy dog that my sister named Scamp. When he was first presented to us he was just like a ball of wool that fitted into the palm of my father's hand. Like all puppies he had those deep, soulful, black eyes and needle sharp teeth; he was very playful. He gave Valerie and me hours of enjoyment; we petted him and stroked him, gave him treats and, against my father's instructions we generally spoilt him. The pup was about eight weeks old when he was presented to us and my mum and dad very soon had him house trained, but not before my dad had come into the kitchen, one Sunday morning in his pyjamas, bleary eyed, yawning and barefooted after his once a week lie in and stood in the still warm, puppy poop. I heard my dad utter words, that morning, which I had never heard fall from his lips before.

Our little puppy, after a few months, became listless and started to have coughing fits; he wouldn't eat, there was discharge from his eyes and his nose was runny, he vomited and had diarrhoea. We wrapped him up at nights and fed him warm milk but after a few days he died of a catarrhal infection known as distemper. Val and I, as young children, didn't know what a veterinarian was and besides, even if we had, the family would not have been able to afford the bills for such treatment that was needed and we all hoped the precious little dog would recover after the loving attention, nursing and care we gave him. The puppy died after a short illness and after the little dog's death, Valerie and I were distraught; tears flowed undammed.

Distemper, I believe, was a notifiable disease and had to be reported to the relevant authority. My father shovelled up the little corpse of the puppy and placed it in the coal hole and put a sack over it, he then made a phone call to the Manchester Council at the Town Hall. The council then sent a man in a small refuse truck to pick up Scamp's body. The puppy's corpse was picked up by the council worker and thrown unceremoniously into the back of the truck and taken away for disposal. Dad said he would buy us another puppy at Christmas, but to two grieving, upset children who understood the loss of a pet more than they understood the loss of a grandparent, it was a hollow gesture and so we received the usual Christmas presents of toys and games of the times. A week after Christmas the New Year heralded the start of a new decade; the fifties. We did not get another dog until I was twelve years old. That dog was a golden Labrador called Shep, but that's another story.

Canine distemper, which killed Scamp, is a viral infection; it was once thought to be caused by neglect, impure food or lack of hygiene, which were things that Scamp never suffered. Young puppies are more susceptible to the virus and are more likely to die from it; older dogs, with the right treatment, can recover from the disease. It is caused by inhalation and can be caught by sniffing other animal's faeces or eating or drinking from a source where an infected animal has been. Canine Viral Distemper (CDV) occurs among domestic dogs and many other carnivores including foxes. The development of a vaccine in the early 1960's has led to a dramatic reduction in the number of infected domestic dogs.

Chapter 2

ROBBERY, HORSE DRAWN
VEHICLES AND CHILDHOOD GAMES

The 1950's

The 1950's as a decade were a time of great achievement and celebration with some sadness. There were numerous memorable events, a few of which I will mention here. At the opening of the decade, almost a month after my fourth birthday, on the 23rd of February, 1950, after a General Election the Labour Party were returned with a majority of only five. The 29th of August saw British troops arrive in Korea to assist the United Nations peace keeping force and in October, Legal Aid was first introduced. Bertrand Russell won the Nobel Prize for literature on the 10th of December. In 1951 on 3rd of May The Festival of Britain was officially opened and later in the year in June, the two spies, Guy Burgess and Donald Maclean defected to the USSR. There was a re-election on the 25th of October which the Conservatives won with a small majority and two days later Winston Churchill became Prime Minister. In the same year John Wyndham's *The Day of the Triffids,* was published. January 24th 1952 saw the killing of over forty Egyptians by British soldiers during riots in the Suez Canal Zone and on the 6th of February, Princess Elizabeth became Queen Elizabeth II after the death of her father George VI. On the 29th September 1952, John Cobb was killed on Loch Ness when his vessel, Crusader, disintegrated after hitting waves at over 200mph. The 20th of October saw a state of emergency in Kenya following attacks by the Mau-Mau. In November Dwight D. Eisenhower won the US presidential elections and during the run up to Christmas, London smog killed over 2,000 people. On the 5th March 1953 Joseph Vissarionovich Stalin died of a cerebral haemorrhage.1953 was also a great year for mountaineers as on the 29th of May, Edmund Hillary and Sherpa, Norgay Tensing conquered Mount Everest and they became the first men to reach the summit of the highest mountain in the world. Four days later was the official Coronation of Queen Elizabeth II in Westminster Abbey. The abbey was full with eight thousand people inside, an estimated three million people lined the streets between Buckingham Palace and Westminster Abbey and twenty million people watched the BBC coverage of the event. There were street parties all over Great Britain with fireworks displays and great joy. A general celebratory mood gripped the country. Also in 1953 the first James Bond book, *Casino Royale*, by Ian Fleming was published. 1954 was a great sporting year for Britain with Roger Bannister breaking the four minute mile; his time was three minutes, fifty nine point four seconds which he achieved on the 6th of May. The 2nd of July 1954, brought the end of food rationing. In 1955 on the 5th of April, Winston Churchill retired and Anthony Eden became prime Minister and on the 26th of May a General Election re-elected the Conservatives. Thirteen was truly an unlucky number for Ruth Ellis that year when she became the last women to be executed in Britain on the 13th July 1955. James Dean the Rebel without a Cause died on 30th September 1955, in a car crash. On the 26th of November, a state of emergency was declared in Cyprus. On16th August 1956, Bela Lugosi, the American actor died. He was buried in his Dracula cape. The Suez Crisis lasted from August through to November. 1957 started with Anthony Eden's Resignation over Suez and it was just two days prior to his resignation that he made the speech stating *'Let us be frank about it: most of our people have never had it so good.'* Harold Macmillan then became Prime Minister. On October 4th 1957, Russia launched Sputnik 1, the world's first man made satellite. The beginning of 1958 was to make it a sad year when on the 6th February the Munich air disaster occurred. The crash killed twenty three people including eight of Manchester United's Busby Babes. On the 17th of February, the Campaign for Nuclear Disarmament was launched with Bertrand Russell as its President and during August, the Notting Hill riots made the news. Parking meters were introduced to the streets of Britain on 10th July 1958 and on the 5th December; the Preston By-Pass, Britain's first section of Motorway was opened. In the last year of the decade on the 8th

January 1959 Charles de Gaulle became the President of France, replacing Rene Coty. Christopher Cockerel's invention, the hovercraft, made its first crossing of the English Channel on the 25th of July and in August the Mini, designed by Alec Issigonis went on sale at an original cost of £496.95 and £537.00 for the deluxe model.

Although I only casually glanced at the news back then, there was one story that really stuck in my mind and that is the story of Captain Carlsen and his ship, a freighter called The Flying Enterprise. I believe that I remember this story because of the sheer heroism and fortitude shown by the Danish captain. It was the stuff that boy's adventures are made of. The ship had left Hamburg on Christmas Day 1951 and was bound for America with a cargo of antique furniture, cars and pig iron. It experienced massive seas passing through the English Channel and into the Atlantic. Eventually the seas proved too much and the vessel's hull was cracked. On the bridge was Danish Captain Henrik Kurt Carlsen. The cargo of pig iron slipped and caused the ship to list at sixty degrees and she was taking on water through the hull. Two American vessels came to her rescue and took off the passengers and crew. Carlsen made the decision to stay with his ship in the hope that it could be towed to safety. Eventually on January 4th 1952 the tug, Turmoil pulled alongside and cast a hawser to Carlsen to make secure. Carlsen was having difficulty making the tow secure and so the Turmoil's mate, Kenneth Dancy leapt aboard the Flying Enterprise to assist and between them they made towline secure. Fifty seven miles out from Falmouth on the 10th January 1952, the hawser snapped and Carlsen and Dancy had to leap into the sea where they were picked up by Turmoil. Shortly after the hawser had snapped the Flying Enterprise went to her watery grave.

Carlsen and Dancy were hailed as heroes. Carlsen was inundated with offers to tell his story to the press. Money was offered for television appearances and film rights. Captain Carlsen refused all offers and said that he was only doing his duty and what was expected of him as a captain. He died in 1989.

The 1950's also brought about a new generation of authors and playwrights; writers who wrote about life as it was. They were known as The Angry Young Men and included the poets Ted Hughes and Philip Larkin along with novelist and poet John Wain whose first novel 'Hurry on Down' was published in 1953. Then there was Playwright Arnold Wesker who wrote 'The Kitchen, [1957] and 'Chips with Everything,' [1962]. Kingsley Amis wrote his book 'Lucky Jim' which was published in 1954, the same year as William Golding's *'Lord of the Flies.'* Then there was John Osborne whose play *'Look Back in Anger'* was published in 1956. The next angry young man was John Braine who's *'Room at the Top'* was published in 1957 and in 1958 Alan Sillitoe's *'Saturday Night and Sunday Morning,'* was released. Sillitoe's next classic was published in 1959, that being *'The loneliness of the Long Distance Runner.'* 1959 was also the year that saw the publication of Keith Waterhouse's *'Billy Liar.'* Most of those tales by those authors were turned into films, mainly shot in black and white; they were earthy, gritty, raw and stark. Of course, there was not only the male of the species that could write in that vein. In 1957 Shelagh Delaney, a Salford girl, started to write a novel called *'A Taste of Honey,'* before the novel was completed she decided to turn it into a play which, when finished, was accepted by Joan Littlewood, a famous director, and it opened in the East end of London in 1958. This was later turned into a black and white film which starred Rita Tushingham and made Shelagh Delaney one of the most famous playwrights of her time.

A Fall into Criminality

I recall that, at that time in my life, I think it may have been in 1951, my mother, Valerie and I were out shopping. It was on a Saturday; shops didn't open on the Lord's Day back then; the Sabbath was still kept as sacred. We had been on Newton Heath market just off Church Street and had made our way down to Oldham Road to look in the shops along there. Being the youngest child I held onto my mother's hand as we walked along the streets. Close to the junction with Church Street, just past the Duke of York public house was a grocer's shop called Siddall's and as we passed I noticed that the window in the door and the door itself were in a state of ill repair and Mr Siddall, dressed in his long, brown duster, serving coat, with a pencil tucked behind his ear was answering questions directed at him from two constables whilst he gave instructions to a glazier and another man who had come to repair the lock and door. I looked at the policemen and at Mr Siddall and the workmen and as I looked, Mr Siddall turned and gazed at us before saying 'Good morning Mrs Driver.'

I turned to my mother and asked, 'Mum, what's happened there at Siddall's?' 'Shh,' she replied 'be quiet! I don't know what has happened.' and with that she nodded in response to Mr Siddall's greeting and promptly ushered Val and me away from the scene.

It wasn't until many years later that the truth of what had happened came out and that was when I heard two of my uncles, John and Walter, who were a little tipsy after a few beers, at a family do, reminiscing about the past. Apparently, in those long gone days, they had both been laid off from their places of work and were desperate to feed their families. There was no money going into their households and what could be pawned had been. In desperation they hatched a plot by which they resorted, due to necessity, to thievery. That plot was to be executed after midnight on the following Friday night/Saturday morning. They recruited my father to act as a lookout, which, with some reluctance he did and in the dead of night they broke into Siddall's grocery shop.

As it happened, my father's presence was not really needed, as unusually, on the normally busy road, no other persons passed by that way on the night in question; there were no homeward bound revellers or policemen and very little traffic passed by that way. That was just as well because my uncles were not the most adept or capable of burglars. As they reminisced, a tale of their clumsiness and gross ineptitude came to light. They knew that nobody resided in the property and that the upstairs rooms were used for storage and office space. They had *'cased the joint'* on their numerous visits to the shop in the past. They had discovered that the shop did not have a burglar alarm but did have bars at the windows. It transpired that on that night of vandalism and petty larceny, Uncle Walter was leading the way up the steps to the door of Siddall's shop, jemmy in hand, when John who was following and carrying a leather hold all to take away the booty and looking nervously to his rear, tripped on the bottom step and fell into the leading robber who, in turn, fell into the door of the grocer's shop. As he fell forwards Walter instinctively put out his hand to save himself. That was the hand that held the jemmy which, under the forwards momentum, came into contact with the pane of glass in the door, shattering the window. My father, upon hearing the noise of the fragmented pane of glass and the tinkling of the falling shards, ran up to see what was going on. He found my two uncles arguing rather loudly about who was at fault. The crooked end of the jemmy had become caught in the pocket of Mr Siddall's coat which hung from a hook behind the door. As he tried to retrieve the jemmy it became caught on the profusion of safety bars behind the window and my Uncle Walter was shaking and rattling it about in an attempt to extricate it from its entanglement. There was enough noise to awaken the dead as metal banged against metal and more shards of broken glass, from the window were shaken to the floor.

My father gripped an arm of each of the noisy, inept burglars and explained to them the need for quietness and a little more stealth and he thus, generally calmed things down before quietly disentangling the jemmy from the bars in the shop door window and returning to his look out point. The door was then jemmied open by the two miscreants and as the lock and the door jamb gave way to the pressure applied, the creaking and cracking of the splintering wood was multiplied to the loud resonance of a nearby thunderclap due to the quietude of the immediate surroundings. Once inside, John turned on the torch that he had brought along and the beam of the flashlight danced around in and out of the shop as it shone through the plate glass window and the door and upon the inventory of provisions within the Aladdin's cave of gastronomic delights. There before them was a cornucopia of comestibles; myriad munchables; a multiplicity of mouth-watering morsels; tinned peaches, pears and pineapple chunks; Spam, sardines and soup; corned beef, baked beans and a mountain of other edible delicacies and viands to tempt the palates of epicureans, gourmands, gourmets and hungry, out of work men.

The two, bungling, would be larcenists made their way further into the well stocked retail emporium, standing on the broken glass that had fell from the door. The glass cracked and crunched, with exaggerated loudness, under their heels. John stood on a piece of glass from the broken window which slid beneath his weight. As his leg shot forward and he started to fall backwards he attempted to grab hold of the shop's serving counter to save himself. He missed that which he sought. The counter had, balanced upon its surface, numerous preserve jars stacked into a pyramid, which John's wayward arm crashed into and brought the whole pile tumbling down with him as he fell to the floor. The noise of the crashing jars carried to my father who was still stood at his lookout point. He shook his head in disbelief and brought his hands up to his forehead in despair and ducked back deeper into the shadows.

Everything went quiet for a few seconds, the torch was turned off, and both outside and inside the shop there was silence and stillness. The two burglars had paused in their felonious undertaking; they held their breath until they had regained their composure and then, when they were sure it was safe, they resumed their nefarious activity and looked further around the store. They were spoilt for choice but they picked carefully the aliment and provender that they needed and after a few more minutes and more banging, clanging and cursing the duo of plunderers approached the door of the shop, they glanced up and down the roadway and seeing that the coast was clear they came dashing out of the shop, down the steps and towards my father, giggling like a pair of schoolchildren who had gotten away with a childish prank. Walter's arms and pockets were full of stolen provisions of epicurean pleasures; whilst John carried the bulging, leather hold all which was full of tins and packages of victuals, viands and various edibles. My father noticed that neither of the purloiners had, amongst their booty, the implement used to gain entry to the shop; the crowbar or jemmy. He asked them where it was and upon being told that it lay on the floor by the door he told the pair to wait in the shadows while he went back to retrieve the tool which would have served as evidence against them, had it been left in the shop to be found by the police.

After the retrieval of the jemmy all three made their way back to our family prefab, taking care only to traverse the quiet back streets. Their journey back to the prefab took them past the Newton Heath Steam Laundry and over the Manchester, Leeds Canal and from the wooden bridge that spanned the waterway the jemmy was cast into the murky waters, never to be seen again. Their journey then took them past Jackson's Brick Works which was in complete darkness. The robbers moved like wraiths, barely noticeable in the blackness of the night. They stumbled and fell as they crossed the rough brickyard, loath to use the torch in case they were spotted. Walter dropped cans and packages and fumbled in the darkness to retrieve them. They came on to the semi lit thoroughfare known as Mitchell Street which was lined with prefabs, each and every one in darkness. Mitchell Street led up to Briscoe Lane which they crossed over onto the unlit croft adjacent to the tripe works. They passed the tripe works and the cemetery on Orford Road, keeping as much as they could in the shadows. They then made their way up the un-illuminated Taylor's Lane to the rear of our prefab. The booty was stored at our family abode, to be shared out the following day. It was only stored at the prefab because that was the closest abode to the scene of the crime. Walter and John made their way to their respective homes to await the divvying up of the spoils on the following day. My father took nothing.

Why the robbers opted to burglarise Siddall's in the first place is a mystery to me. Siddall's stood on the busy A62 main road between Manchester and Oldham, very close to a much used and popular public house, The Duke of York, where the would be crooks had sat, nursing a pint apiece, until closing time on the night of the burglary. The A62 thoroughfare is usually well used both during the day and into the night, but being the week end it was quieter than usual. Upon reflection, if I had have been an out of work felon bereft of the wherewithal to buy provisions to feed my family, I think Sarson's grocers on Seabrook road would have seemed a better proposition in the case of breaking and entering for the purpose of robbery and self survival. Sarson's like Siddall's was a lock up shop but it was set back from the road and had no other properties adjoining it. It was a free standing building with no lighting to the rear on a very quiet suburban street and no further than four hundred yards from our prefab. Still, being a law abiding, upstanding citizen, what do I know?

My uncles only appropriated the rations and provisions that they required and although that was no excuse for risking their liberty for their breaking of the law, it temporarily lifted them out of the poverty trap into which they had fallen. They both found gainful employment shortly after their escapade into criminality, which is a good thing because their careers as felons, due to their incompetence and gaucherie, would have been very short, lived. They were, by sheer luck, never apprehended although they regretted their nefarious exploit for a long time after the event and they frequently tried to redeem themselves with Mr Siddall by offering to do odd jobs, free of charge. Siddal must have wondered why those regular customers, who he had known for a long time, were suddenly offering their help whenever the opportunity arose. I have no wish to make excuses for my relative's actions, they were wrong, but all concerned are now deceased and what is done is done.

Visits to Grandma's

When our family visited Granny Annie's, or when our grandmother looked after us during school holidays especially in the summer, we children would make for the top of the back garden, past the then overgrown vegetable plots, to the far left hand corner, where grew a large rhubarb patch. Since the passing away of Grandfather George the vegetable plots had not received the care and attention due to them. Upon reaching the rhubarb my sister and I and Cousin Bobby would snap off a couple of the larger stalks, discard the leaves, peel the stalks and take them into Grandma's kitchen. There we would wash the fibrous stems under the cold water tap and then dip them into the sugar bowl and relish the convergence of the sweet sugar against the sour rhubarb dancing across our taste buds, playing tippy-toe across our tongues. We would then go back and raid the rhubarb patch for more; such pleasure indeed, until later in the day when we suffered intense stomach cramps, which in turn, called for numerous visits to the smallest room in the house. The rhubarb worked wonders to keep us regular and had a much better taste than the Ex-Lax Chocolate or syrup of figs which children were force fed in those days to regulate the movements of the bowels. If we suffered from any other ailments whilst at Grandma Annie's we would be given a Fenning's Little Healer, some of which she always had in stock and which were claimed to cure coughs, colds, bronchitis and influenza and were thought by some in those days to be a universal panacea.

In Grandma's back garden there also grew a black currant bush which, at a certain times of the year, had the caterpillars of the Cabbage White butterfly crawling about them and later the chrysalises which would metamorphose into the adult Cabbage White butterflies. There was also a gooseberry bush which had the caterpillars of the gooseberry sawfly on it at certain times of the year. We would pick and eat the fruits straight from the bushes without washing them. Grandmother Annie took great advantage of her limited stock of fruits. She would gather them, prepare them and then produce, with her nimble fingers and culinary expertise, the most wonderful tasting rhubarb and black currant or gooseberry crumble which would be served with her home made, hot, thick, creamy, vanilla custard.

The cooking at Grandma's was done on a big, black, cast iron, back to back oven made by a company called Ure, which I believe was a Scottish firm, that specialised in iron fire grates, wood burning stoves and ovens. The massive range, which was heated by the multi fuel, front room fire, had four hot plates, a spacious oven plus a warming oven and a swinging kettle or pan holder by the fire; it also contained a back boiler which supplied the house with hot water. Grandma's speciality on this range was a nutritious thick pea soup and ham shank, made with a cheap cut of meat and steeped peas which were soaked overnight with a tablet of bicarbonate of soda. That was the staple diet at Grandma's house and it was one meal that stuck to your ribs. She also cooked hot pots and stews with suet dumplings and numerous pulses such as barley, split peas, lentils etc, again using cheap cuts of meat.

When it came time to clean the range, Gran would bribe Bobby, Val and me with a penny to polish the range and fire grate with a black lead compound, which I think, was called Fire Black. We kids ended up blacker than coal and certainly blacker than the range we had cleaned. The Fire

Black compound ended up on our clothes and on our hands and faces and in our hair, until we looked like Al Jolson impersonators. We all enjoyed doing the cleaning and polishing of that big, old fireplace and cooking range and a penny, a whole penny, to us, was a king's ransom which, after we had cleaned ourselves up a little, we would take to the corner shop and rummage through the 'up to a penny tray,' which held such delights as Blackjacks at four for a penny and spearmint sticks and ha'penny chews; there were liquorice roots and colt's foot rock and large gobstoppers that changed colour as you sucked them, and a host of other sweet delicacies.

In those days we lived on a diet of staple foods and hung on a hook by the side of the fireplace in the front parlour was an extendable, three tined toasting fork. After playing out at Grandma's house we would enter the house and Gran would have a plate of bread, sliced thickly off a large loaf. She would pierce a slice of the bread with the toasting fork and hold it over the glowing coals in the fireplace. When one side was nicely browned to the point of turning black she would turn it round and toast the other side. Once done she would spread it with beef dripping and sprinkle it with salt. She would then cut the round of toast in half, diagonally and place it on the plate before picking up another slice of bread and repeating the process. Grandma Annie would occasionally let one of us hold the toasting fork but she kept a watchful eye over us. Sometimes we would argue about whose turn it was to hold the fork but Grandma would make the final decision.

Depending upon how many of her grandchildren were present there would be a dash and scramble for the toast, everyone wanting it while it was still piping hot, especially the end crust. Not very often and when things were looking up we were given the rare treat of real, best butter on our toast and as an extra treat we were given homemade, black currant preserve, spread lightly over the melting butter on the piping hot toast. Bread browned under the grill never tasted as good as that browned in front of an open fire.

Dripping, from cheap cuts of beef such as brisket was never thrown away. Other cheap cuts that we survived on were scrag end of mutton and breast of lamb plus the offal such as hearts, kidneys and livers of various beasts. We also thrived on such delicacies as cowheel stew, pig's cheeks and a titbit known as brawn which was a meat paste made from pig's head in jelly. When a roasted joint of meat was removed from the roasting pan one of our favourite culinary delights was to dip a round of bread into the hot, residual fat and savour all the flavour of the meat as it ran from our mouths and down our chins. That fatty delight was known as a dip butty and was full of saturated and cholesterol inducing fat and remnants of slightly charred meat, but it never seemed to do us any harm. The residual fat in the roasting tin was also the base for the gravy which Gran made by adding flour to thicken and that juice complemented any meal where gravy was a requirement.

Just around the corner from Gran's house there was a row of shops. There was a newsagent on the corner and then there was a grocer's and a green grocer's. There was a small butcher's shop and hardware shop, but best of all there was a fish and chip shop. When Val and I were being looked after by Gran and when my mother could afford it she would leave money with Grandma for a Fish and Chips dinner and we would join the queue at the chip shop and wait our turn to buy our four penn'orth of chips and a fish with a penn'orth of scrapings. If my memory serves me correctly, plaice or cod and chips with the batter scrapings was 1/3d which equates to approximately seven pence in decimal coinage. The same fish and chips now costs nearly a fiver.

Next door to my Grandmother at number sixteen lived the Yates' family which consisted of Mrs Yates who was approximately the same age as my Gran plus her two sons, Norbert who was about twenty years old and Bernard who she had later in life and was about two years older than me. There was no Mr Yates, perhaps he had been wounded close to the end of the war and died later, or perhaps he had left the family home or like my Grandfather, maybe one of the illnesses that blighted the working class had taken him. Bernard, now and again, but only occasionally, played childhood games with Bobby and me but generally he was a bit of a loner.

Next door on the ginnel side of Grandma's house, at Number twelve, lived a strange old woman called Mrs Hennessy; she was a crooked backed harridan who put the fear of God into any child that ventured close to her property. She lived alone and no one ever visited her, save for the rent man or the doctor. She had a large, hooked nose with a very prominent and hairy wart on its side, sat on the bridge of her nose were tiny wire rimmed spectacles. She wore a black, crocheted shawl over a long skirt and a blouse and cardigan and she wore her hair in an old fashioned snood which she sometimes covered with a headscarf. She walked bent forwards and with an obvious limp using a crooked and knobbly walking cane for balance which she gripped with a prominently blue veined, knotty and arthritically gnarled hand. That walking stick was regularly used to lash out at any child that wandered within striking distance. She would constantly harangue children playing in the road close to her house. She would berate Valerie, me and Bobby whilst we played in the back garden at our Grandmother's. Making a noise in the ginnel was something we dared not do. If a child's ball was accidently kicked or thrown into her garden that was the end of that. No child would dare to venture to retrieve it and when she was ready, Mrs Hennessy would come out and plunge a knife into the ball and throw it in her dustbin. When Mrs Hennessy was out and about she would shuffle along talking and cackling to herself. Local children were convinced that she was a witch and that any transgression towards Mrs Hennessy would result in a curse being put upon the transgressor. Children from a few streets away, who she did not know but who knew her, would follow her at a safe distance and call her names and throw things at her but they would not go close to her or her abode.

Sometimes Grandma would send Bobby and me, she never sent Valerie, to the corner shop to get the accumulators for the radio recharged. When we reached the rear of the shop one of us would make sure the coast was clear and then climb over the wall and pass up to four empty lemonade bottles over to the other. We would take the empties along with the accumulators into the shop where we were given the deposit money for the return of the empty bottles, with which we would buy sweets. When we returned later to pick up the charged accumulators we would do the same thing. We very rarely bought any lemonade but we always returned empty bottles.

In the summertime, during the school holidays, when the temperatures soared, kids would play in the streets. We would ask, beg and pester; we would implore with doe like, pleading eyes, until our Gran submitted to our entreaties and bought us ice lollipops from the corner shop or from the passing ice cream cart. It seemed that all the other children pestered their guardians or parents for ices as we would all sit on the kerbside eating our sweet, sticky ices until we were left with an empty, wooden lollipop stick. The construction of Rosebank Road, where we played and sat to eat our lollies was that of a concrete thoroughfare with bitumen expansion joints between each 20 ft length of concrete.

The summers of my childhood were occasionally so hot that the sun would melt the tar in the joints and kids, including me, my sister and cousin Bobby, would sit on the kerbside and push our lolly sticks into the soft, black, glue like compound and twist them around until we had a round, sticky, black blob of bitumen on our sticks. It wouldn't be long before the first stick, with its gooey, glossy globule, was thrown into the air; the weight of the black, bituminous, bulbous blob would cause that end of the stick to fall to earth first. After the first stick was thrown other kids did the same and then a battle royal would ensue as blobs of tar were thrown at each other. The tar would stick in the long hair of the girls and sometimes in the shorter hair of the boys. Most of the kids involved got some of the black, viscid mess on their clothes or on their bare arms and legs and when it set hard it was almost impossible to get off. Later girls could be seen with clumps of hair cut from their crowning glory, other kids had their skin scrubbed raw in an attempt to remove the tacky mess. The raw skin was almost as painful as the red marks received by way of the spankings we received from parents or grandparents, but we never learned. Clothes had to be boiled in an attempt to remove the coagulated tar, but it always left a stain.

It was on one of those summer days during the holidays that we were playing in the street when I noticed that a couple of the cast iron, drainage grids in the gutter of the roadway had been removed, probably stolen by tinkers looking for a weigh in. I ran to my Granny's to tell her and she told me 'Keep away from the holes where the grids were because it's dangerous and you might get sucked down into the sewers. Now play in the garden while I walk round to the council yard and report it.'

Of course, being children with inquisitive natures, curiosity got the better of us. At the time there was a young girl of about six or seven years of age named Sandra from number six Rosebank Road playing with a couple of her pals and one of her elder brothers. They had a skipping rope and were playing skipping in the roadway. Sandra came from a large, poor family, always scruffy and renowned for their rowdiness. When they saw my sister, Cousin Bobby and me poking sticks, with tar on the end, down the hole, they came over to see what was happening. 'What're yuh doin'?' asked Sandra.

'There's a florin down there and we're tryin' to get it.' I replied.

'Get outa the way and let's 'ave a look.' demanded Sandra.

Not wishing to offend her I said, 'Alright.' and I and the others moved out of the way. Sandra got down on her knees and leaned into the gaping drain. Both of her arms, her head and shoulders were down the hole as she tried to reach the elusive coin. Her elder brother, not realising the consequences or how stupid an act it was, came up behind Sandra and placed his plimsolled foot on her behind and pushed. Sandra slipped, ever so gracefully forwards, into the drain, her legs in the air and her skirt about her waist, 'Yuh bastards! 'Get me out!' she shouted in a tearful and angry voice, but the other kids were laughing and pointing at her and one said 'Look at Sandra; she's got no knickers on!' Hearing all the noise and shouting Sandra's mother and a few other adults came out of their houses and Sandra was pulled to safety. She was filthy her hair was streaked with greasy, thick, smelly sludge from the drain. She was a mess and she was crying but her right hand was closed tightly around the florin. The next day the Council workmen arrived to put new, cast iron grids over the gaping drain holes.

Sandra wanted to be a pal to Cousin Bobby, Val and me but we were told, by Grandma, to keep away from her and her siblings because 'they're a rough lot,' but we still kept her acquaintance when we visited Grandma's and that didn't stop Sandra coming round to the prefab a couple of years later. She came one Saturday morning with Cousin Bobby and he, Val, me and Sandra went to play in Tetlow's woods. We were playing Hide and Seek and Valerie was the seeker. As she counted to a hundred with her face against a tree, the rest of us ran off to hide. Sandra followed Bobby and me and she suddenly stopped and said, 'These bushes look like a good place to hide and there's summat I wanna show yuz.'

We all went into the bushes and I asked Sandra, 'What is it you want to show us?'

To which she replied 'Show us your willies and I'll show you mine.'

Well, being inquisitive children, Bobby and I looked at each other in bewilderment then we both smiled and a tacit agreement was formed. We each hoisted a leg of our short pants and pulled out our weenies. After looking at them for a few seconds, cocking her head from side to side as if in appraisement of what she saw, Sandra lifted up her skirt to reveal her pudenda and once again she wore no drawers. Bobby and I were staring at her genitalia when we heard Valerie close by shouting 'Come out, come out wherever you are. I give up, I can't find you.' The calling shook us out of our mode of curiosity and voyeurism and we all adjusted our clothing and walked, seemingly innocently, out of the bushes. We were actually ashamed and red-faced but Val didn't suspect a thing and we carried on playing various childhood games. Before we knew it my mum was shouting us in for dinner and it was time for Bobby and Sandra to return to Rosebank Road.

My sister Valerie and I were the only Grandchildren left that lived locally except for Cousin Bobby who still lived at Grandma's. In Gran's front room was a black wooden cabinet stood on four spirally twisted legs, which were shaped like barley sugar sticks. When the lid was lifted a turntable and space to store old 78rpm records was revealed. On the right hand side of the cabinet was a winding handle with which to wind up the turntable before adjusting its speed. Around 1954 we began to take an interest in that antique phonograph and Valerie, being the eldest was appointed as the one to handle the records and place the phonograph arm containing the needle upon the discs. We grandchildren would play such records as Music, Music, Music by Theresa Brewer, This Old House by Rosemary Clooney, How Much is that Doggie in the Window by Lita Rosa and other songs by Perry Como, Jo Stafford, Frankie Laine, David Whitfield, Eddie Calvert and many more. Those old shellac 78rpm records belonged mainly to Auntie Annie and Auntie Joan and consisted of the popular music of the day. That middle of the road music would have to suffice until Rock 'n' Roll came upon the scene. After we left Newton Heath for Blackley, Auntie Annie and her husband Harry purchased a more modern electric gramophone and a separate radio, but when we visited we were not allowed to touch the record player. Both instruments had valves and not transistors.

Visits to see Other Relatives, TheLovely Fireplaces and Sunday school

As a child of about four or five years of age I, with my parents and my sister and Uncle Bob and Aunty Joan and Cousin Bobby, would travel by bus to visit various aunties and uncles. I remember one particular Saturday; we were to visit Aunty Elsie's and Uncle Harry's flat in Wythenshawe. My Mum and Dad and Joan and Bob were going out that night with my aunty and uncle, to the Naval Club on Brownley Road, Wythenshawe where they would meet Uncle George and Aunty Elsie Hampson who lived in Woodhouse Park. Uncle Harry was on the committee at the Naval Club. We were to stay at the flat for the night where Cousin Margaret, who is nine years older than me and her elder sister Iris, were to baby sit Val, Bobby and me.

When my mother was getting dressed up to go out there was a ritual that had to be adhered to. In those early, post war day's nylon stockings were expensive and hard to come by, so my mother, like a lot of other young women of the time, after shaving her legs, would smear them with gravy browning to darken them. My father would then use mother's eyebrow pencil to draw a seam down the back of her legs to give the appearance of fifteen denier stockings. The drawing of the seam had to be done by someone else because it was impossible for the lady to reach behind her and draw her own seams in a straight line. I had visions of young women being followed by sniffing, inquisitive dogs which would attempt to lick off the gravy browning. When my mother could afford a pair of nylons she would treat them with the utmost care, she would keep her toenails well trimmed to avoid putting a ladder in her nylons and if a run or a ladder should appear she would stop its journey with a dab of nail polish.

On the way to Wythenshawe we had to pass through Moss Side where Aunty Hetty and Uncle Peter Flanagan lived. We took a bus from Newton Heath into the centre of Manchester where we boarded a bus from Piccadilly bus station to Moss Side where we alighted and called round to see Hetty and Peter. At their house Hetty and Peter had another visitor; Peter Flanagan's Brother David, a very fine Irish Fiddle player. After a couple of hours and cups of tea and sandwiches and numerous renditions of old Irish ballads we left and made our way to Princess Road to catch the bus to Wythenshawe. As the bus progressed along Princess Parkway, approaching Chorlton, I looked to my right through the bus window where something had caught my eye. I then turned to my mum and dad and said 'Look at all those lovely fireplaces. Aren't they pretty and nice and shiny?' Mum and dad started laughing as did all the other passengers that heard my comment. Those lovely fireplaces were white marble and granite tombstones; we were passing Southern Cemetery.

That Saturday night when the adults had gone out to the Naval Club Bobby, Val and I and our baby sitters, Margaret and Iris were entertaining ourselves with colouring books and coloured pencils and watching the searchlights from Ringway Airport when there was a knock on the door of the flat. Iris went to answer the door and came back into the living room with a youth of about sixteen years. The youth sat down and after while he asked 'Would you like to hear a scary ghost story?' We all nodded in the affirmative.

He then said 'Right, for effect, let's turn the lights off and I'll begin.' So in the darkness of the living room, with only the luminescence from the Ringway searchlights occasionally shining through the curtains, he started his chilling tale of spectres and ghosts. We sat there enthralled and not just a little frightened when he came to a part in his narration whereupon he said 'and the door creaked.'

At that precise moment the living room door creaked as it opened. Bobby, Val and I jumped up and ran behind the settee where we sought refuge and where we stayed until Margaret turned on the lights. We slowly came out from our hiding place to find a second youth had joined the group and he was laughing. Actually he had entered the flat at the same time as the storyteller and he had stayed in the hallway until the requisite moment. The whole thing was contrived to scare us youngsters witless. It worked.

The flat in Wythenshawe was a three bedroom abode and when our parents arrived home from their evening of conviviality and not quite completely sober, sleeping arrangements had to be sorted out. The adult men shared one bedroom and the adult women another. Valerie shared a bedroom with Margaret and Iris and Bobby and I slept on the settee in the front room. The next morning the women arose first and cooked breakfast for every one. Once breakfast was out of the way and the dishes washed and the house was tidied it was close to ten thirty so the males, Bobby and I, my father and Uncles Bob and Harry, donned our coats and walked to the perimeter fence of Ringway airfield to watch some take offs and landings. Upon returning to the flat it was close to Sunday opening time and so the men deposited us at the door and went for a couple of pints in the nearest pub. They returned home around two o'clock and we all sat down to Sunday lunch, prepared by the ladies. At about four thirty, we put our coats on, said our goodbyes and made our way to the bus stop to begin the journey home, arriving home at about six o'clock in the evening, tired and ready for an early night.

During the early 1950's, Valerie and I and some other neighbourhood children started to attend Sunday school. The Sunday school that we attended belonged to and was run by All Saints Church at their annexe on Culcheth Lane, virtually opposite to the Soap Box public house and Christ the King Catholic School. The Sunday school building was a large wooden structure, like an over sized garden shed, which I believe was used as a pre-school nursery through the week. I believe the reason that my mother sent us to the Sunday school, as well as to get a basic understanding in religious education, was to get us out of the way so that we would not be under her feet, whilst at the same time knowing where we were while she did her housework and prepared the Sunday roast. The Sunday school being a church run establishment, there were religious connotations to everything that went on there. We played games, there were religious overtones, we had readings, there were religious overtones, we made things in arts and

45

crafts, and there were religious overtones. The Sunday school teachers were strict and they tried to instil their religious discipline into us wayward kids. I was baptised into the Protestant Church and therefore a Christian but after a few weeks I started to make excuses as to why I should not attend Sunday school and quite soon I had found other things to do on Sunday's. I believe that Sunday school discipline never did me any good and to this day I am a devout atheist.

Asbestos and its Dangers

In those long gone days of innocence, nobody knew, or more to the point, nobody was made aware of the dangers of asbestos, be it of the blue, white or brown variety. If the authorities did know, they kept it close to their chests. Workmen in the asbestos related trades were told nothing of the dangers and, indeed, were not even required to wear masks or breathing apparatus to filter out the air borne filaments which were and are responsible for so many deaths from Mesothelioma, asbestosis and its varied complications. In those days personal Protective Equipment, (PPE), was the responsibility of the worker who could not afford such equipment and so went without. Nowadays it is the responsibility of the employer to supply such equipment, from safety boots and hard hats to Hi-Viz vests and breathing equipment. Masks and respirators are now mandatory when employed and working within close proximity of asbestos and indeed, companies that specialise in the removal of asbestos have come into being and they need to be registered with the government to work with asbestos, so much as Health and Safety in the Workplace changed. I believe that the Health & Safety within the Workplace laws were not brought in to protect the working population but rather to protect the employers from liability and prosecution. The working class are a secondary consideration and have always been deemed expendable by the ruling and upper classes and profits for the bloated industrialists always came before the welfare of the workforce.

Asbestosis is a chronic inflammatory medical condition affecting the lungs and usually occurs in individuals who have had long term exposure to asbestos. It is classed as an occupational lung disease. Sufferers have severe shortness of breath (Dyspnoea), and are at an increased risk regarding different types of lung cancer especially and including Mesothelioma.

Mesothelioma is a rare and virulent form of cancer that is almost always caused by exposure to asbestos. It can lie dormant for between twenty and fifty years after the asbestos fibres that cause the disease have been breathed in, thereafter it can raise its ugly head in a life threatening form. It can affect the lining of the lungs, the lining of the abdominal cavity and the lining around the heart. Mesothelioma like asbestosis is now classed as an occupational disease and numerous people are seeking compensation for what they see as their employer's negligence. Unfortunately a lot of sufferers have died before their claims for compensation have been realised and as far as I know, up until recently there was no retrospective compensation, but I believe that that has recently changed and sufferer's families will get the compensation that is due to the deceased member of their family.

The roofs of the prefabs were made of corrugated asbestos sheets which overlapped and were bolted to the roof trusses. The outer skin of the shed in the back garden of our prefab which was oblong in shape with a flat roof, was constructed completely of corrugated asbestos sheets over a metal frame, held together where they overlapped by nuts, bolts and washers, as were all the other sheds in the back gardens of the prefabs. The buildings also had asbestos guttering and downspouts. As children, my cousins and I and our friends played in and around the shed and climbed onto its roof and those of our friends. We would sometimes scratch or cut ourselves accidently on the edges of the asbestos sheets and obviously, asbestos fibres must have made ingress into the cuts and abrasions.

I remember my cousin Freddy, who was full of derring-do, one weekend, despite being implored not to, climbing up the drainpipe of the prefab and clambering onto the roof. There was a gap of around five feet or a little less between the prefab and the shed; the shed being somewhat lower than the living accommodation. Once Freddy, who was a little older than me, was on the roof he said, 'I can jump across to the coal shed from here.' Then he demanded, 'Hey! Do you think I can jump the gap or not?' There were a number of noes and a few ayes; a number of shakes of the head and a few nods from the kids gathered around when cousin Freddy, full of bravado, said 'Right, watch this!' and with that he backed up the slight incline of the prefab roof. He then took a large inspiration, mustered up all his courage and took a run to the edge of the roof and with much intrepidity and bravado he launched himself into space and across the intervening gap, to come crashing down, feet first, onto the roof of the shed.

Unfortunately, corrugated asbestos sheeting is not manufactured to take the weight of an airborne eight year old coming in to land. The moment his undercarriage touched down there was a loud splintering and cracking noise and Freddy plunged bodily through the newly made hole in the roof and into the shed, from which a second crash resounded as he landed, in a heap, on the pile of coal within the shed. Luckily he fell between the steel cross members that made up the frame of the shed and gave it its rigidity and fell clean through the asbestos.

Panic spurred us in to action and we all ran to the door of the shed, fear obvious on our wide eyed faces, terrified of what we might find, I flung open the door to see Freddy lying in the twisted position into which he had collapsed. He was moaning and his trousers were torn and his shirt shredded. There was blood, mingled with coal dust and shards of broken asbestos sheeting on his arms legs and face and his eyes were closed. As we gazed upon his bloody, inert form he opened his eyes and with an insouciance borne of naivety said, 'See! I told you I could jump the gap.'

Fortuitously, my mother, after hearing the crash came dashing from the kitchen to ascertain what all the noise was about. She was dressed in what was the norm for working ladies and washerwomen in those days; she had a brightly coloured, floral pinafore over her dress with a scarf, tied in a turban style on her head. After she had recovered from the initial shock of the sight that greeted her, she took control. She checked Fred over and helped him to his feet and took him indoors to clean him up; she bathed and dressed his cuts and sewed and repaired his trousers as best she could. She gave him one of my shirts to wear because his own was beyond repair. By that time he had stopped moaning and he appeared none the worse for his crash landing experience, except for the cuts and bruises; he had looked in a much worse condition than he actually was, but my mother's pinafore was utterly filthy, covered in asbestos and coal dust and besmeared with Freddy's blood. Once they had been washed, both Freddie's shirt and my mum's pinafore were consigned to the rag box for when the rag and bone man came around.

On the following Monday my father phoned the council who, after a few days, came out to repair the roof of the shed. The Council Maintenance Yard, which occupied approximately an acre of land, was situated behind Sarson's grocer shop off Seabrook Road, just 300 yards from our domicile. It was full of all the things that were needed to repair and maintain council houses and of course the council prefabs. There were stacks of corrugated asbestos panels and pebble dashed panels for the repair of the prefabs and coal sheds, rows of cast iron grids of various shapes and sizes for use on the highways, byways and for domestic drainage purposes. There was all manner of goods to be used in building maintenance and repair such as roof tiles, slates, guttering, fire grates, downspouts and different gauges and lengths of cast iron piping. There were paving stones and kerb stones and there were large mounds of sand and different grades of stone. To the left of the compound was a large, long building which housed the yard foreman's office plus storage room for all the maintenance goods that were of a fragile or perishable nature and could not be stored outside or that were easy to steal and carry away such as external and internal doors, gates, kitchen and bathroom fixtures, bags of cement etc.

I do not know whether the council made a charge for the repair to the coal shed roof as it could not be explained away as an ordinary accident. We, as children, had already been warned of the dangers of climbing onto the fragile roofs of the two buildings and we were banned from doing so, but after Freddy's little, foolish accident we were very seriously rebuked and the ban on climbing was reinforced. Fred who at the time of this writing was in his late 60's, has never suffered any asbestos related diseases as has anyone else I know that lived in the asbestos roofed prefabs of the early post war years. Apparently, the asbestos used in component parts of the prefabs was bonded with other materials and was of no danger unless it was broken into small pieces and the ensuing air borne filaments were breathed in.

Horses and Carts, Traders and Childhood Games

There were friends aplenty, with whom to play childhood games, when I was between four and nine years of age. The types of games that we played changed as we got older and included Hide and Seek, Hopscotch, British Bulldog, Rallivo, Kick-can, Tag, Marbles, Jacks and many more. We had sticks and hoops and whips and tops and we played out until the street lamps came on. Those lampposts were originally fed by mains gas, which had to be lit by a lamplighter, to supply light. They were going through a process of conversion to electricity and so the lamplighters, whose job it was to light the lamps at dusk and extinguish them at dawn were becoming redundant. The lampposts on our prefab estate were electrically powered but retained the style of the old gas lamps and were installed before we moved into our new home.

The cast iron, Victorian style, lampposts of the day had cross members just below the glass lamp housing to which we would tie a rope and use it as a swing, usually with an old bicycle tyre attached to the rope. The games we played were often of the rough and tumble type and yet I cannot remember anybody getting badly injured. Minor injuries were common; scraped knees and shins, cuts and bruises, the occasional bloody nose and numerous banged heads. I don't remember any eviscerations, decapitations or amputations; the very worst that happened was that someone would break a limb.

Whilst we were playing, in the summertime, a peel of bells would herald the coming of the horse drawn ice cream van. There were a number of the horse drawn ice cream vans that came from the "Little Italy" area of Ancoats. I remember Pandolfo's, Giovanni Cabrelli's, Granelli's, Sivori's, John Pessagno's, Marco Rea's and Scappaticci's amongst many others. There names were musical as they tripped off the tongue but they also sounded like a list of Mafia Hit Men. I think that they all had their own areas but crossed over into their rivals areas. All the horses wore blinkers and all had a nosebag constantly attached. All the ice cream carts were brightly painted, small, two wheeled vehicles with just enough room to carry the ice cream tub and the cornets wafer biscuits and chocolate flakes and raspberry juice and room enough for the vendor to do his job.

In the city centre, when I went with my parents, I seem to remember hand pushed or pedal driven ice cream carts, usually with the name Ben's Ices or Gerard's Ices on the tub. Ben's Ice's was owned by Bernardo Scappaticci and Gerard's Ices was owned by Gerado Scappaticci. The pedal driven type had two wheels at the front with the ice cream tub situated between them. Behind the ice cream tub was the handlebars and the saddle where the ice cream man sat to pedal and steer and directly behind him was a single wheel. They were really just oversized, wrong way round tricycles adapted to carry the ice cream tub. They would be seen at Lewis's Arcade and in Piccadilly Gardens and various other parts of the city centre, selling their produce. Besides the big stores and smaller shops, they had to vie with another mobile trade, around Piccadilly Gardens and Lewis's arcade and those other traders wore shorter, tighter skirts than were the norm for the day, with fishnet stockings, high heeled shoes and heavy make up, they were the prostitutes that hung around that area of Manchester. The ice cream that those Italians sold was delicious and firm. It was pure white and in my opinion it was far superior to the likes of Wall's and Lyon's and the floppy gloop of Mr Softee or Mr Whippy. I remember Granelli's and Sivori's had ice cream parlours in various parts of the city. The wares that those scarlet women sold I had no knowledge of.

The two wheeled horse drawn cart, in those days, was used by other traders as well as the ice cream man and it was a bugle call that heralded the approach of the rag and bone man. The rag and bone men were almost always bearded, dirty looking individuals who usually wore army greatcoats whatever the weather. Across his shoulder attached to a lanyard was his battered, brass trumpet, full of dents and badly tarnished. The rag and bone men were known as tatters or totters and there were one or two of them that worked the Newton Heath area. One, we used to avoid because all he gave in exchange for a bundle of old clothes was a donkey stone for cleaning the front steps and window sills of terraced houses, public houses and shops etc.

We didn't live in a shop or a pub or even a terraced house and in our new Prefab there was no call for donkey stones and so we would wait for the rag and bone man who had balloons tied to the back of his cart. This man also gave out goldfish which he kept in a water filled tank on the rear of his cart. The fish would be taken from the tank by the use of a little net attached to a handle and placed into a water filled plastic bag which would then be handed over to his customer for a bundle of rags. He also gave various little playthings such as whips and tops but mainly he would give out bows and arrows made of bamboo cane which all the boys clamoured for, for the sole purpose of bursting the balloons that the girls received. It was a minor miracle that no one lost an eye as did King Harold at Hastings in 1066; cane arrows were flying around as thick as arrows at Crecy or Agincourt.

October 14th 1066 was the date of the Battle of Hastings between King Harold Godwinson of the Anglo Saxons and Duke William of Normandy. The Normans invaded England and the battle was fought at Senlac, re-named Battle, close to Hastings. Harold's army was defeated and William became the first king to rule over England and Scotland. Crecy was one of the most important battles in the Hundred Years War, taking place on 26th August 1346. The English, under Edward III were victorious over the French, pitting the English longbow against the French crossbow. Agincourt was another battle in the Hundred Years War where the English longbow men, under Henry V won a decisive battle against the French on October 25th 1415, when they were vastly outnumbered.

On a warm summer's day, during the school holidays, when I was maybe six or seven years of age, I was sat at home alone while mum nipped to the shop, my sister was playing out and my father was at work when I heard the rag man's clarion call. I went to the box where mother used to store old clothes and rags that were no longer fit for use and were kept for the rag man, it was empty but for some ragged underwear, which I left. I scoured the house searching for old clothes that were no longer of any use but I couldn't find any, let alone enough to warrant a bow and arrow.

As I dashed past my parent's bedroom I noticed that my mother's wardrobe door was ajar and I skidded to a halt and entered the chamber and approached the wardrobe and opened it wide and saw that there were numerous garments hanging there. I looked through them and picked one of my mother's older, but well preserved, winter coats off the hanger. I now had enough to justify a bow and arrow, my weapon of choice. I rolled the coat into a bundle and then ran to the tatter man and exchanged the coat for the cherished weapon of my desire. I now think that the coat may have ended up being worn by the tatter's wife rather than ending up with all the other rags for sorting and what a well dressed lady she would have appeared.

It was not until later in the year after a few months had passed and the weather started to turn a little inclement and the mornings greeted us with a coating of hoar frost and a bitter wind that my mother noticed that the coat was missing. She came into the living room and asked 'Has anyone seen my winter coat? I mean the black one with the big silver buttons. I can't find it anywhere.'

My father replied, 'You must have took it out with you one day and it probably got a little too warm and you may have left it somewhere; in a café or at your mothers house.'

'Don't be daft, Gus.' she replied 'I wouldn't do that. Do you kids know anything about it?'

Val and I looked at each other as if we didn't know what she was talking about, well actually, Valerie certainly didn't and she said 'If it's not in the house and you have looked everywhere, dad must be right, you must have left it somewhere.'

My mother walked out of the room shaking her head and muttering to herself but nothing more was heard of the missing winter coat. Dad bought her another coat; a brand new one from Stewart's Clothiers of Oldham Road, Miles Platting. The new coat was paid for on the never-never and payment was made to the company's collector who called for the money on a weekly basis, usually on a Saturday.

There was also a man that came round with his horse and cart to sharpen lawn mower blades, garden shears, knives, scissors, chisels etc. His cart was a four wheeled contrivance and was covered with a greased tarpaulin over a steel frame. The tarpaulin was lifted and drawn back to reveal a seat and a big, treadle driven grinding wheel fixed to the floor of the cart. There were numerous oilstones and whetstones fitted into slots on a shelf; they were used for fine honing. On the shelf was an oil can for lubricating the whetstones. In construction the cart was a forerunner of modern tilt trailers albeit a lot smaller and similar to the Western covered wagons that transported the pioneers across America. As Kids we would stand and watch, in amazement, as the sparks flew, like fireworks, from the grinding wheel as the man pushed up and down on the treadle and the wheel went faster and faster and the sparks flew further and further as he honed the household implements to a razor sharp finish. The knife sharpener also mended metal jugs and buckets with threaded contrivances of different sizes and lined with rubber. He would put one piece, rubber facing the hole, to either side of the receptacle to be repaired, a bolt would be threaded through and a nut attached to the other side when tightened it would seal the hole and thus stop any leakage.

There was an elderly, one legged man that lived on Seabrook Road in Newton Heath. Everybody knew him as Peg Leg Pete and he wore a wooden leg with a hollowed out cup at the top, much like the one-legged pirates in the swashbuckling films of the day and he used to peddle bundles of firewood or kindling from door to door. He had lost his leg and I do not mean that he had misplaced and could not find it, no, he had lost his leg during the First World War after being wounded on the Western Front at Verdun. He was invalided out of the forces and after the war he set up his little woodcutting business because he could not find any other kind of gainful employment due to his disability. He had no wish to be a burden on the state and could not live on an army pension and so set up his own little business. He would salvage, or purchase, for the lowest price he could, old pine furniture and any other salvageable timber. He would dismantle the furniture and saw the component parts into lengths of approximately six inches and chop the lengths into kindling which he would bind with baling wire. In his yard, just off Briscoe Lane, he had an old tree stump on which he would saw and chop the wood. To either side of the tree stump were two off-cuts which were used as seats. There were numerous saws and axes and pairs of pliers stored in a shed in his yard. Next to the chopping stump was a small cable drum which held the wire with which he bound the bundles of wood using the pliers to twist and cut the wire. In one corner of the yard was a grinding wheel for sharpening his axes. Peg Leg also had a fixed wheel, specially constructed bicycle which he used to ride from his home to his yard and back, it only had one pedal which was on the left hand side; it looked like a ladies bike with a step through frame and was of the fixed wheel type to facilitate his riding it. Because there was no downward stroke on the right hand side the fixed cog helped the wheel rotate until his left leg reached the apex of its stroke and he could then push down on the only pedal allowing him forward movement. His mounting and dismounting, however, was a more complicated procedure especially if he had removed his wooden stump. The bike had to be leaning against a fence or gatepost to enable him to get on and off and his speed, timing and judgement of distances had to be spot on. Peg leg was fortunate insomuch as the journey to and from his yard was over fairly flat terrain.

For his deliveries Peg Leg Pete had a small two wheeled cart which was pulled by a well cared for donkey which was stabled at his yard along with his cart. He would advertise his presence, when out selling his wares, by ringing a large hand bell and yelling 'Get yur kindlin' here! Firewood for sale, a tanner a bundle!' On Saturday mornings, when we were about seven years old and when we were needed, Pete would employ Cousin Bobby and me to chop the sawn pieces of wood into firewood and bundle and tie them and stack them on his cart ready for delivery. He would pay us one shilling each for our labour. Of course Health and safety would not allow such practises and exploitation of children nowadays, although Bobby and I did not view it as exploitation but rather as a way of earning extra spending money. The axes that we used were sharp enough to take a misplaced finger off with ease and one day that is exactly what I almost did. As Bobby and I were sat on the two logs on opposite sides of the chopping block, working industriously, I brought the axe down too close to the edge of the length of wood that I was working on. The axe struck a knot in the wood which sent the sharpened edge sideways towards where I held the wood. I pulled my finger away, but alas I was too slow and the blade of the axe caught my left index finger at the first knuckle and sliced down to the second knuckle and down to the bone. I dropped the axe, jumped to my feet and ran out of the yard holding my injured hand in my good hand and screaming in pain with Bobby close on my heels. I didn't stop running until I reached home, leaving a trail of blood spots behind me. My mother dressed the wound and my father took me to Ancoats hospital where the laceration was sutured with five stitches and I was given an anti tetanus injection, Bobby came with us to the hospital. That bloody and painful day was also the end of the extra earnings and entrepreneurism for Bobby and me as our parents stopped us chopping wood for Pete ever again, although he soon found other children to perform his cheap labour for him.

Yet other traders that used the humble horse and cart were the milk delivery men from various dairies. Our milk was delivered, in glass bottles by a Co-op milkman and his horse and cart, although the equine power would shortly be replaced by the electric milk float. Our family used the Co-op because we got a dividend on everything that was bought from the Co-operative. A few carters still used horses and carts in the 50's; the railways still had a few horses which were being slowly replaced by the Scammell mechanical horse which was first introduced in the 1930's. A company called Hanson's in Manchester city centre was reputed to be the last carting company to use horses and carts and did so until the mid to late 60's.

As children, we didn't have a lot of proper or expensive toys, just cheap wooden playthings. My father acquired, I know not from where, some steel moulds for the casting and manufacture of lead soldiers from around the Crimean and Peninsula war eras. He obtained a number of those moulds and each mould came in two parts. When the two parts were put together, lined up by way of spigots and reciprocating holes, two grip clips were placed one at each end to keep them firmly together. Each mould made two soldiers and the soldiers were in different poses and positions. There were lancers, riflemen, grenadiers, guardsmen and there were even moulds with which to cast horses and soldiers sat astride their mounts.

Father would bring home, from his place of work, stubs of solder and off cuts and castaway pieces of lead and lead piping. Those pieces of scrap metal he would melt in a ladle on the open fire, (Later he used a small metal pail in a tilting stand, which he fabricated himself at work, he would place the metal stand and pail over one of the gas rings on the stove). The moulds had, at their upper ends, two orifices; one for each soldier and into those orifices was poured the molten lead which would fill the hollow shapes of the figures. Once inside the mould the lead soon cooled and solidified and within a few minutes the grip clips could be removed. My father would then break open the moulds and remove the lead figures. He then lined them up along the hearth until they were cool enough to receive a coat of paint. Sometimes the figures would come out not quite whole and father would return them to the ladle or the pail, re-melt them and try again. When he had produced about ten figurines and they had cooled down he would paint them with Humbrol modelling paint; blue or black trousers with a red stripe, red tunics, green tunics for the riflemen and black bearskins or Busby's for those that wore them. Over time we had built up a regular little army and some of the lead figures my father painted in opposing armies' colours. I spent many a happy hour playing with my little lead soldiers.

War Games

As kids we had all heard of the allies and enemies in the war. We knew of Guy Gibson and the Dambusters. Indeed Bobby and I went to see the film The Dambusters starring Richard Todd as Guy Gibson in 1954. Montgomery was a name we all knew along with The Desert Rats and their opponent in North Africa, Irwin Rommel. Winston Churchill was renowned as the great leader in Britain. We knew that the Americans were our allies and so we had heard of Patton and others. We had heard of the atrocities perpetrated by the Japanese and the Germans, we knew all about Adolph Hitler and his cronies through the rhyme that was doing the rounds at the time which went: *Hitler has only got one ball, Goering has two, but they are small, Himmler has something similar and Goebbels has no balls at all,* and was sung to the tune of Colonel Bogey's March. We had heard the name of Mussolini; knew he was leader of the Italian military but that was all.

The wartime souvenirs that one owned dictated which side one would be on as we played out our war games. We must have put forward an amusing sight with helmets falling over our eyes and chinstraps hanging three or four inches below our chins. We looked more moronic than Teutonic, more dummy than Tommy. Those that owned German helmets and other German relics had to get used to being on the losing side. Our arms, when stretched out to the sides, became the wings of Spitfires' and Hurricanes, whilst others became Messerschmitt's, Junker's, Stuka's, Heinkel's or Fokker's. Wooden bayonets were fixed onto wooden or toy rifles with bits of string, but no one was injured. I always wanted to be the driver supplying ammunition etc; to the troops, driving my imitation army truck which seemed to run on two spindly legs. No one ever seemed to oppose me in that desire.

As children we had few toys to play with but whichever gender one was determined, then as now, what toys one played with. Boy's toys were usually the type of playthings that could be associated with violence or warfare. We had cap guns modelled on the Colt .45 Peacemaker for when we played Cowboys and Indians, for which we also had bows and arrows. Another imitation firearm that we played with at the time was the 'spud gun.' The business end of the 'spud gun' would be forced into the flesh of a potato and then prised out, leaving a pellet of potato in the end of the barrel of the gun. When the trigger was pulled a small blast of air would propel the pellet from the gun towards its intended target; quite safe unless the pellet hit you in the eye. Other imitation weapons of violence that we played with as children were plastic knives with retractable blades which when stabbed into the intended victim, the plastic blade would slide into the hollow handle, giving the appearance that the knife had penetrated the body. Dads bought their lads punch bags and boxing gloves and taught their sons how to look after themselves. As we matured in years air rifles replaced cap guns and spud guns and sheath knives and switchblades replaced plastic knives. Girls, on the other hand, pushed along the streets, prams containing little dolls. Indoors they would dress and undress their little charges or play with cookery sets and other playthings that were allied to future homemaking, no doubt to prepare them for motherhood in the distant future.

To the rear of our prefab was the home of the Rogerson family. The children of the family, both boys, were named Thomas after his father and Terence. They were always well dressed because Thomas senior was a tailor by trade. The Rogerson's stayed in their prefab for another five years after we moved out of ours because they were same sex children. On occasions I travelled to Newton Heath to see them, but lost contact when they eventually moved. There was another friend, Albert Edwards, who lived in the prefabs opposite to the local graveyard on Orford Road. Two doors down from Albert lived the McCullough's who had two sons, Kevin and Barry. Kevin, the youngest, had lost one of his eyes, whether through disease or accident no one seemed to know or dare to ask but it had been replaced with a glass eye.

Kevin never talked about the loss of his organ of sight and he did not seem be bothered about the fact that he only had one eye but he was always threatening to take out the glass orb to scare us all. Sometimes he would wear a pink plastic eye patch with a wad of cotton wool or lint beneath it and other times he would not. I never found out the reason for the occasional patch; perhaps he wore the patch when the glass eye was removed because it became uncomfortable after a while or if it needed a good cleaning. One day Kevin approached me with a maniacal grin on his face, the eyelid of the false eye firmly closed and something obviously clasped tightly in his right hand, he chased me around the garden and the shed and out on to Taylor's Lane. I ran because I didn't want him touching me with his glass eye which I thought was clenched in his right hand and which I perceived to be slimy and horrible. When he eventually caught up with me he opened the closed eyelid to reveal the unseeing eye, he then pushed his clenched fist close up to my face and opened it to reveal.......... a bull's eye marble. We laughed so hard we almost cried although I doubted that the laughter would have brought a tear to Kevin's glass eye.

Just across the road at number six and slightly lower down from our prefab, which was number three Elbain Avenue, lived the Crossdale family who had a son called David, who was friend of mine and a daughter called Barbara who was a friend of my sisters. The Crossdales moved to Blackley, a few years later, but about a mile from Plant Hill where our family moved. We kept in touch for short while but soon found new friends to take their place.

There were many other young friends and acquaintances. We used to play a game, which went by the soubriquet of Black and White Rabbit or sometimes Knock and Run, whereby someone would pinch a reel of cotton from his mother's sewing box. One of the gang would sneak to the front door of a neighbours house and quietly lift the knocker, tie the cotton to it and then lower it back in place and make his way back to where the rest of us were hiding, unreeling the cotton as he made his way to the hiding place.

From our hiding place, usually behind a privet hedge, the cotton would be pulled, thus raising the knocker. The cotton would then be released. This was done three or four times in quick succession, causing the resident to believe someone was knocking at the door. The front door would open and the resident would look up and down the street, see no one and then close the door. The same thing would be re-enacted until, after two or three times the resident would get wise and find the cotton and snap it. Oh, how easily we were entertained in those long ago, innocent days.

There was a second version of that game which entailed one of the gang, picked by losing out at Scissors, Paper, Rock, who would, warily, sneak down the path of the house of choice, lift the knocker manually and slam it down two or three times in rapid succession and run back to where we were hiding. That was the most daring version of the game because if the householder opened the door before our brave champion reached the hiding place he was caught out. The rules of the game dictated that he would not give the rest of us up and if caught he would be marched home to suffer the wrath of his parents alone whilst we, in our hiding place, giggled quietly behind hands, held close to our mouths, at his misfortune. At other times we would all wait at the end of our victim's path whilst one of our gang would go and knock on the door and we would all run away together.

By the side of our prefab was a patch of uncultivated, rough, grassland bordered by an unpaved public footpath known as Taylor's Lane which ran from Seabrook Road and along the side of Christ the King Catholic School's playing fields, up to Culcheth Lane, where on the corner stood a pub which my parents occasionally visited. I cannot remember its proper name but it was and still is known locally as the Soap Box and Taylor-Eagle Brewery beers were sold there. It had a bowling green to its rear where our parents would take us, sometimes, during the summer months and we would be bought a packet of crisps and a glass of lemonade, dandelion and burdock or cream soda whilst they enjoyed their occasional socialising as we sat besides the bowling green watching the older clientele roll their woods towards the Jack. Another place that our parents took us to during the summer time was Brookdale Park. Brookdale is a large municipal park on the borders of Newton Heath and Failsworth. It has a Victorian bandstand and numerous leisure facilities. The park is used by birdwatchers, dog walkers, people out for a leisurely stroll and no doubt, the occasional flasher with his long, beige coloured, gabardine mac. We enjoyed our visits to the park.

Tetlow's Woods and Pond

Further back down Taylor's Lane, quite close to our prefab, was a small woodland which ran part way along Taylor's Lane and then along the other side of Christ the King's playing fields. The lower end of Taylor's Lane ran past the back gardens of the houses on Seabrook Road. The small woods came to an end at a little pond; both were on the land of E.D. Tetlow; the local coal merchant, known to his customers as Eddy. Above the pond standing in its own grounds was Tetlow's house, it was the biggest house I'd ever seen and was officially accessed from a drive off Seabrook Road.

E.D. Tetlow owned a couple of drop side, bonneted, Bedford two tonners for his coal deliveries, they were probably ex war department, petrol powered, vehicles of the WLG models with the side boards removed but the tail boards left in place. Anybody who burned coal in the area, and that was almost everybody, bought it from E.D. Tetlow. Some other coal merchants in the surrounding areas still used horses and carts for delivery purposes. Small businesses such as Tetlow's that only ran within a few miles radius of their yard escaped the Nationalisation of inland transport which was introduced a few years earlier in 1948, by Clement Attlee's Labour Government, 1945-1951, which led to the formation of the nationalised railways and waterways and of British Road Services (BRS), which took in around two hundred and fifty haulage companies.

As children, especially in the summertime, when the dappled sunlight filtered through the foliage and branches of the many trees, casting mottled shadows on the woodlands floor strewn with twigs and mosses, we would play in the small woodlands, climbing trees, and falling out of them, playing hide and seek and other games. We would fish for sticklebacks in Tetlow's pond and catch newts there and carry them home in a jam jar with string tied around it fashioned into a carrying handle. We would remove our shoes and socks and wade into the pond up to our shins looking for various amphibians. Besides the efts there was an abundance of toads and frogs to catch and numerous types of insects like the daddy longlegs, the water boatman and iridescent dragonflies. Earlier in the year we would gather frog spawn and take it home and watch the tadpoles emerge and gradually change into frogs. E.D. Tetlow, or others members of his family, as I remember, regularly chased us off their property. Although we knew we should not have been there, we were not causing harm or damage of any kind. We were just kids of our time, doing what kids did.

Our family purchased coal off Eddy Tetlow, as did my Gran, but to a young family it was very expensive and so my father occasionally bought a bag of coke from the Bradford Gasworks at the bottom of Briscoe Lane, for a few pence a bag, to eke out our coal supply. Bradford Gasworks, which was nationalised, with all other gasworks, in 1948, was fed from the coal from Bradford, Clayton and Moston Collieries. My father would balance the sack of coke, which was sealed at both ends, over the cross bar of his fixed wheel bicycle and because it was almost impossible to ride whilst balancing the coke, he would push it home. That was a somewhat awkward task because of the fact that the bicycle was of the fixed wheel type and for every revolution of the rear wheel the pedals also completed one revolution. If my father was not careful the pedals would catch the back of his leg, causing him to stumble or fall and I am sure that, at least, on one occasion my father suffered from that problem. He came home one day and after depositing his bike and the coke in the shed he walked into the prefab. The knees in his trousers were ripped and the bloody skin beneath could be seen through the tear. He changed into something more comfortable and my mother cleaned and dressed his minor injuries with antiseptic balm and band aids and then repaired his pants by patching them before we sat down to our evening meal.

Coke was a by product of coal from which the gas had been extracted and it burned very hot. Coal was used to produce gas by removing the volatile constituents including water, coal gas and coal tar by baking in an airless oven at temperatures as high as 1,000 degrees Celsius, thus producing coke which was silvery grey in colour, hard and porous. When burnt in a domestic fireplace it would leave big clinkers in the fire grate, which had to be raked out when the fire had gone out and prior to re-lighting.

Coke was approximately half the weight or less than coal by volume and it was the first smokeless fuel. The other alternative was to burn coal bricks which were made of coal dust mixed with cement and bound together with water, moulded into a brick shape and then dried. There was also coal eggs which I presume were made of the same constituents and moulded into the ovoid shape and dried in the same way. They were crap but poorer people had no alternative because they were cheap. Those bricks and eggs also left big clinkers in the fire grate. It wasn't long, or so I heard, before Tetlow tendered for the coke rights from the Gasworks and although it was cheaper than coal he held the monopoly and charged a premium rate for it.

In those days when every household burnt solid fuel, the residual deposits from the fireplace had to be raked out and deposited in the galvanised steel dustbin to be carted away by the dust cart. The dustbin men (some people still called them the midden men) came around once a week to collect the household rubbish and up to fifty per cent of the household rubbish was ash and clinkers from the fireplace. The dustbin men would walk down the path of the household, hoist that heavy steel bin to his shoulders and carry it to the dust cart where he would tip the contents into the cart and then carry the empty bin back down to where the bin was stored and put it back in its rightful position. Not like the bin men of today who do not have to lift anything and do not even tote the wheeled, plastic bins to the footpath. The bins are emptied by way of a hydraulic lifting mechanism and then the bin men deposit them on the pavement anything up to twenty five yards from the household from where they were collected.

The Bookie and the Runner

Granny Annie Hampson, who looked after Bobby, Val and me when required, had liked a flutter on the horses when her husband George was alive and this minor gambling addiction continued after his death and after a couple of years it was Bobby and I who were sent to place her bets and, very occasionally, pick up her winnings. Her stake was always a tanner (6d or 2 ½p), each way and usually on long odds. There were no legal bookmakers, except on the racecourses, until Harold McMillan's Conservative government legalised bookmaking on May 1st 1961. After gambling was made legal, bookies opened up at the rate of one hundred per week to accommodate those that liked a little flutter.

Prior to the gaming act illegal bookmaking flourished in pubs and various other establishments and those Bookmakers had no compunction about taking money from minors such as Bobby and me, aged six or seven. The Bookie that my grandmother used was situated in the back entry behind the Phoenix pub, on Briscoe Lane. He operated from a garden shed which had been erected against the fence at the top of his back garden, a hole had been cut into the fence directly opposite the window in the shed to enable bets to be passed through the aperture, from the back entry and through the shed window and into the Bookies hand. The hole in the fence, when closed, was disguised by way of a shutter or some other contrivance to make it less obvious what it was used for. Once the bet was placed the Bookie would then issue the punter with a betting slip stating all the relevant information; the odds given, the name of the horse, the time of the race and the stake placed, etc.

The Bookmaker would employ a person known as a Bookie's runner who would drum up business for the bookie by taking bets in the local pubs where the landlord's of those pubs would turn a blind eye and maybe even have a bet themselves. Bets would be taken on street corners or any other place of convenience. The runner would issue betting slips and then take the bets and stakes to the Bookie. He also served as a lookout for the Bookie and would warn of the approach of the police. At times the runner was expected to divert the law enforcement officers away from the Bookie's clandestine and illegal activities by running away from or distracting the officers by some means of duplicity. This could lead to the bookie's assistant occasionally being apprehended, arrested, charged and prosecuted and if the worst came to the worst the Bookie would pay the fine for his man. It was for these reasons that the bookie changed his runner on a regular basis. He did not want him to become known to the local constabulary.

Bobby and I quite often watched the actions of the runner in his efforts to divert Mr Plod away from the illicit and prohibited turf accountant's affairs. Those shenanigans gave us cause for a great deal of amusement. Often, the runner would have a bicycle which he would mount and pedal away with the law enforcement officers in hot pursuit. If he drew too far away from the cops he would slow down to tempt them and give them false hope of catching him, he would then pedal away again, thus avoiding capture and allowing time for the bookie to secrete away his bookmaking equipment and paraphernalia and close up shop. On those occasions the long arm of the law probably wished its arms were just a little longer, although not all chases ended in failure for the police.

One time, after slowing down and allowing the police to get within striking distance, the runner missed his footing as he attempted to reach the pedals of his bicycle. As he endeavoured to evade capture, he swerved from side to side as he tried to avoid running into the shoppers and other pedestrians who in turn attempted to dodge away from the wayward cyclist. The out of control runner/cyclist then wobbled as he tried to control his steed. Complete loss of balance was inevitable and he fell to the ground with the bicycle on top of him and his legs entangled in the machine. Various denominations of coinage fell from the runner's pockets and his bag and rolled in all directions. Before he could extricate himself from the encumbrances of the crossbar, pedals, wheels and chain the policemen were upon him, truncheons at the ready and he was quickly seized. His face was pushed onto the pavement, distorting his features and his arms were pulled around his back and handcuffs placed upon his wrists. He was arrested by the boys in blue and marched away. What coins could be found were picked up by one of the policemen and when they had left the scene Bobby and I searched for more but only found a couple of pennies. We were very fortunate, however, never to be caught placing those little, illicit, monetary stakes for our grandmother. Whether the bookmaker had to make good any bets taken by the runner before his arrest, I do not know.

The Coalmen and the Householder

I remember, when I was about seven years old, going round to call for a friend, one cold, snowy winter's day, just as Tetlow's coalmen had delivered two hundredweights of nutty slack to his house. That friend, whom I was calling for to play out, was Raymond Wood; he was in the same class as me and he lived on Ascot Road, Newton Heath. Ascot Road ran parallel with Rosebank Road and Ray's house, like most of the houses on Ascot Road had a cellar. Outside the front door of his house was the round, cast iron cover over the external entry to the cellar. The hole beneath the cast iron cover was known as the drop. The cast iron cover was removed and the coal was tipped or 'dropped' down the hole and into the basement. As I arrived to call for Ray, his mother was at the front door arguing with the coalmen about payment. Voices were raised on both sides as each party attempted to give credence to their argument. I stayed out of sight and watched and listened as the quarrel progressed. Mrs Wood did not have the money to pay for the coal until the weekend. Tetlow's men would hear none of it; if she could not pay there and then the coal would be recovered. Mrs Wood pleaded and begged them to leave the coal and told them that her husband would be around to pay for it on the Friday when he received his pay.

Whether it was E.D. Tetlow's policy to exact payment immediately or to refuse credit, or whether his men did what they did of their own volition, I don't know. Most traders, whether it was the never, never man or the man from the newsagents or the coalman had a collector man who went around on Friday evenings to collect any outstanding payments. Whether they had experienced difficulty getting payment from Mrs Wood in the past, I don't know, but without further ado one of the coalmen removed his leather back protector and climbed down into the subterranean vault. His mate passed him down a shovel. Shovelsful of coal began flying upwards through the hole and the second man, with another shovel, started re-filling the sacks which had previously bore the coal that was now being returned.

Once the sacks were full they were placed onto the scales on the flat bed of the Bedford lorry. Every coal truck or cart carried scales and coal weights of 28lb or 56lb; I believe it was a legal requirement. The sacks of coal were weighed to ensure that not an ounce more than there should be had been taken. The man in the cellar handed back his shovel to his workmate and then climbed back up to ground level and donned his back protector. Mrs Wood was, by then, on her knees, in the snow, her pinafore held to her face, dabbing at the tears that were streaming down her cheeks in rivulets. Her slight frame shivered and shuddered as she pleaded, in a tremulous voice that was full of desperation, with the coalmen, to leave her the wherewithal to heat her humble abode. At one point she let go of her pinafore and gripped one of the coalmen's legs as she pleaded. He tried to take a step away but the poor, unfortunate woman was dragged along, clearing a path in the snow as she was pulled through it. It wasn't until the coalman forcibly removed her hands that he could make his way to the coal truck and make good his escape, leaving the distraught woman kneeling on her snow covered path, crying. From my place of concealment I had witnessed enough; all thoughts of asking Mrs Wood if Raymond could come out to play on that cold winter's day were banished from my mind and I turned around and walked back home. I never mentioned what I had witnessed to Raymond.

Horse Manure, Fruit & Veg and Immigrants

Times were hard and things such as coal were precious commodities and any nuggets of the black, carbonaceous rock that fell from the coalman's truck were soon snapped up by the householders. The men of the poorest of families would walk along the railroad tracks in search of coal. Likewise any dung that was deposited on the roads by the workhorses that pulled the rag and bone man's, the ice-cream man's and the knife sharpener's carts was soon shovelled up to be used as manure on vegetable plots in people's back gardens or carried to gardener's allotments. It was a case of first come first served with the horse droppings and the first person out into the street with a bucket and shovel won the treasured but malodorous prize. Of course, those that lived in the back to back terraced houses and who had no gardens to speak of missed out on the benefits of horse manure and indeed, missed out on the whole concept of growing their own vegetables which, of course, led to them having to pay out more of their weekly pittance to feed their families.

Those people that had the means and the wherewithal, in those frugal, post war days grew as many vegetables as they could to save on the expense of buying what were rare and expensive commodities and the horse manure was a smelly, graveolent, but free method of ensuring a fine crop of edible leaves, fruit and tubers. Greengrocers survived, however, because people could not grow enough to feed the large families of the day. There were also new types of foods coming into the shops. Before the war not many people had seen or tasted a banana or some of the other more exotic fruits and vegetables that were coming on the market such as pineapples, melons, yams and sweet potatoes, etc, and during the war and after, there was a positive dearth of those fruits and vegetables. Besides vegetables, those that had the room, also kept a couple of chickens and I remember my father telling me of one household that kept a large sow. They only kept it until it had reached the correct size and weight to go under the butchers knife and then certain joints of pork were given in payment of debts and others were shared amongst the family. Not much was wasted.

The strange, exotic, foreign foods arrived, and not by mere coincidence, with the influx of people from the Caribbean and other far flung countries who came over to the British Isles in the early 1950's to fill the many jobs which were left vacant due to the ravages of the recently past conflict. The working class had been decimated because most of the fighting Tommy's were from that class of people, once again deemed expendable so that our great country could survive. A great many of those people who came from British protectorates and other parts of the old empire around the world were willing to do some jobs that were considered menial or below that which an Englishman would consider and so those immigrants were a massive benefit to a post war Britain that had lost a generation to conflict. Of course Britain, at the time had people heading for a new life in places such as Australia or New Zealand where one could go as emigrants from Britain via the ten pound passage and become known as Ten Pound Poms. Other countries that English people emigrated to were Canada or the USA and the balance between émigrés and immigrants would be balanced.

Jamaicans, Trinidadians, Barbadians and those from the Sub Continent took jobs on the buses and on the railways; they took lowly paid and mundane labouring jobs. Britain was not then the cosmopolitan melting pot that it has since become but new fruits and vegetables and the curries from the Asian continent added to our somewhat, bland diets of the day. Pakistanis and Indians opened or took over corner shops, Indians and Chinese opened restaurants adding more to the multi-culturism. There was, however a hard core section of people who were against those newcomers to our generally, tolerant country and that intolerance is still very noticeable today with the advent of the skinhead culture and the BNP. Britain itself is a country of immigrants since we were invaded by the Vikings or Norsemen, the Saxons and Angles from Northern Germany and Southern Denmark and later the Romans. The French invaded in 1066. Some Spanish people settled here. It is hard to believe that there is such a thing as a definitive Englishman. The problem that arose with the immigration after the Second World War was one of colour. Never before had Great Britain seen such an influx of coloured people and it seemed that a lot of Briton's could not come to terms with or understand it.

Those immigrants from India and Pakistan and the West Indies had been granted British Citizenship via The Nationality Act of the 30th of July 1948. The modern state of Pakistan, officially The Islamic Republic of Pakistan came into being on August 14th 1947, when Muslims of the Sub Continent gained their independence from British rule. Their leader was Quaid E Azam Muhammad Ali Jinna, the recognised founder of Pakistan. From 1947-1956 Pakistan was a Dominion in the then Commonwealth of Nations. It became a republic in 1956 and has had numerous leaders since then. Pakistan split into two separate entities, on opposite sides of the sub continent, in 1947 becoming East Pakistan and West Pakistan. In 1971 East Pakistan became known as Bangladesh. It was from Pakistan, amongst other countries, that we accepted numerous émigrés into Great Britain. Indians, Pakistanis, Barbadians, Trinidadians and many more from the West Indies came for a new life in Great Britain.

It is a different story today with the opening of the European borders, we have Czechs, Poles, Albanians, Hungarians, Bulgarians and various other East Europeans including those from the ex communist countries. On top of those we also have emigrants from a lot of the African Countries such as Somalia, Ethiopia, Sudan, Kenya where civil wars and famine are rife. Those from the Middle Eastern countries who come over here to benefit from our education system and that come from some of the Muslim states that have no freedom of speech in their own countries, where women are banned from education and treated as second class citizens and are occasionally stoned to death for what we would consider to be minor offences. Some of those aforementioned people are so committed to peace and integration in their new country that they will demonstrate and call for the beheading of the British Infidels in our own country.

I, personally, welcome those that come here to work and pay their taxes. The Polish people have some of the best trade's people around and will work hard in their adopted country, as will a lot of other East Europeans, but there seems to be some who come to this country because they see it as an easy touch, which sadly it is. These people, from various places around the world, do not understand the concept of *'When in Rome do as The Romans do.'* They ignore our culture and customs and set up their own ghetto's where some can live on the money the state hands out to them whilst they live in the houses provided for them by the state. Some of these people cannot even be bothered to learn the language of the country that they so desire to live in. It has been shown in the newspapers that we have allowed, into this once great country of ours, convicted murderers, rapists, pimps, people traffickers and drug peddlers. Is it any wonder that the average Briton is fed up to the high teeth of the way consecutive governments handle the situation? Consecutive governments are now run by nothing more than a bunch of career politicians who accept free junkets to foreign climes and make the most of the expenses available to them so much so that it borders on criminality. The politicians, it seems, are in the job only for what they can get out of it and bugger the electorate. There is no longer any philanthropy associated with politicians and it has become a case of *'do as I say, not as I do,'* with our elected political ministers. It seems to me that there may be one or two Member's of Parliament who are there for the good of the country and their fellow man, but it appears that they are in the minority.

Chapter 3

HOSPITALS, CINEMAS, TELEVISION AND A BRUSH WITH DEATH.

My last days of Nursery School

At the age of five I had moved up from the nursery school, which I had attended since I was three years old and was enrolled into Briscoe Lane Primary School. Cousin Bobby and I were in the same class. I have only scratchy recollections of attending the nursery which was, generally, a place where working mums dropped their offspring while they went to whatever occupation they worked at. However there is one incident that sticks in my mind before my move to the primary school. I recall being sat, with others, on a summer's day, on benches in the nursery school when everybody held their noses and people were saying things such as pooh, smelly pants, cacky kecks and the like. The female nursery attendant walked amongst us asking 'Has someone had an accident?' I slid along the bench, to disassociate myself from the little boy that I had been sat next to who had fouled himself to no small amount and who as a consequence, stank to high heaven.

His mother, before going to her part-time job as a cleaner or waitress or whatever it was she did to earn a few extra shillings to keep the wolf from the door, had dropped him off at the nursery in his little short, grey flannel pants, shirt, grey woollen socks and sandals; he was supposedly toilet trained, as were the rest of us and so without a diaper in place. He was found out; he had committed the ultimate childhood error; he had shit himself and he immediately burst into tears as the attendant gripped his hand and marched him to the toilets to try to rectify his mistake and to clean him up prior to contacting one of his relatives to take him home. I can still remember him walking away towards the toilets, holding the attendants hand, ambling with that rather strange gait with which a child perambulates after such a mishap and with watery brown sludge trickling down his legs to his socks.

Education and erudition were limited at nursery school. Rather, we played games and listened to and recited nursery rhymes. There was one about a rather rotund chap who fell off a wall and broke himself to pieces and another about three mice that were already blind and had to suffer the further indignity of having their tails chopped off by a farmer's wife. There were other tales of cruelty such as the four and twenty blackbirds that were baked alive, in a pie, for the king. There was a nursery rhyme of the plague (ring-a-ring o'roses) and rhymes about poverty and penury like Old Mother Hubbard and the Old Woman who was very prolific in childbirth and lived in a shoe. There were rhymes about personal injury such as Jack and Jill and many more dire ditties. Did children's pleasure and enjoyment know no bounds?

Children's minds are considered to be not fully developed, especially infants, but even I realised how stupid and ridiculous the rhymes were. Cat's and fiddles, cows capable of jumping over the moon, dishes running away with spoons, all nonsense lyrics which made no sense because their roots were never explained to young children. Those lyrics, I later learned, had their basis in English, mediaeval history and were used to parody royalty and the parliament of the day where direct dissent may have been punishable by death. Nursery rhymes are OK but their origins should be taught alongside the rhymes.

A Nasty Burn and Scarlet Fever

The move to the primary school was a very welcome change to me, insomuch as I could escape those tales of innate cruelty and poverty. I had been at the primary school for just over a year when I suffered quite a serious accident whereby I suffered burns to my left leg which caused me a lot of pain and anguish and gained me admission to the burns unit in Ancoats Hospital.

That misfortune befell me one morning after my father had left for work. He had lit the fire to warm up the prefab before he left. The fire was an open coal fire and the device used to light it was a gas poker; this was a hollow steel tube with holes drilled into its lower quarter. The hollow, metal pipe was attached to the gas outlet by way of a brightly coloured orange, rubber tube secured to the gas poker via a jubilee clip. A jubilee clip also held the bright, orange, rubber tube to the gas outlet by the side of the hearth. My father made the gas poker; he also made them for other people. He also made ordinary pokers with which to prod and poke the coals within the fireplace. He sold these implements, which he made at work in his spare time from materials and off cuts, to supplement his wages.

When the gas was turned on at the outlet, by way of a tap, the pungent smelling, highly inflammable coal gas made its way down the rubber tube to issue from the holes in the poker where it was ignited by way of a match and flames then took the place of the gas which emitted from the holes. The lighted gas poker was then inserted beneath the coals and kindling made from rolled up newspaper within the fireplace and it would quickly ensure a blazing fire within the fire grate.

On that morning before he left for work my father took my mother a cup of tea and made sure that she was awake; he then returned to the living room and turned off the gas poker and laid it in the hearth to cool down. The coals and kindling within the grate burnt with intensity, the fossil fuel in the fire hissed and spat as the multi coloured fingers of flame reached upwards and were drawn into the chimney. Father put the fireguard in front of the open fire and then he donned his coat, picked up his haversack which contained his sandwiches and departed, believing that he had done everything in the name of safety.

The slamming of the back door and the noise as he took his bike from the shed as my father left for work awoke me and I arose before my mum or sister and went through the living room and into the kitchen where I took a bowl from one of the cupboards. I then took a box of Bird's Grape Nuts from the food cupboard and poured a helping into the bowl. Grape Nuts were the preferred, healthy, breakfast cereal in our household in those days. Next, I opened the fridge and took out the ice cold milk which I poured over the Grape Nuts. I replaced the milk in the fridge, took a spoon from the draw and wandered back into the living room with my breakfast. Father had left the radio on and I sat on the floor in front of the fire to listen to it. My legs were stretched out in front of me and onto the hearth. At the time I was still a little sleepy-eyed and not quite aware and in my drowsy state I didn't realise, that the bottom of one of my pyjamas legs had come to rest over the still hot gas poker which was on the outside of the fireguard. I sat there entranced by the movements of the flames and the smoke, imagining strange animals and other weird, bizarre and grotesque beings prancing and dancing within the swaying, flickering red, orange, blue and yellow tongues of fire. Mesmerised and enchanted by the wavering movements within the fireplace I failed to notice the left leg of my pyjamas smouldering before it burst into flames. The sudden outbreak of flame shook me from my reverie and caused me to leap to my feet. Grape Nuts, milk and the spoon and cereal bowl flew into the air. The bowl tumbled to the floor where it smashed into numerous pieces, milk and cereal littered the floor and the ensuing screams of terror and pain, as I slapped at the burning material, brought my mum dashing from the bedroom. She found me jumping up and down and waving my arms about frantically, with the left leg of my pyjamas ablaze and my agitated movements serving only to fan the flames. She immediately grabbed a coat from the back of the door and wrapped it quickly around my lower half to smother the flames. If it hadn't have been for my mother's quick thinking that morning, Things could have been a lot worse for me.

My sister, by this time, and after hearing the shouting and screaming, had come into the room. She stood there; mouth agape and eyes wide open in shock. My mother, although desperately worried stayed cool and calm and she sent Valerie next door for assistance. She ran, still in her pyjamas, to the next door neighbour's to inform him of what had transpired and in those long ago days, long before mobile phones and when only the rich and well off could afford telephones in their homes, the neighbour ran the two hundred yards to the nearest public telephone box to call an ambulance. My mum, meanwhile, had carried me into the kitchen where she sat me on the wooden draining board as she turned the cold water tap on. She tore the charred pyjama leg and held it above my knee. The cool water cascaded onto the burnt area of my limb which stretched from knee to ankle and which my mum held under the faucet. The running water eased the pain a little, but I continued to scream and shout hysterically. My father, after my accident, fabricated a holder in which the hot gas poker could be placed so that it would no longer compromise safety, something like locking the stable door after the horse has bolted.

An ambulance arrived within a few minutes and I was laid on a stretcher and put into the rear of the vehicle and taken, still in hysterics and crying loudly, to the local hospital at Ancoats where my burns were assessed and treated and I was allocated a bed. The bed had a metal frame under the covers and over my legs so that I wouldn't feel the pressure of the blankets upon my burns. The burns were covered in a gauze which itself was impregnated with a foul, yellow, stinking balm. The balm was most efficacious, as it happens and because of the impregnated gauze the need for skin grafts was avoided. I was given an injection and some pain relief; I don't know what was in the injection that was administered or what the pain relief consisted of but within minutes of receiving both types of medication I was quickly embraced in the arms of Morpheus; sound asleep and feeling no pain.

The following day I heard the doctor who treated me and who had a rather stentorian voice, state to my mother that skin grafts may be necessary and that the donor site would most probably be my buttocks and that slivers of donor flesh would be peeled from my bum and adhered to the burn site. He said those things using rather more technical jargon, but I got the picture. I am really grateful that the smelly gauze had such curative qualities as, despite the analgesic medication that I was given, I still suffered a great deal of pain from the burned area of my leg and I had no requirement for pain from my posterior at the same time. That coupled with the fact that I would not be able to sit or lie on the donor site was a little off putting, even to someone of such a tender age, standing all day did not seem to be the answer to me.

After some time in Ancoats Hospital and when I was well on the road to recovery and looking forward to be being sent home and even looking forward to my return to school, because my burns were almost healed, although still rather raw and tender I contracted Scarlet Fever. My throat was sore, my speech was hoarse and my tongue developed a white coating which peeled off leaving it looking like a strawberry as it turned a bright red, I developed flu like symptoms with nausea and vomiting and developed an all over red rash. After the diagnosis I was removed from my bed, placed on a trolley and taken to an ambulance in which I was transferred from Ancoats Hospital to Monsall Isolation Hospital, approximately one and a half miles away.

The cell or chamber, within Monsall Hospital, in which I was incarcerated, was an isolation room with a large viewing window. The large viewing window was there by reason of the fact that I could not receive visitors due to the highly contagious nature of the disease. So when my family came to visit, they looked through the window and waved and gestured to me. I can especially remember my aunty Annie tapping on the window and saying 'Coo-ee our Laurie, it's your aunty Annie.' As if I didn't know who she was. Family members pointed at me and waved; I felt like a monkey in a cage or some kind of sideshow attraction, 'Roll up, roll up, come and see the world famous red boy,' 'Look but do not touch.' There may as well have been a sign on the door saying 'Please, do not feed the animals.'

Scarlet fever or Scarlatina as it is also known, is caused by the streptococcus bacterium and develops only in people who are susceptible to the toxin produced in the body by the streptococci bacteria. I had become quite susceptible due to the fact that my resistance was at an all time low and I was totally run down by the after effects of being quite seriously burnt. It is, typically, a childhood disease but it can also occur in adults. If the disease is not treated quickly it can attack the vital organs; liver, kidneys, heart and arteries. Complications include pneumonia, throat abscesses, meningitis, blood poisoning and toxic shock syndrome. It is normally treated with antibiotics, particularly, at that time, with penicillin.

Penicillin was the antibiotic of choice and it was with that drug that I was initially treated. It was when the penicillin was administered to the debilitated and weakened, bed ridden child that I had become that the fact that my body was intolerant to it was discovered. I suffered an allergic reaction that caused alarm within the hospital. I went dizzy, sweated profusely, felt nauseous, wheezed and suffered difficulty in breathing and I closed my eyes and fell backwards into my pillow as I drifted into unconsciousness, my face the colour of china clay.

That little episode caused quite a bit of panic and confusion; my mother became alarmed and was blurting out questions, which at the immediate time, went unanswered. Consultants, specialists and all manner of medical experts ran around and consulted with one another in an attempt to find some drug or other that would set me on the road to recovery. A drug was found to counteract the effects of the penicillin, I believe it was a form of anti-histamine, and then I was treated with another antibiotic called erythromycin to lessen the effects of the Scarlet fever and after a couple of weeks, I left Monsall Hospital, to return home, a much better, fitter and less red child.

These early memories are somewhat fragmented due to the passage of time, but they are as I remember them.

Our First Television

Not long after my discharge from Monsall Isolation Unit and while I was still not fit enough to re-commence my school attendance, some time in 1952, my father purchased our first television. My mother had been granted unpaid leave from her job at the Steam laundry in Newton Heath and was at home tending to my needs when there was a knock on the front door; she went to answer the knocking and gave entrance to a man carrying, what to a young boy, was a large box. He opened the box, pulled out all the supplementary packaging and lifted out the Pye television set which had a fourteen inch screen. His job was to deliver, install and make sure the set was in fine working order before he left. We had had an outside 'H' shaped aerial fitted to the chimney the week prior to the delivery of the TV, by the same company from whom we had purchased the set.

The casing for the TV was made of a hard, brittle, mottled brown plastic known as Bakelite named after its inventor Leo Baekeland (1863-1944), a Belgian Scientist and inventor who first made Bakelite in 1907 from phenol and formaldehyde. Bakelite was the first commercially viable plastic and it seemed that it was used for most domestic appliances in the 1950's such as the outer casings for radios and TV's, Knife handles, combs and telephones. It was also used in the manufacture of paints and varnishes and as an insulator as on electric plugs and anywhere that a hard plastic, impervious to heat could be used. The only plastic available before Bakelite was celluloid which was not a very viable product; it easily caught fire, it melted at low temperatures and it cracked easily, its fragility was its downfall, although it had been used to make shirt fronts and detachable collars and cuffs.

After its removal from its packaging the television was fitted with a thirteen amp, Bakelite plug by the deliveryman. It was then placed on a table in a corner close to where the aerial wire came through the wall and which my mother had positioned in such a location that it was possible to view the set from anywhere in the room except from behind. The fitter/ deliveryman then plugged it into the mains socket and switched the set on and inserted the aerial wire; of course in those days of valves and cathode ray tubes it took about five minutes for the set to warm up.

Once the valves and the tube had reached their operating temperature the screen was completely filled with frenetically furious, trembling horizontal and zigzag, black and white lines. The installation man then commenced to twiddle with the buttons at the rear of the goggle box; there was the horizontal hold, the vertical hold and the contrast button which he turned slowly backwards and forwards like a safecracker trying to open a vault. As he fiddled he related to my mother that once the television was set up it was just a matter of turning it on and waiting for it to warm up and it should spring into life, but if the frenetic lines reappeared it was a simple procedure to disperse them and achieve a clear picture.

Mother and I waited in anticipation and with eager expectation when, all of a sudden, in glorious black and white and various shades of grey a clear picture came into view. The first program I ever saw on our own television was Rag, Tag, and Bobtail, one of the tales of Watch with Mother, which, as it happens on that day, is exactly what I was doing for the first time. Other programs in the Watch with Mother Series were Andy Pandy with Looby Loo and Teddy, The Woodentops, Bill and Ben the Flowerpot Men and Picture Book which was introduced by Patricia Driscoll who also played Maid Marian to Richard Greene's Robin Hood in the TV series. On all of those shows, except Robin Hood of course, one could see the strings that operated the puppets quite clearly. Watch with Mother was a follow on program from the radio show Listen with Mother and was the first television program aimed at educating and entertaining very young children. Television sets in Britain, at the time, could only receive BBC and it was not until late 1955 that commercial television became available.

Another children's television programme of the time was a fortnightly, Saturday afternoon show called Whirligig which featured Francis Coudrill with puppets Hank and Mexican Pete the Bandit. The show was introduced by Humphrey Lestoq with a puppet by the name of Mr Turnip and also featured a young Rolf Harris. Whirligig alternated with a show called Telescope and later Saturday Special introduced by Peter Butterworth. In 1953 Harry Corbett debuted on Saturday Special with his glove puppet Sooty. He was an immediate hit and introduced another puppet called Sweep, a dog with a sausage fetish; they became regulars on the programme. Other children's escapism came in the form of an equine marionette named Muffin the Mule and all his friends introduced by the late Annette Mills, sister of John Mills the actor. I also remember a show introduced by Michael Bentine which featured puppets known as the Bumblies. There was also Mick and Montmorency starring Jack Edwardes and the diminutive Charlie Drake who went on to star in his own show, The Worker. There was Mr Pastry starring Richard Hearne and shows such as Crackerjack that allowed youngsters on stage to compete for prizes whilst appearing on television. The kids of the day even had their own talent show, introduced by Huw Wheldon and called 'All Your Own' which ran from 1952 until 1961 in which talented and sometimes not so talented children demonstrated their skills in a range of activities. Billy Bunter based on the Frank Richards stories was a show that ran from the early 50's to the early 60's. The series starred Gerald Campion as the Fat Owl of the Remove at Greyfriars School where the headmaster was a Mr Quelch. Gerald Campion was twenty nine years old when he first played the young Billy Bunter and almost forty years of age when he finally gave up the role. Johnny Morris was another children's entertainer who had his own show 'The Hot Chestnut Man', whereby he told stories from behind a hot chestnut barrow, it ran from 1953 until 1963. There were many, many more children's shows of the day; some that ran for years but too many to mention here.

When he had finished adjusting and setting up the television, the deliveryman cum fitter then asked my mother to sign the consignment note for the delivery, which she did and also gave him a few pence as a gratuity. He thanked her graciously wished us goodbye and was gone. Oh what joy to have our own 'idiot's lantern' on which to watch our favourite programs, no more begging the neighbour's if we would be allowed into their houses to watch their televisions. A few days after the delivery of the 'goggle-box,' I was recovered and fit enough to return to my primary school education.

At the time I did not realise how lucky I was to be receiving an education. It was only a few decades earlier that education was something only the wealthy and privileged received. To educate the masses may have sown the seeds of anarchy so the working class was once again subjugated by the rich. It was only the advent of the ragged schools and later the education act that allowed for working class children to receive what should have been a basic right for all.

My favourite programs on the television during those innocent days of the early 50's to the mid 60's were the westerns of the day; The Lone Ranger, starring Clayton Moore and Jay Silverheels as the Ranger and Tonto respectively was a series about the sole survivor of an ambushed troop of Texas Rangers. He was found and nursed back to health by Tonto, a Native American who became his sidekick. He adopted the mask as a disguise as he hunted down his ambushers and any other wrongdoers. He used silver bullets in his six guns. The Lone Ranger's Horse was called

Silver and Tonto's horse was Scout. The theme tune to the series was Rossini's William Tell Overture and the Ranger's catchphrase was 'Hi, Oh Silver, away.' At the end of each episode, as the Ranger and Tonto rode away into the sunset someone in the cast would ask 'Who was that masked man?'

Clayton Moore was dropped for one season of the Lone Ranger over a supposed argument about pay. The part was taken over, for that one season, by an established actor called John Hart who later went on to play Nat 'Hawkeye' Cutler in the 1950's television show *Hawkeye and the Last of the Mohicans*. The show was loosely based on James Fennimore Cooper's series of novels known as the Leatherstocking tales which includes *The last of the Mohicans, The Deerslayer* and *The Pathfinder*. The hero of the books was Hawkeye whose given name was Natty Bumppo. John Hart's co star in the TV series was Lon Chaney Jnr who played Chingachgook a Mohican chieftain. Clayton Moore was later re-established into the role of The Lone Ranger and one presumes that the pay dispute was settled.

The Range Rider starring six feet four inches tall Jack or Jock Mahoney as the eponymous hero and Dick Jones as his trusty sidekick Dick West was a favourite of mine. The series was first aired in 1951. The Range Rider's horse was named Rawhide and Dick's was called Lucky. The Range Rider wore fringed buckskins and moccasins and a white Stetson and was deadly accurate with his six shooter revolver. His sidekick Dick dressed in black. The theme tune to the show was 'Home, Home on the Range, where the deer and the antelope play.' Born Jacques O'Mahoney he was of French, Irish and Cherokee descent, he died in 1989 age seventy.

The Cisco Kid, a character devised by the American author O. Henry in his collection of short stories entitled 'Heart of the West,' in a story called 'The Caballero's Way,' published in 1907, was played by Duncan Renaldo and his partner Pancho was played by Leo Carillo. The horse that Cisco rode was Diabolo and Pancho's horse was named Loco. The pair operated like latter day Robin Hood type characters and were classed as outlaws but they were always on the side of the downtrodden. They dressed in rhinestone studded or embroidered attire and wore broad brimmed sombreros. In O. Henry's original story Cisco was a non Hispanic, cruel outlaw.

There was a number of western series on evening television during the mid to late 50's and early 60's such as Wagon Train which told the tales of the early pioneers crossing America from Missouri to Sacramento, California to claim land in the west. It starred Ward Bond as Major Adams the Wagonmaster and Robert Horton as the scout, Flint McCullough. Each episode was the story of one of the travellers with the train. After Ward Bond's death John McIntyre took over as the Wagonmaster, Christopher Hale and when Robert Horton left the show Robert Fuller, who had starred in Laramie, became the wagon train's scout under the guise of Cooper Smith. Throughout the series the cook, Charlie Wooster was played by Frank McGrath.

Gun Law starring James Arness as Marshall Matt Dillon and Dennis Weaver as Chester Goode was originally entitled Gunsmoke in America. It was as I remember set in Dodge City. It featured The Long Branch saloon, owned and run by Miss Kitty Russell, played by Amanda Blake. Burt Reynolds was also featured in a number of episodes from 1962-1965 as the half caste indian blacksmith Quint Asper. Gunsmoke originally aired, with a different cast, on American radio, with William Conrad playing the part of Matt Dillon. Conrad later had his own TV detective show called Cannon.

The Restless Gun starred John Payne as a wandering cowhand/gunslinger and ran for 78 shows, it was shot in black and white and ran between the years 1957-59. Payne played the main character who went by the name of Vint Bonner. The show was based on an earlier radio show called The Six Shooter starring James Stewart and was produced by David Dortort who went on to produce Bonanza starring Lorne Green as Ben Cartwright the patriarch of the Cartwright family who owned a massive ranch called the Ponderosa. Ben had three sons, Adam played by Pernell Roberts, Eric (Hoss), played by Dan Blocker and Little Joe played by Michael Landon.

Rawhide (1959) was a series about cattle drives across America from San Antonio in Texas, along the Sedalia Trail to Sedalia, Missouri and starred Eric Fleming as Gil Favour the trail boss ably assisted by his hot-headed ramrod Rowdy Yates played by a young Clint Eastwood. The chuck wagon was manned by the cook known as Wishbone who was played by Paul Brinegar and his assistant known as Mushy. Sheb Wooley who was a country and western singer and actor; he wrote and recorded the novelty rock'n'roll song "The Purple People Eater," played the trail scout, Pete Nolan. There were such guest stars as Lon Chaney Jnr, Elijah Cook and Victor McLaglen and Linda Cristal amongst others who appeared in Rawhide.

Have Gun–Will Travel was a rather far fetched western starring Richard Boone as Paladin, a Gentleman gunfighter. He is a well travelled person in the series, having been to India where he gained respect as the killer of man eating tigers. He was West Point trained and served in the Union Army in the American Civil War.He spoke numerous languages; he lived in the Carlton Hotel in San Francisco where he dressed in formal attire and regularly attended the opera. His calling card had a Knight Chess piece on it and he operated as a gun for hire; a bounty hunter or mercenary in the old West.

The Life and Legend of Wyatt Earp was a western series starring Hugh O'Brien as the famous lawman. Unlike the real Wyatt Earp, O'Brien did not sport the famous moustache and he wore a flat brimmed Stetson hat. The series was loosely based on the legendary lawman's life from Ellsworth in Kansas to Dodge City and finalising with his time in Tombstone and the infamous Gunfight at the OK Corral. The series was first shown in America in 1957. In the series Earp made great use of a gun called the Buntline Special invented by Ned Buntline but it is a disputed point whether, in real life, Wyatt Earp ever used such a gun.

Then there was The Rifleman Starring Chuck Connors as Lucas McCain and Johnny Crawford as his son Mark. The Rifleman series was the brainchild of American director, Sam Peckinpah who went on to direct such films as The Wild Bunch, The Getaway and Major Dundee. In the series Peckinpah used character actors who would later star in his big screen films such as Warren Oates, L.Q. Jones and R.G. Armstrong amongst others. Johnny Crawford went on to record a number of 50's hit records including Cindy's Birthday and Rumours.

Connors went on to make another western series in the 60's, entitled Branded about a US cavalry captain, Jason McCord who is cashiered from the army for cowardice. The charge is, of course, untrue and each episode shows McCord having to prove that he is a man and not a coward. The Dakotas was another western series starring Jack Elam as Deputy J.D. Smith to Larry Ward's Marshal Frank Ragan. Frank Ragan had two other deputies and the series revolved around them trying to keep order in Dakota Territory. Elam became well known for playing the villain in numerous western films.

Lawman starring six feet four inches tall, ex US Marine John Russell as Marshall Dan Troop and Peter Brown as his deputy Johnny McKay was a half hour, weekly series shown between 1958 and 1962. The series revolved around the mentor/protégé theme between the two stars keeping law and order in Laramie town in Wyoming and most of the action was centred on the Birdcage Saloon, owned by Lily Merrill, portrayed by Peggie Castle.

Cheyenne was yet another western series and its star was Clint Walker as the eponymous Cheyenne Bodie an ex cavalry scout who drifts around the west taking temporary jobs as a ranch hand, law enforcer and occasionally returning to his scouting roots. Walker walked out on Warner Brothers and the series in a dispute about remuneration; he was temporarily replaced by Ty Hardin as the character Bronco Layne. When Walker's dispute was settled and he returned to the role of Cheyenne Bodie, Warner Bros made Ty Hardin the star of the spin off series entitled Bronco Layne which alternated with Cheyenne. In the spin off series Bronco Layne is an ex confederate officer who drifts around the old west meeting such notables as Wild Bill Hickock, Belle Starr, Billy the Kid, Jesse James, Cole Younger and John Wesley Hardin.

Maverick starring James Garner as Brett Maverick was an unusual western insomuch as it relied mainly on comedy. At first Brett was the only Maverick and then a brother, Bart, played by Jack Kelly was introduced into the series followed by a cousin Beau played by Roger Moore. Later, another brother, Brent, was introduced. Brent Maverick was played by Robert Colbert who bore a striking resemblance to James Garner. They all dressed similarly sporting well tailored frock coats and trousers, fancy waistcoats and the flat brimmed, flat crowned, black Stetson hats that had become synonymous with western gamblers.

Laramie was an early 60's series about a ranch cum stagecoach station and starred Robert Fuller as Jess Harper. Other stars of the show were writer, singer and composer Hoagy Carmichael, Robert Crawford and John Smith. Then there was the Virginian, which was loosely based on the Owen Wister novel of the same name with James Drury playing the Virginian and Doug McClure playing Trampas. In the series Trampas was one of the heroes, whereas in the Wister novel he is the villain of the piece. The Virginian was the foreman on The Shiloh Ranch which had four owners through the series.

Laredo was a mid 60's series about the Laredo Rangers, a law enforcement agency and part of the Texas Rangers and starred Neville Brand as Reese Bennett. There were other lesser series like The Big Valley starring Barbara Stanwyck, Lee Majors and Linda Evans, and Tenderfoot starring Will Hutchins as an Easterner who goes west to study law. The 50's and 60's were the heyday for the western genre on television and there were others, too many to mention, some good, some bad. Some of those western shows, notably the Cisco Kid, Gunsmoke and The Lone Ranger started life as radio shows in America and although a lot of them started on television in the early to mid 50's, they ran on into the 60's.

Around about the same time as I was watching the children's programs mentioned my parents watched other shows in the evenings. Although my father liked to watch the westerns he also watched Weekly Playhouse which showed dramas by the playwrights of the day performed live on TV. Fabian of the Yard was one of my father's favourite series. It starred Bruce Seaton as the eponymous Robert Fabian a real life police inspector at Scotland Yard and it chronicled the cases in which he was involved. In 1954 the BBC produced an outstanding series on aerial warfare, comprised of fifteen, half hour shows made from footage from the Second World War. My father, an ex RAF man watched the series avidly. It was probably his favourite TV show of the day. That show was entitled 'War in the Air.'

The Saturday Matinee

When I was six years old and old enough to go to the picture house, for the Saturday matinee, I went, sometimes, with my sister Val, but more often with my cousin Bobby and one or two more friends. The admission fee, back then, was sixpence; six old pence, (2 ½ p), known in those days as a tanner, and the show started at 2.00pm. Prior to going to the pictures we would go to Sarson's grocery shop on Seabrook Road, where we would spend our sweet ration coupons on goodies to suck on and chew throughout the two and a half hour show. Those goodies included colt's foot rock, blackjacks, liquorice roots, gobstoppers and tiger nuts. Sweet rationing finished in 1953.

The cinema that we frequented was called the Magnet Picture House, situated next to the Rochdale Canal on Church Street. Where the Magnet cinema once stood there is now a Lidl Store. It was a marvellous way to spend a Saturday afternoon, watching cartoons of Heckle & Jeckle, Woody Woodpecker, Tom & Jerry and Mighty Mouse. There were also cartoons of Mickey Mouse and Donald Duck, Daffy Duck and Bugs Bunny etc. The main feature would usually be a western featuring Roy Rogers (Leonard Slye) and his wife Dale Evans and their four legged friends Trigger, the golden palomino and Bullet the German shepherd; Dale Evans' horse was called Buttermilk. Roy Rogers originally found fame as the lead singer in his country and western group, The Sons of the Pioneers, founded in 1933.

Hopalong Cassidy (William Boyd) and his horse Topper was another favourite. Bill Boyd in the guise of Hoppy dressed in black and wore silver spurs and ivory handled six shooters. He wore a big, black 10 gallon hat similar to the style of hat favoured by Tom Mix, another early film cowboy who died in a motoring accident in 1935. His films were shown at children's matinees for years after his death. Tom Mix's horse was called Tony. Hopalong's sidekick and comic relief was Red Connors played by Edgar Buchanan. George 'Gabby' Hayes played another of Hoppy's sidekicks, Windy; he also played the sidekick to Roy Rogers, Randolph Scott and others. Gabby Hayes also starred in major feature films alongside John Wayne. Other western heroes of the kid's matinees were Rod Cameron, and Lash La Rue. Those old westerns, all shot in Black and white, dated from the 30's and 40's.

Gene Autry whose full name was Orvon Grover Autry had a long time sidekick and comedic relief in his films named Smiley Burnette, real name Lester Alvin Burnett. Autry was a notable singing cowboy and had numerous hit records including Here Comes Santa Claus, which he wrote, Rudolph the Reindeer and Frosty the Snowman. His signature song was, Back in the Saddle Again. The equine star in Gene Autry films was Champion the Wonder Horse. The horse went on to have its own TV show Made by Autry's own production company, 'Flying 'A' Productions, which was also responsible for the Range Rider and a number of other TV western programmes. Autry founded the Museum of Western Heritage in California in 1988. It is now known as the Autry National Centre of the American West. Gene also had his own record company and label. Gene Autry and Roy Rogers, the two most famous singing cowboys, died within three months of each another in 1998.

There was another singing cowboy, Woodward Maurice Ritter, (1905-1974), better known as Tex Ritter. Ritter was a Texan born in Murvaul, Texas. He, like Gene Autry and Roy Rogers, starred in numerous B Westerns from the 1930's through the 1950's. I do not remember seeing any of his films and he is most probably best remembered for his rendition of 'Do Not Forsake me Oh my Darling,' sang over the opening credits to the 1952 film, High Noon, starring Gary Cooper and Grace Kelly. That was another great western that my father took the family to see.

Lesser known western heroes that we saw at the Saturday matinees were Ken Maynard, Hoot Gibson and Bob Steele who together made a series of B western shorts known as the Trailblazer series containing such films as 'Arizona Whirlwind' and 'Sonora Stagecoach,' which were made in the early and mid 1940's but were still doing the rounds in the 50's. Then there was Tim McCoy, Johnny Mack Brown and Buck Jones who made western B movies in the 30's and 40's that were still shown in the 50's. Buck Jones died in 1942 four years before I was born but I remember seeing films of his in the fifties and also reading picture comic books of Buck Jones' adventures.

There would be shorts of the three stooges in all their reckless glory and a fifteen part serial of Superman, the man of steel, played by Kirk Alyn and whose catchphrases were "Up, Up, and Away" or "This is a Job for Superman" usually spoken with some gusto before he leapt out of a window, probably to land on a mattress on the other side. The role of Superman was taken over by George Reeves for the television series. George Reeves was no relation to the late Christopher Reeves who played Superman in later Superman films.

The fifteen part serials which were part of the Saturday cinema entertainment and which finished with a cliff-hanger at the end of each instalment, to guarantee that you would come back the following week, if not Superman was Flash Gordon battling against Ming the Merciless played by Larry (Buster) Crabbe and Charles Middleton respectively. Ming was the emperor and ruler of the planet Mongo, he was evil personified and used such weapons as ray guns and death rays. The series featured The Clay people who lived in subterranean tunnels, The Birdmen who lived in Arboria and various other strange characters. Flash, of course, was the ultimate sci-fi hero of the day, as big, at the time, as Captain Kirk, Buck Rogers or Luke Skywalker are today. Buster Crabbe wasn't only known for his role as Flash Gordon; he was also one of the many actors that portrayed Tarzan on the silver screen.

Another of the fifteen part serials was The Blackhawks who were a quasi-military Squadron of World War Two pilots that fought against communism and Nazism led by Bart Hawk (Blackhawk), an American of Polish extraction played by Superman actor Kirk Alyn. His band consisted of a mixed group, of various nationalities including Andre who was French, Olaf a Norwegian, Chuck an American from Texas, Hendrickson a Netherlander, Stanislaus a Pole, Chop-Chop a Chinaman and Zinda (Lady Blackhawk) from USA.

I remember whilst watching the westerns, that the goodies mostly wore white hats and light coloured attire, the exceptions to this rule were Lash La Rue and Hopalong Cassidy who dressed all in black. The baddies wore black or dark clothing. When the goodies were in pursuit of the baddies all the males in the audience would stand up and whistle and cheer when the heroes were on screen and boo, hiss and stamp their collective feet when the outlaws were shown.

On the way home we, in our minds, became the heroes of the films we had just watched, especially the westerns, and we would run along slapping the flanks of our imaginary horses to make them run faster as we pointed our imaginary six shooter revolvers at the imaginary baddies who were trying to get away. Those imaginary six shooters looked remarkably like fingers. A lot of the films we saw had a vintage of at least ten years or more and although I didn't know it then, I now realise that quite a lot of them were made as anti Nazi, propaganda films.

My first trip to London

I was still in my seventh year when an envelope dropped through the letter box of the prefab. The letter had imprinted, over the postage stamp, a postmark stating the missives town of origin which happened to be our capital city, the Big Smoke, London and it was addressed to my father. My mother placed it on the dining table and left it unopened for my father. Upon his return from work my mother handed him the letter and we all gathered around while he opened it. Bleedin' 'ell!' he exclaimed, in surprise 'It's from Uncle Joe and Aunty Mary from the Elephant and Castle. She has been wondering what had happened to me and she got our address from my mother. They want to see us all and they've invited us down to the Smoke for her sixtieth birthday party.'

Arrangements were made to travel to London and we were to stay at Aunt Lou's house on Stoke Newington Common, just off the A10 Cambridge Road. The place names that were mentioned like Stoke Newington, Bermondsey and The Elephant and Castle sounded very exotic to me; I had never heard of them before. We travelled down to London on a steam train which my father told me was called The Mancunian and it ran, non stop, from Manchester, London Road to London Euston in just over two and a half hours. London Road station, where we boarded the Mancunian had numerous platforms where stood numerous steam trains venting their pent up power with belching smoke and steam under the massive arched canopies of which the station was made, As we made our way down the platform for our train we were enveloped in a thick fog and people emerged wraith like from the mist created by the plumes of smoke and steam.

I remember, whilst travelling on the corridor train from Manchester, pulling the leather strap on the window of a door situated between two carriages. I poked my head through the open window but had to pull it back in immediately as the train rapidly approached a tunnel. Once we had passed through the tunnel, I stuck my head out again. It was such innocent joy to feel the rushing wind in my face and hair. That was until a piece of hot ash from the locomotive's funnel hit me on the lower eyelid, it stuck there and I rubbed it causing more damage than if I had left it alone. I was left with a nasty little burn which did not heal until we had returned home to Manchester. It did however, have the effect of curing me from sticking my head out of the windows of fast moving steam trains. The Mancunian with its numerous coaches seemed very long. It was like a winding serpent and as it made its way southwards on its sinuous track it gobbled up the miles like a voracious reptile issuing smoke and sparks from its insatiable head as it sped towards its destination.

We arrived at Euston Station and caught a connecting local train to Stoke Newington Station where Uncle Bill Bellini picked us up and conveyed us to the big house on Stoke Newington Common where he and Aunt Lou and cousins Billy and Beryl lived. We were made very welcome and shown to our rooms. We freshened up and dined with our hosts before we retired leaving the adults to enjoy some drinks and adult conversation. The next day we travelled down to the Elephant and Castle where we met my father's guardians from years before. Joe would have been in his early sixties and it was Mary's sixtieth birthday that we were there for. There was plenty of hugging, kissing and hand shaking and tears of joy on both sides. We spent a couple of days with them and went to see a lot of the sites and attractions of London including Tower Bridge which, just as we arrived, started to rise. My dad said 'You don't realise how lucky you are, me and my mates used to wait here all day just to see the bridge opening and you waltz up for the first time and up it pops.'

On the second day we went back to Joe and Mary's nice, cosy little home where Aunty Mary asked Val and me if we wanted to freshen up. Well, we had had a wash that morning and so declined, Aunt Mary with a knowing smile and a wink towards my dad said 'I understand, only dirty people wash, don't they?'

It was there that guests to Mary's sixtieth birthday party started to arrive. We all had a wonderful day. My dad's sister, Aunt Lou and her hubby, Uncle Bill along with My Grandmother Nellie were there but all too soon it was time to say goodbye. There was more hugging, kissing, handshaking and tears as we said our goodbyes for the last time. It was then time to escort my father's mother, Grandma Nellie, back to her home. I cannot remember exactly where she lived at the time but it was not far from the Elephant and Castle junction. Nellie's second Husband, Benjamin (Benny) Mills had died in 1949, the same year as Granddad George Hampson.

My father must have been a very forgiving man for he treated his mother, the mother that had ill treated him and given him up as a child, with the utmost respect and politeness, never once mentioning the hard times that he had suffered as a child and I must admit I found Grandma Nellie to be quite a nice person. Perhaps time and circumstance had changed her. She came out with us when we visited Trafalgar Square; she even treated Val and I to ices and bought the monkey nuts with which to feed the Trafalgar Square pigeons. Even though we were staying at Aunt Lou's house for free we could only afford a week in London and soon enough it was time to make the journey home. For the return journey to Manchester we travelled on a different train which seemed to stop at all the major towns and cities on its passage north, consequently the trip took much longer than the southward expedition.

My father, for whatever reason, invited Nellie to travel back up North with us. Perhaps he hoped to repair the damage and heal the rift that had been opened in his early life. Nellie did come back to Manchester and stayed with us for a week. My mum and dad gave up their marital bed to accommodate his mother and they slept on the floor on the cushions off the three piece suite. Nellie had a terrible habit of going to bed with a bag of barley sugar, boiled sweets. That was not the worst of it; she would fall asleep whilst sucking on one of those hard boiled sweets and in her sleep would dribble all over the pillows and sheets, staining the linen with sticky yellow saliva. When Nellie returned to London the bed linen which she had used was disposed of.

While she was in Manchester Grandma Nellie along with my mother took Valerie and me for a full day at Manchester's Belle Vue, Zoological gardens where we had a wonderful time we went all the funfair rides that were suitable for children of our age and we viewed all the wild animals. We visited the monkey house where we watched gibbons at play and chimpanzees. We saw baboons doing things they ought not to do in front of children and we saw the big silverback gorillas. We also visited the aquarium with its tropical fish and the aviary where we saw brightly coloured, exotic birds. We also visited the reptile house where we saw massive boa constrictors and numerous types of venomous snakes and various lizards. Dinner was bought and paid for by Nellie who also treated us to candy floss on sticks.

I Almost Drown

I was seven years old when disaster struck one day in the depths of winter. That disaster caused me to miss the matinee at the picture house. Cousin Bobby, myself and three or four other friends decided that, one Saturday morning, we would go and ride the clay trucks, a regular but somewhat dangerous and forbidden pastime, at Jackson's Brick Works. Jackson's was one of the major brick manufacturers and their works, kilns and clay pits took up numerous acres behind Briscoe lane and alongside the Rochdale canal and Mitchell Street. They had their own fleet of red liveried lorries and I regularly watched them and the occasional BRS truck being loaded up with bricks for deliveries near and far.

The clay trucks that operated between the clay pits and the brick making works were little tipping hoppers mounted on bogies that brought the clay for making the bricks from the clay pits to the manufactory on a circular, narrow gauge rail line. The bogies had hooks on the bottom which caught on a chain which drew them up into the brickworks. We would sneak into the works and when the trucks had tipped their load of clay we would jump into them and ride them down to the working clay pits where we would jump out, our clothes smeared with the residual clay from the hoppers and run away from the loaders who always, half heartedly, gave chase but never caught us. We would stop and taunt them shouting, 'One, two, and three, you can't catch me. Two, three and four, chase us some more.'

On that particular freezing, winter's Saturday morning we were all dressed alike; short grey trousers, down to our knees, long grey socks, pulled up to our knees, shirts, pullovers and jackets or windcheaters. We all probably wore vests with liberty bodices over them, although we would not readily admit to it. When we had outrun the workmen from the working clay pits we took a walk around the disused pits which were steep sided, full of water and of which there were three which were approximately twenty feet deep and were waiting to be filled in. The water in the pits was frozen over.

Upon reaching the disused pits we circumnavigated each one and when we had walked around them and we were stood by the edge of the biggest I said 'Come on, lets slide on the ice.'

'No way!' replied the others in unison, 'it's too dangerous.'

'Are you frightened? Have you got the willies?' I asked and without waiting for an answer I said 'watch me, you scaredy cats,' and with that I foolishly and with reckless abandon ventured onto the ice and started sliding around the perimeter of the pit like Richard Button the 1952 world figure skating champion. Bobby yelled 'Gerroff before you fall through!'

To which I responded 'Don't be soft; it's all right, look.' And with that I jumped up and down on the ice to prove my point.

'Please Laurie, come off, it's not safe,' pleaded Bobby. I ignored his pleas and those of the others and went a little further out where, unbeknownst to me, the ice thinned out. As I nonchalantly slid along the ice there came, without warning, an eerie creaking sound, cracks appeared in the ice around me and started to spread like cracks in glass, water seeped up through the fissures. I was, for a second, frozen to the spot and then, in panic, I attempted to run to the edge of the pit. My feet could gain no purchase on the glistening, wet, slippery surface. The splits in the ice widened and the frozen surface beneath my feet opened up and I plunged into the icy water below.

I could not swim and I kicked frantically with my legs and thrashed wildly with my arms in a struggle to keep my head above the chilling, sub zero water. I could feel my sodden clothes hindering me and dragging me down. 'Help me!' I shouted, 'Get me out; I don't wanna die, please, help me!'

It was so cold that I could scarcely breathe after my first plea for help. As I strove to reach something solid I noticed that Bobby was on his hands and knees and then he lay flat on his belly and made his way out the few feet to where I struggled in the icy water. The others held on to his ankles and just as I was about to go under he reached out to the edge of the broken ice and gripped my hand and pulled. Those holding on to Bobby's legs pulled him backwards and I came out of the water, breaking more ice as I was pulled forwards and dragged to the edge and on to the frozen ground and relative safety. I was, by then, in tears, I was saturated and I was freezing and I had nearly lost my life.

To get home from the clay pits meant making our way to Briscoe Lane school and squeezing through a gap in the fence separating the Primary School from Jackson's Brickworks, crossing the snow covered grounds and playing fields of the School which we all attended and climbing over a high, steel, perimeter fence with spikes along its top at the Briscoe Lane boundary of the school.

The best and easiest place to climb over the fence was in the corner where the fences that separated the Primary school from the nursery met at a right angle. I, still in tears and shivering uncontrollably, was helped up the fence by the pushing and shoving of the others. Upon reaching the top I stood, wobbling, feet between the spikes and then I bent my knees and lowered myself until I could grip the spikes with fingers stiffened by cold. I then, slowly and ever so carefully, turned myself around so that I could lower myself down the outer side of the fence to the icy pavement below. I was trembling with both fear and cold.

Unfortunately, as I lowered myself down the fence, one of the spikes of the fence went up the front of one of my soggy trousers legs. Being in a somewhat distressed state and with my eyes misted over with tears and my body numb with cold, I did not notice until, under the strain and pressure, the metal spike tore through the rapidly stiffening, sodden grey flannel of which my pants were made. As it came free it ripped the material from knee to groin, I tumbled backwards and downwards out of control onto the frozen sidewalk, to land on my back on the snow and ice covered paving stones. The impact with the pavement knocked the wind out of me and I banged my head. I was in terrible pain and I rolled over onto my side and pulled my knees up to my chest in a foetal position. I started to breath more normally and my sobbing was renewed and I cried uncontrollably. Perhaps because it was such a cold day it seemed that not many people had ventured forth into the outside world. Such being the case no adults came to enquire as to my welfare or offer any help. It was one of the few times as a child that I craved and needed an adult's attention.

My companions climbed over the fence in record time, unrestricted by tear filled eyes, frozen extremities and rapidly freezing clothes. When they reached me and picked up the shivering, sobbing, downhearted, wreck that I had become, from the floor, where I lay in the snow, crying like a baby and uttering 'I-I-I w-w-want m-m-mi m-m-mum,' through chattering teeth and lips that had turned blue with cold; all the bravado that I had exuded as I pranced about on the ice was gone, I was shown up for what I was, a terrified, young child with not an ounce of courage.

As we made our way home, Bobby ran ahead to inform my parents of the bad luck that had befallen me. There was panic in the prefab as my mother grabbed a blanket and her coat and followed Bobby back along the road that he had earlier bounded along with the bad news. My father ran along at her side and they finally met us near the tripe works, at about half the way home. My mother wrapped me in the blanket that she carried then my father swept me into his arms and carried me the rest of the way home. I was covered in goose bumps and I swear that there were snotty icicles depending from my nose and my trousers had hardened to a solid state and could have been snapped. I was shivering unrestrainedly with the cold; I was very close to being hypothermic.

Upon reaching the prefab, all of my friends especially Cousin Bobby were thanked profusely by my mother and father. Bobby was given some of my dry clothing to replace his wet ones and my dad walked my friends to their homes and explained to their parents what misfortune had befallen me and to praise and thank their children for the presence of mind that they had shown that day. Lastly, he took Bobby home to Rosebank Road and told his mum of the day's adventure and how her son had surely put his own life at risk to save his young cousin's life.

Back at the prefab my mum, whose emotions had gotten the better of her, shed tears in abundance. Globules of the salty, lachrymal fluid rolled down her cheeks in rivulets. She cried tears of relief and gladness that I had not drowned and tears of anger and exasperation at my stupidity. She clenched and unclenched her fists; she squeezed me and shook me. She uttered words that I was unable to understand. She was in turmoil, she did not know what to do or think and I was sure that she didn't know whether to give me a cuddle or a wallop for being so empty headed. Luckily for me she settled for the embrace.

She ran a not too hot bath for me, which I luxuriated in; enveloped in its warmth I slowly thawed out. After a while my mother lifted me from the warm water and I was dried off, dressed in clean underwear and wrapped in a robe and then sat by the fire with a cup of hot malted drinking chocolate. The drinking chocolate was a brand called Milo made by Nestlé's; it came in a green tin and was named after the famous ancient Greek athlete Milo Of Croton, renowned for his legendary strength and prowess as a wrestler. It wasn't until the next day that I was read the riot act by my father. He was fuming and shouting at me, instilling into me how stupid I had been. Some fathers may have hit their children but my father's anger and raised voice were enough to reduce me to tears. My mother came to the rescue and calmed my dad down, telling him that enough was enough and that she was sure that I had learnt my lesson. She was right; I never went near the clay pits again. I was banned from going near the place, as were my friends of the day, although a ban was totally unnecessary as we had all learnt a very harsh lesson that day. And that's how I came to almost die and to miss the Saturday afternoon matinee at the cinema.

Chapter 4

ANOTHER NEAR DROWNING
AND LEARNING TO RIDE ON TWO WHEELS

Crossing the Locks & Leeches

On the way to the cinema, on the Saturdays that I did go, we would sometimes take the route along Taylor's Lane to Culcheth Lane, turn left and walk towards Church Street and past All Saint's Church; the church where I was christened. Outside the church, mounted on the pavement, opposite Briscoe Lane and on the corner of All Saint's Street was a blue Police box, the same type of box that is now used in Dr Who as the TARDIS, although I doubt that the internal dimensions matched those of the TARDIS. It was approximately eight feet tall and the telephone handset was mounted outside the box. The external handset was for public use to summon our defenders of justice or any other emergency service. There was a door that allowed entry to policemen who carried a universal key which would open any blue police box. The inside was set up as a miniature police station where the Bobby could do his paperwork and any other relevant crime orientated work or it could be used as a temporary holding cell for drunks or those of a violent nature apprehended whilst in pursuance of their misdoings, until reinforcements or a black Maria arrived.

We would carry on down Church Street passing the pubs and shops until we came to the corner where Fred Gosling's white tiled, wet fish shop stood. Gosling's wet fish shop also sold rabbits and hares and various types of poultry which were hung on hooks around the shop. Sometimes, the counter hand behind the stall at Gosling's would give us the rabbit's tails and feet but the prized pieces of deceased fauna were the feet of dead chickens with the tendons still attached, this allowed us to pull and release the tendons causing the chicken claws to open and close. The boys would chase the girls with those chicken claws, making them scream and even cry, as we grabbed their hair with the dead talons; such fun we had.

We would then go around the back of the shops, near Newton Heath Market, which was open for business on Saturdays and Wednesdays and which catered for patrons from near and far. There we could gain access, by scrambling over a low fence, to the towpath which ran alongside the canal. The canal and towpath, even back then were disused, no barges or narrow boats, commercial or otherwise floated along that stretch of water. Years before and to allow the level of the canal to drop and to pass under Church Street there was a set of working locks. Those locks, at the time were disused and permanently closed, and they had to be crossed to get to the Magnet cinema. Of course one could go back onto Church Street and by pass the locks, but that would result in being called a mard arse or a sissy, so out of bravado we crossed the locks; this was no mean balancing feat for unsteady youngsters.

On other days we would take a different route; we would go via Orford Road, across Briscoe Lane, up Mitchell Street and past Jackson's Brick works where we would join the canal and turn right to walk along the towpath to the locks. At the point where we joined the towpath there was a wooden bridge that straddled the canal to join a cobbled roadway which ran past a row of ancient terraced houses, the Newton Heath Steam Laundry and some other commercial enterprises before continuing through to Oldham Road. As we navigated the path alongside the navigation we would look for flat stones or slivers of brick and skim them along the water to see who could make the most bounces or try to bounce the stones off the water onto the opposite bank.

During spring time, one Saturday afternoon, as we approached the locks on the way to the picture show, a young lad of about eight or nine years of age, was crossing the water barrier, being cheered on by his mates. He stopped at the half way point, where the two lock gates met and where water spurted and gushed, under pressure, from the narrow fissures between them before cascading into the five feet deep, black, foul smelling water below, causing a certain amount of rippling turbulence. The young lad, an obvious show off and extrovert, started to clown around and show off. He let go of the handrail that ran across each lock gate and balanced on one leg, he shouted 'Look! No hands.' He spun around on one leg and then grasped the hand rail, then he attempted a second pirouette but, as he reached for the handrail, he missed and promptly lost his balance and his footing; he slipped and plunged headlong about twelve feet into the deep, murky, rubbish strewn water below.

He disappeared momentarily beneath the dark waters and came up spluttering and coughing. We all ran down the towpath and underneath the bridge to where he had surfaced. It was completely in shadow down there, no matter what time of the day it was, the sun did not penetrate that black and sinister place. There was an overflow culvert that ran by the side of the towpath and emptied back into the canal below the bridge, causing the water to bubble and swirl, creating numerous little eddies as it mixed with the water tumbling from above. The plummeting acrobat who, as luck would have it, had learned how to swim had reached the edge of the water and was clinging desperately to the large, granite paving slabs which lined the side of the canal and the towpath and he was crying for assistance.

The water into which he fell was once the locks chamber where boats would wait whilst the chamber filled but the second set of lock gates had long since been removed. As I hark back to those long gone days I realise that if the incident would have happened today there would, most probably, be quite a different outcome. Instead of wind blown rubbish such as newspapers and the like the lock would now, no doubt, be filled with supermarket trolleys and discarded bedsteads and bicycle frames as well as empty pizza boxes and other debris. The youth that fell would, more than likely, have been the recipient of a broken back at worst and broken limbs at best.

On the day in question, someone had the presence of mind to dash to the blue police box to summon the emergency services, namely the police and an ambulance. The youngster who had fallen from the locks was pulled from the inky black, stinking and stagnant water and laid on the towpath. He was wearing short pants and one of his shoes was missing, sucked off by the water, his socks were down around his ankles and on his legs were numerous leeches, some were thin and flat whilst others had sated themselves on his blood and were fat and bloated, there was one sucking on his neck, it seemed to pulsate as it fed on his blood.

We didn't know what to do, we were scared due to the situation that we were in and we were frightened of the leeches which, when in the brackish water, appeared to be black in colour but whilst feeding on their host they appeared to be a greenish brown, not unlike slugs. We stared in disbelief at the lad who was hosting the leeches for their gory, afternoon snack and who was shivering and crying. In-between sobs he pleaded for someone to remove the bloodsuckers from his limbs and other parts of his body.

As a crowd gathered a middle aged man came along, he was smoking a cigarette. He immediately assessed the situation and then bent down by the side of the trembling, prostrate figure of the young lad. He spoke soothingly to the boy explaining what he was about to do and asked him to lie still. He then closely examined the leeches. Those that were round and sated were flicked off. Those that were still flattish and sucking, he touched the glowing end of his cigarette to. The leech that was on the boy's neck was one that was still snacking and so the man touched the glowing end of his cigarette to it which caused it to release its sucker and shrivel up much like a slug when salt is put on it. The man flicked the leech off and one of his young audience kicked it back into the canal. A trickle of blood flowed from the boy's neck due, apparently, to the anti coagulant in the leech's sucker. The guy was attacking another with his cigarette when we heard the ambulance bell and the screeching of brakes above us, but he with the glowing fag carried on removing the water worms.

Within a couple of minutes two ambulancemen carrying a stretcher and followed directly by two policemen, arrived. The young lad that had fallen into the water was placed onto the stretcher and carried to the cream coloured, Bedford ambulance which then sped off towards Ancoats' Hospital. The rest of us young cinema goers didn't have the sense to run away and so the policemen rounded us up. Because we hadn't broken any laws, except, maybe, the law of trespass and because the policemen knew that we were going to see our once a week picture show they gave us a severe tongue lashing accompanied by some good advice about using the roadway and keeping away from the canal and locks before sending us on our way. We stood there, heads bent forward and took the admonishment in silence; we were genuinely frightened of figures of authority back in those days, especially the police and crossing the locks was then and for a number of weeks, considered taboo.

The police also talked to the guy with the cigarette and thanked him for his assistance and prompt actions before they departed. The rest of the young crowd, including me, carried on to our afternoon's enjoyment at the flicks with the eldest amongst us saying 'They didn't frighten me, them coppers.' But the rest of us knew better.

Gillibrand's Hairdressers

Behind Newton Heath Market and running parallel with Church Street was Droylsden Road. On Droylsden Road close to The Oddfellows Arms was the barber's shop that my father favoured. The proprietor was a man named Gillibrand and his name was over the shop to the side of the red and white barber's pole. Gillibrand, although I did not know it until the day of the following episode, wore a ginger hairpiece.

While I was a youngster I would go, once a fortnight with my father, to Mr Gillibrand's Gentleman's Hairdressers, for a short back and sides. My father would have his own hair trimmed by the tonsorial artist, on the same occasion. Mr Gillibrand had an assistant and they must have both been quite adept at the art of hairdressing and haircutting for there was always a queue of gentlemen awaiting a shave or haircut.

It was on a cold, blustery, winter's day that my father and I were sat; glad to be in the warmth of the hairdresser's shop, waiting our turn to sit in one of the two barber's seats, when a strong wind blew the door of the shop open. It banged against its stopper, the glass rattled in the frame. Customers shivered as the heat left the premises, ousted by the cold wind. Gillibrand, who was working the chair nearest to the entrance, made his way to the door to shut it when another strong gust blew in and plucked his ginger wig from his head in the manner that the autumn winds plucked the leaves from the trees. The toupee flew across the room like a red squirrel jumping from branch to branch, to land on the floor and skid for a couple of feet. It came to rest beneath the furthest chair from the door, amongst the hair clippings. In his embarrassment, Gillibrand's hands flew to his bald, shiny, white pate and he chased his hairpiece across the room to where it had come to rest. He went down on all fours under the seat, nudging his fellow barber out of the way and came up, a few seconds later, with the wig upon his head but somewhat askew. Another customer, by that time, had closed the door and I was laughing out loud when my dad nudged me and put his forefinger to his lips in a gesture that meant 'Be Quiet!' It took a few moments for me and a couple of others within the shop who found it amusing, to stifle our laughter. Gillibrand, strange though it may seem, soon regained his composure, he stood in front of the mirror and straightened his hairpiece and combed it into his normal style with a centre parting. He then made his way back to the customer who was sat in his chair with the half completed haircut. He picked up the tools of his trade and continued where he had left off, plying his trade with the usual banter and small talk; 'Would you like something for the week-end, sir? 'Have you been away this Year?' but nothing was mentioned of the incident of the wind borne wig that had just occurred.

Riding on Two Wheels

It was around that time, when I was nearly eight years old that my father decided it was time that the stabilisers were removed from my bike, which I had outgrown and had not used for a couple of years. It was time to learn to ride it as a two wheeler. My sister Val was already quite adept at riding her two wheeled bicycle and had learnt a couple of years earlier and I was quite jealous of her being adept at something of which I was totally bereft.

My stabilised bike was brought from the shed into the back garden where the stabilisers were removed and the saddle and handlebars were raised to their highest position. I was then instructed to mount my iron steed while my dad stood behind me holding the rear of the saddle. On his word I started pedalling along Taylor's Lane while he ran behind still gripping the saddle. Upon reaching what he perceived to be the requisite speed he let go of the rear of the bike and I carried on going forward in blissful ignorance. I just happened to take a backwards glance to see my father stood some distance to my rear.

The realisation that I was no longer being held steady caused me to lose my equilibrium; whatever it was that had held me upright failed me completely and my unsteadiness caused me to lose control and sense of direction. I swerved unbalanced and erratically from one side to the other before tumbling from the two wheeled conveyance and to the ground. The last thing I saw before impact was the footpath, seemingly rushing up to meet me. I landed roughly, spread-eagled on the rough terrain, scraping skin from both knees and hands. There was no other damage done and so, after drying my eyes and wiping my nose, the lessons resumed until after about two days tuition I found myself propelling the bike along Taylor's Lane unassisted. I had mastered the art of conveying myself via the two wheeled velocipede.

After a couple of weeks, on a Sunday morning, whilst my mum and dad were having their once a week lie-in, I arose, got washed and dressed and went outdoors. I had decided that I was a big boy and would like to ride a big boy's bike, so unbeknownst to my father; I unlocked the shed and wheeled his bike out. It was much too big but I somehow managed to mount it with the assistance of the garden gate. I could not sit on the seat and reach the pedals so I sat, somewhat painfully, on the crossbar. I pushed myself away from the gatepost and swaying with uncertainty, from side to side I managed to make a few complete revolutions of the pedals and then I stopped pedalling. Big Mistake!

What had slipped my mind was that my dad's bike was of the fixed wheel type and as I stopped pedalling the pedals, pushed forward by the momentum of the rear wheel with its fixed cog lifted me upwards and forwards. As I discontinued the act of pedalling, my involuntary representation of a bird began; I proceeded to fly over the handlebars. I flapped my arms wildly as I flew forwards to land ahead of the bike in a heap on the stony path that was Taylor's Lane. I was no longer a big boy on a big boy's bike but a fledgling aviator fallen painfully to earth.

Luckily, my dad's bike appeared to have sustained little or no noticeable damage and so after I had picked myself up and checked it over, I examined myself for personal damage, which consisted of a number of small lacerations and abrasions on my hands and knees. I considered remounting the bike but that thought was soon rejected and cast from my mind and so I pushed it the short distance back to the shed where I placed it in the closest approximation to its original position. I then wiped it down with a piece of cloth that was at hand and closed and locked the shed door very gently; I then re-entered the prefab and hung the key on its hook.

I crept stealthily through the kitchen and living room and down the hallway to the bathroom without being heard. There, I cleaned myself up; I sauntered back to the living room and turned on the television and sat there watching until a few minutes later when both mum and dad arose and came into the room. The scratches that I had sustained were quite noticeable but young lads, at any time and as a matter of course had any number of lumps, bumps and scratches about their person. Nothing was suspected and there was no mention of my unsuccessful attempt at riding dad's bike but on the morning of Christmas Day that year I woke up and gazed over the end of my bed where hung my Christmas stocking containing Clementines, nuts and chocolate coins, etc. There, leaning against the wall beneath the window was the present that I had pleaded and begged for. I had received the brand new and more adequately sized two wheeled cycle that I had been asking for.

A couple of days after that Christmas and sometime between Boxing Day and New Year, I was out early on my new bike, pedalling along without a care in the world. I was enjoying the pleasure of riding my new racer; no hobby horse or boneshaker was my new pride and joy. On that day the weather was crisp and cold but dry; there was no snow on the ground even though it was the depths of winter. Being quite new to cycling and a complete novice to cycling on proper roads, I kept close to the kerb, too close as it happens for as I propelled myself forward, nice and slowly, my front wheel dropped into one of the grooves in a roadside grid and the bike came to an abrupt halt. I slid off the saddle and in my efforts to stay upright I dropped my feet off the pedals and to the floor. Unfortunately I landed heavily, groin first on the crossbar. My gonads took the full impact and I uttered a profanity, a profanity I had heard in the playground but which I had never uttered or used before. I exclaimed one word and one word only: FUCK!!! My eyes started to water and I felt nauseous. I initially looked around to make sure that no-one had seen my little mishap. Seeing that I was alone I painfully climbed off my bicycle and as I lifted my leg over the crossbar there came a shooting pain like a red hot needle through my testes and into my lower stomach. I carefully laid my bike down on the kerb and I then sank slowly to my knees as the tears started to flow and a long, low moan escaped from my mouth on a visible, steamy exhalation.

How long I knelt there, rocking back and forth as I cradled my ballocks in my hands, I don't know. It was not a great length of time but during that span no other person appeared on the street. After the pain had subsided a little I struggled to my feet, picked up my bike and pushed it home where I put it away in the shed. I wiped my eyes and nose, took a deep breath and entered the prefab, walking as close to normal as I could manage, although there was a tendency to throw my legs out slightly as if to walk around my hanging bits. I greeted my mother and father and went straight to the bathroom. I dropped my trousers and underpants to survey the damage I had executed upon myself. My goolies had turned a dark purple blending into black and the pain had subsided into a nagging dull ache around the nether regions.

The day passed with me in a rather subdued mood. I told my parents that I didn't feel too well and made excuses to have an early night. I asked my mother if I could take a bath before I retired, to which she acceded. While I was in the bath I undertook further and closer investigation of my scrotum, testicles and the surrounding area. Besides the extensive bruising there was a distinct swelling around my groin and lower stomach.

I gently prodded the swelling at the base of my belly and it felt spongy and a small, round indentation, like a dimple appeared and then slowly that disappeared; it was like sticking one's finger in rising dough. I finished bathing and dried myself off, taking extra care when it came to my bits down below. I donned my night-time attire and took an Aspro painkiller from the medicine cabinet and swallowed it with a glass of water and then I retired to the comfort of my bed before the rest of the household and I slept fitfully. When I awoke next morning the pain had all but disappeared and so I thought to myself that the damage must not be too serious. The swelling gradually decreased until after a week it had disappeared. The bruising stayed for about a month, constantly changing colours, going from black to purple and then a mixture of tints and hues from blue through brown to yellow until it finally vanished leaving me none the worse, but a little wiser, for my painful experience.

Radio, Comics and The Bayko Building Set

During the late 1940's to the late1950's when a lot of homes had no television to view, other forms of family entertainment had to be pursued. The radio was the most obvious form of entertainment for families when they would gather round the set to listen to Dick Barton Special Agent which ran from 1946 to 1951. Another popular radio show was Valentine Dyall's The Man in Black. Dyall was the narrator of the BBC horror series, Appointment with Fear. He also parodied his part as the Man in Black in guest appearances in the Goon show.

The Goon Show ran from 1951 until 1960 and starred Spike Milligan, Peter Sellers, Harry Secombe and Michael Bentine. The goons used zany and surreal humour and strange noises and in some ways were the forerunners of later television shows like The Goodies and Monty Python's Flying Circus. There were, of course, numerous other shows that provided a healthy escapism for both adults and children such as Beyond Our Ken featuring Kenneth Williams which was the forerunner of Round the Horn with Kenneth Horn. There was also the 'Cheerful' Charlie Chester Show. The Billy Cotton Band Show featuring singer Alan Breeze was a Sunday dinnertime show which ran from 1949 until 1966. Guest artists included Russ Conway, Kathie Kay and many more the show always started with ex racing driver Billy Cotton bellowing WAKEY- WAAAKEY!! to his audience. The show transferred to a Saturday evening on TV in 1956.

Worker's Playtime, which ran from 1941 until1964, was another light entertainment show that was broadcast, three times a week, from worker's canteens in factories up and down the country. Such stars as Peter Sellers, Tony Hancock, Charlie Chester, Frankie Howerd and Anne Shelton appeared on the show. Of course, I only heard the program during school holidays.

Comic books were another mode of entertainment for children in the 50's. A lot of the comics that I read were the American DC products of which most carried advertisements for *'Daisy BB rifles'* and characters in the cartoons wore lapel badges and buttons with the slogan *'I LIKE IKE,'* alluding to the popularity of Dwight David Eisenhower, thirty fourth President of the USA from 1953-1961. The DC Comics included The Adventures of Superman and all its offshoots. Superheroes were a firm favourite of youngsters even though they were established in the USA in the late 1930's and early 40's. Superman appeared under his own title and also in The Justice League of America and Action Comics titles.

Superman was created in 1932 by American writer Jerry Seigel and Canadian born artist Joe Shuster, while they were both living in Cleveland, Ohio. They sold their character to Detective Comics in 1938 and the Superman Character first appeared in Action Comics in the same year. Superman, in the early comics, was not able to fly but he could leap over tall buildings in one bound. He was known as the Man of Steel and could run faster than a speeding bullet and was more powerful than a locomotive. He was a much darker character in the early stories, often taking the law into his own hands and using violence against lawbreakers.

There have been numerous adaptations of the Superman story from radio to television with both live actors and as a cartoon feature and from newspaper comic strip to comic book and to film telling how baby Kal-el was sent to Earth by his father Jor-el just before their planet Krypton exploded. How he was discovered by Martha and Jonathon Kent, in the mythical town of Smallville, Kansas and brought up by them and instilling their principles of righteousness, integrity, honesty and goodness into the youngster. The Kents, (Ethan and Sara Kent in the early film and television programs), called their new found son Clark and he grew up to be Clark Kent, the mild mannered reporter for the Daily Planet in the equally mythical city of Metropolis Clark Kent was the alter ego of Superman, The Man of Steel.

An alternative to Superman was Captain Marvel and the Marvel Family. Captain Marvel's alter ego was Billy Batson who, upon shouting the word SHAZAM, was transformed into the indestructible Captain Marvel, imbued with the same powers as Superman. There was also Captain Marvel Junior and Mary Marvel. There were a lot of problems and litigation against The Captain Marvel series from the publishers of Action Comics and DC who believed that Captain Marvel was a rip off of their Man of Steel Superhero. Nyoka the Jungle Girl, Wonder Woman, The Blackhawks and Batman and Robin all featured in the comics of the day and most of them transferred to film or TV, either as live action films or as cartoons, at one time or another.

Marvelman was the hero of a British comic and was a virtual copy of Captain Marvel, brought about by the lawsuits that were happening in America. Marvelman was, in essence a transformation of Captain Marvel, created in 1954 by writer/artist Mick Anglo for UK publisher L. Miller and Sons. A young reporter named Micky Moran, who to become his alter ego, uttered the word Kimota (phonetically atomic reversed; rather than Shazam, as uttered by Captain Marvel). He had all the powers that Captain Marvel had and even had a similar family, i.e. Young Marvelman etc, all, in my opinion, based on the ultimate superhero, Superman.

Batman and Robin are probably the most recognised superhero's, after Superman. Co-created in1939 by artist Bob Kane and writer Bill Finger, Batman first appeared in Detective Comics in the same year. They are based in the mythical American city of Gotham. Batman's alter ego is millionaire Bruce Wayne who, after seeing his parents gunned down, during a robbery, swears to fight crime. He does so in the guise of a bat. Unlike the other superhero's he does not actually possess super powers but relies on physical fitness, scientific devices and intimidation to fight the villains who go under such names as The Joker, The Riddler, Catwoman and The Penguin. His Young sidekick, Robin is actually his ward Dick Grayson. Batman and Robin are helped in their endeavours by the family butler, Alfred and they make use of The Batplane and The Batmobile as modes of transport. Batman was parodied in the 1960's in a rather camp show that became something of a cult and starred Adam West as Batman and Burt Ward as Robin.

Other publications were more of an educational tool as opposed to means of escapism. Classic's Illustrated released, on a monthly basis, individual comics that were précis of all the popular classic stories including James Fennimore Cooper's The Last of the Mohicans and titles by Alexander Dumas, Jules Verne, Charles Dickens, Robert Louis Stephenson, Mary Shelley amongst many more and including the Greek classics The Iliad and

The Odyssey by Homer. I bought Classic's Illustrated on a regular basis and that whetted my appetite to read the full and unedited versions of the classics, turning me into an avid reader. I actually collected the Classic's Illustrated comics and went out of my way to acquire titles that I did not already have. I would offer two or three other comics for a title that I didn't have. I collected them for years but never managed to get the complete set. In my endeavours to get rare titles I actually gave twelve almost new comics for a rather beaten up copy of Mary Shelley's Frankenstein.

Another series of comics that was around in the 50's and 60's was Movie Classic's Illustrated which did much the same as Classic's Illustrated but concentrated solely on films of the day and earlier. Although somewhat less than educational they were still a form of healthy escapism. Popular in the 50's were war comics telling of heroic deeds in the Second World War. Most of those war comics were American publications which told the story of how the Yanks won the war. There were also the soft paper titles such as the Dandy and the Beano, The Eagle, the Knockout, The Topper, The Beezer etc; and those that had fewer pictures and more of the written word such as the Hotspur and the Wizard. Unless an individual collected certain titles, the glossy, higher priced comics were swapped amongst friends for comics that one had not already read.

There also was a genre of comics in the 1950's known as Horror Comics; mainly from America. They reportedly gave children nightmares and were similar in content to the horror 'B' movies of the time, although they would not so much as raise an eyebrow nowadays. They were supposedly only to be sold to people over sixteen years of age, but like most things that shouldn't have; they fell into the hands of younger children. The government of the day tried to ban them. There were reports in the national newspapers of children waking up screaming that the Creature from the Black Lagoon or Dracula or Frankenstein's Monster was walking through their dreams.

During the mid 1950's, I wasn't that interested in the news of the day, even though I had learned to read at an early age, but I did glance through the newspapers that we received at our abode. Instead of reading the news I turned to the funnies page for the cartoons. My father being a socialist at heart always bought the Daily Mirror and when he had read it I would take it and read of the adventures of Pip, Squeak and Wilfred. Pip was a dog, Squeak a penguin and Wilfred was a rabbit. The cartoon strip was drawn by Mr Austin B. Payne and the trio of animals had many magical adventures. In the Daily Mirror there was a strip cartoon of a character named Garth whose arrival parallels that of Superman although he did not have an alter ego. He did, however have colossal strength and travelled in time and space. His love interest was the Goddess Astra and his mentor was Professor Lumiere. Jane was another Daily Mirror cartoon strip which featured the eponymous heroine getting into tight corners and having her clothes torn off innocently or accidently. Her love interest was Georgie Porgy and I believe it was my father's favourite strip. Those cartoons mentioned came well before Reg Smythe's Andy Capp and the Perishers.

We also had the Manchester Evening News delivered in those days and when I got a chance to look through it I turned to the cartoons where I would read the Adventures of Fudge the Elf. Fudge was written and drawn by Ken Reid who went on to work for the Dandy and the Beano. The elves' adventures took place in Pixieville and Fudge's friend in all of his adventures was another elf called Speck. There were such grand adventures as Fudge's Trip to the Moon and Fudge and the Dragon.

For adults, when families got together, there was the pack of cards and all the gambling games that could be played whether for match sticks, pennies or higher stakes. For the kids there were board games, from the simple games like Ludo and Snakes and Ladders to the more sophisticated like Monopoly. One form of entertainment that I remember and was particularly fond of in those far away days was the BAYKO Building Set.

My father returned home, with my mother, after a day's shopping one Saturday and beneath his arm and held close to his body was a large flattish box. The box was wrapped in brown paper and tied with string. He placed it on the dining table and started to unwrap it. My sister and I, full of curiosity, gathered close to dad as he removed the wrapping. Inside the wrapping was a brightly coloured box with pictures of little houses, churches and other buildings on it. The lid of the box was removed to show lots of different sized blocks and strands of steel rods of varying lengths. There were bay windows and flat windows, doors and pitched roofs or gable ends, floor plates and many and varied embellishments. The plastic pieces of the set were made of Bakelite, hence the name BAYKO. Besides houses, garages could be built; there were gates, perimeter fences, all made by the Plimpton Engineering Company of Liverpool.

The idea was to start with a base plate or floor and insert the steel rods in the pre- drilled matrix of holes around its perimeter. The brick blocks would then be inserted between the rods, along with doors and windows and finally the roof. It was not unlike the construction of prefabs only on a far smaller and more simplistic scale. There were numerous styles of buildings that could be built, churches, shops, and factories and like Meccano the set could be added to. Whole streets could be built and those streets turned into whole villages or towns. There was no end to the different building that could be built; the only limitations were imagination and the amount of building materials in ones possession. The whole family had hours of fun in a week with the BAYKO Building Set and we had the set and its additions for years, even after the television came into our lives. It was an early forerunner of Lego in a lot of respects. BAYKO was finally sold to Meccano in 1960.

Meccano was another construction toy that I played with as a child. It was somewhat more sophisticated than BAYKO, insomuch as it had to be fastened together using nuts and bolts to join the pre drilled plates and strips of metal. It also had girders, axles, wheels and gears to allow for the construction of working models and mechanical devices to which an engine could be fitted. The Meccano was contrived by a Liverpudlian clerk, Frank Hornby, of model railway fame, who invented the system in England in 1901. It was manufactured in England until 1980 by The Meccano Company Limited. It is now manufactured in France and China. It was more than just a toy; it was quite educational, giving many children a grounding in basic mechanical engineering principles such as pulleys, levers and gears. Meccano came in various sets from the Meccano No1 basic set for making basic things and it got more complex as set number increased. Of course one could inter-mix the sets to make ever more complex pieces of machinery. All that was needed to construct some of the most ingenious designs with a Meccano set were a screwdriver, a spanner, common sense and a modicum of intelligence coupled with manual dexterity.

Chapter 5
Romany's, Fairgrounds
and Teddy-boys.

Caravan Dwellers & The death of a Stallion

There seemed to be a lot of itinerant folk about during the early to mid fifties, what today would be called New Age Travellers, and there regularly appeared, behind Briscoe Lane School, on the land owned by Jackson's Brickworks, a gypsy encampment. Those Romany people lived in caravans and as long as they didn't cause any trouble and did no damage, the management from Jackson's allowed them to stay on their land. At the time the majority of the gypsy caravans were horse drawn contraptions. The horse drawn caravans were of the typical Romany type built of timber with a bow shaped, canvas covered roof, with coach painted designs on the bodywork and etched glass work, others had wooden roofs with a raised centre running the length of the caravan with small windows built into their sides. The caravans were of different designs and sizes. There were one or two more modern caravans towed by motor vehicles. They were usually tandem axle caravans with great expanses of chrome and etched windows. Some of those itinerants, I believe, were not true gypsies but belonged to the travelling fairgrounds of the time.

The caravans that the Romany's used, whether horse drawn or pulled buy a truck, never had fitted inside, any means of running water. It was considered taboo to have running water in their caravans because of the damage that could occur if there was a leak. Caravans, especially the more modern type are very susceptible to damp and the Romany people tried in every way possible to minimise the chance of damp occurring in their mobile homes. The old wooden, horse drawn caravans were just too small to have sanitary fitments. They had, instead, implements in which to convey water such as stainless steel churns and small water barrels, which they referred to as butts, though a true butt was a large wine cask capable of holding one hundred and twenty six gallons. The stainless steel water carriers were like farmers milk churns, but maybe a little smaller, any bowls were also made from stainless steel and they were generally, unless in transit, left outside the caravan. Some caravans were fitted with a wash hand basin which was manually filled; for bathing I suppose that they used the local wash baths. I think that the management at Jackson's Brick Works allowed access to clean drinking water for the caravan dwellers.

The horses that towed the Romany caravans were tethered close to the fence which separated Briscoe Lane School from Jackson's land and at play time children would feed grass to the horses through the fence. Those carthorses were huge, magnificent beasts, slightly smaller than shire horses. Their coats were shiny and their manes and tails smooth, testimony to the care and love that they had lavished upon them. They were tethered to the ground to wooden or steel stakes by a halter of either plaited leather or rope; they had a little room to move about on their tethers. It seemed that it was the duty of the youngsters and the women of the Romany clan to water and feed the horses as one of them would, periodically, bring water in a large urn and pour it into a trough placed there for that purpose. Nosebags would be brought and placed on the horses; I presume that they were filled with oats. I also saw various members of the horse drawn contingent grooming their animals with brushes and curry combs.

One morning as I was about to enter the school gates I saw a crowd of both children and adults gathered. There was a cacophony of sound as they shouted and pushed and shoved to get a view of what was appertaining. I wandered over and managed to get close to the front of the mass and there I saw one of those magnificent equine beasts lying on its side in the back garden of the house adjacent and nearest to the school drive; there was a lot of blood on the ground and the blood appeared almost black, although I could not see from where the blood issued. The horse, a black stallion with a white blaze on its face, was whinnying lowly and would occasionally lift its head and neigh loudly, as if venting its pain with the vapour which issued from its nostrils. It occasionally kicked out its back legs in some distress.

Knelt down by the head of the suffering animal, stroking its cheek and its mane tenderly and talking softly to it was a dark, curly haired, swarthy complexioned man. He looked to be around forty years of age and wore a collarless, striped shirt over which was an unfastened black waistcoat. Encircling his neck was a brightly coloured bandana, knotted at the throat, he wore black, serge trousers with a wide brown belt around his waist, on his feet he wore clogs and he was crying, quite openly.

The horse, it seems, had managed to escape from its tether and in seeking its liberty had made its way out of Jackson's compound and across the Red Rec, (recreation and football ground covered with crushed red brick), and down Ten Acres Lane and onto Briscoe lane where it had been struck by a vehicle. In panic and in fear and pain it had bolted through the open gates of the school and into the garden where it came to a halt and collapsed. The owner of the horse had followed it in an attempt to capture it and return it to the place where it was tied, but, alas he had failed. The halter was still around the beast's head and neck as it lay in pain.

Somebody, I don't know who, had telephoned the relevant authority and as the crowd stood by and watched, a police car followed by a large, motorised horse box, fitted with a winch, drew up; a man, dressed in a brown duster coat, climbed out of the cab of the vehicle carrying a silver coloured case which, I later learned, contained an instrument known as a humane killer. He entered the garden and squatted by the suffering beast and gave it a thorough examination. He then donned a green, rubberised apron; a screen was erected around the tormented animal, there was a few seconds silence and then....... CRACK!!! There was a sharp report like that of a firearm.

The humane killer, a gun to all intents and purposes, was devised to send a steel bolt through the skull of the horse and into its brain, killing it instantly. Teachers arrived to usher away the children and as we went towards the school building I looked back to see the gypsy man whose horse had just been slain. He was a little over six feet tall but his shoulders were rounded in grief and they went up and down as sobs wracked his frame. I silently cried in sympathy. I saw the slaughterman's vehicle reverse onto the drive of the school, I suppose, to take away the dead animal to the glue factory or wherever it was that they took dead horses. When the school bell rang for morning break, or playtime as it was called, there was little evidence to show what had occurred earlier that morning.

Milk Monitors & Miss Lord

At that time, the teacher of the class that I was in was an elderly lady named Miss Lord who, upon looking back, was the archetypal school ma'am of the day with her hair pulled back severely and tied in a bun towards the rear of her head. She used tortoiseshell framed lorgnette spectacles which had a long, tortoiseshell handle with which she held them to her eyes; she wore a business suit with a skirt that came almost to her ankles and she wore black, sensible shoes. She was feared by the children in her care only slightly less than those children feared the bogeyman. The fearful Miss Lord, as my mother informed me, had been a teacher at Briscoe Lane Primary School when my mother herself attended the school and was equally feared by those children long ago.

Miss Lord appointed me to the position of milk monitor, responsible for allocating to each child in the class, at the morning break period, the third of a pint of milk that each child was allowed as part of a healthy diet and which in 1971, Margaret Thatcher the then Tory Minister for Health, and in later years the Tory Prime Minister, in a cost cutting exercise, would stop. She was accused, at the time, of stealing the milk from children's mouths and became known as 'Thatcher the Snatcher.'

In the winter time, as I remember, the milk would be brought into the classroom early and all the children would lay their milk bottles on the radiators to warm up the contents for break time. My job, as the milk monitor, was to remove the bottles from the crate in which they arrived and distribute one bottle per person around the class. I was ably assisted by a second milk monitor in that endeavour. If a bottle was dropped and it smashed, the milk monitor would be removed from his job and that job allocated to another pupil who was, maybe, not so accident prone or clumsy.

One winter's morning as I was going about my job, I squatted down and picked up two bottles from the crate, outside the classroom. The bottles were slippery because of the icy conditions and as I rose from my squatting position one slipped from my grasp and plunged towards the floor. I was about to lose my treasured job, one of great importance and also about to lose any chance of promotion to the elevated position of ink monitor, when instinctively, I brought my knees together and caught the tumbling glassware between them, thus saving me any embarrassment and securing my job for a little longer.

The second milk monitor, a boy named David Middleton, was watching as I dropped and then caught the falling bottle, he pointed at me and then at the bottle between my knees. He then uttered the word 'WOW!' and, immediately, dropped one of the bottles that he was holding which fell between his feet and shattered into smithereens on the concrete floor, splashing both of us with cold milk and slivers of glass. Miss Lord heard the sound of the breaking glass and came marching outside. She looked down at the puddle of milk and broken glass at my companion's feet and then looked him straight in the eyes with a withering gaze. He seemed to shrink under her penetrating stare as she raised her arm and pointed to the classroom door. Not a word was uttered as he slunk inside and made his way to his desk where he cowered in fear. She followed him in and within thirty seconds another pupil came out. I had a new assistant milk monitor to help me. It could so easily have been me that lost the job. Miss Lord then sent me to report the mishap to the caretaker who arrived with a mop, a brush and a shovel to clean up the mess.

Evenings at the Picturehouse

Once a week, in the evening, during spring and summertime, when the nights were light, mother, father, Valerie and I would go to the cinema. As we reached the entrance to the picture house there would be a one legged man sat against the wall with a placard around his neck stating that his injuries were received during the war and that he was unable to work, there was a begging bowl placed in front of him and across his leg, his crutch lay. He was positioned to one side of the entrance, his back against the wall of the movie theatre with one trouser leg pinned up at the thigh. On the other side of the entrance stood a partially sighted man, again supposedly injured during the war; he had a white stick attached to his wrist by way of a leather thong. That man had a tray balanced at his waist and held there by a leather strap around his neck. He was the vendor of matches and shoe laces and various other small but useful items. Rumour had it that after the last show had started and the cinema had closed its doors to any more entrants the match seller, whose tray folded up into a wooden and cardboard carry case complete with handle and who was too proud to beg, packed away his goods and made his way home via shanks's pony, his folded tray in one hand and his white cane being moved laterally in front of him in the other. Meanwhile, a posh limousine driven by a well dressed lady pulled up and took away the one legged, crippled beggar and his takings in positive comfort. I relate this tale to show that, even back then there were those that would do anything rather than work and still be better off than those who chose to do something productive.

We would enter the theatre and my father would pay for the tickets before we entered the actual cinema from the kiosk area. There, an usherette, usually an attractive young lady in crisp uniform would greet us and light our way, by way of her torch, down the steps from the rear of the cinema to our seats. When we reached the row of seats where we were to sit other cinemagoers would have to stand to let us pass. We would struggle past as sweet wrappers, peanut shells and dropped popcorn crackled beneath our feet. Why people always sat at either end of the row and leave the middle seats empty for the latecomers I don't know, but it was ever the case.

All picture houses in those days were referred to as flea pits or bug houses and they usually had seats upholstered in blue, green or red velveteen. If one took the trouble to pat the well worn upholstered seat before sitting down, clouds of dust would erupt upwards from the padding like volcanic ash from Vesuvius. The back couple of rows were fitted with double seats known as lover's seats for courting couples. It was viewed as a treat for Val and me to be taken to the picture show. There was a choice of two cinemas; the Magnet on Old Church Street where we went for the Saturday matinee and about fifty yards distant from the Magnet, on Dulverton Street, was the Pavilion. There was one other cinema locally and that was the Ceylon picture house on Thorpe Road, but it was a rare occasion when we visited that venue. It was usually father's choice which film we went to see and at which cinema, but it was usually the Magnet. In those days, depending on the type of film, the programme would change mid-week. A film would be screened from Sunday to Tuesday and then another film from Wednesday until Saturday. If the films were so called blockbusters, they would be on all week. Prior to the main feature there would be advertisements from Pearl & Dean followed by the Pathé Newsreel, then a minor film or cartoons. During the intermission the screen would be filled with adverts for Lyon's Dairymaid Ice cream and Kia-Ora orange drink and Orange Maid iced lollies sold as the 'drink on a stick,' then the lights would come on and the ice cream lady/usherette would walk down the central aisle and stand beneath the screen to sell her wares which included cigarettes as well as sweets and ices.

I remember seeing two biblical epics starring Victor Mature; those were The Robe and its sequel Demetrius and the Gladiators. I also remember seeing the great western, Shane, written by Jack Schaefer and starring Alan Ladd, Van Heflin and Jack Palance and one of the great American character actors, Elisha Cook Junior. I always thought that Alan Ladd was miscast as Shane. I also remember going to see another Alan Ladd film entitled Hell Below Zero, also starring Stanley Baker. It was based on a Hammond Innes Book. The film is about whaling and the action takes place on board the mother ship in the seas of Antarctica.

One film my father took us to see was, A Lion Is in the Street, starring James Cagney. The story, as I remember it, took place somewhere in the Deep South of the US, especially in Louisiana, during the depression era and was based on the life of Huey P. Long, a lawyer turned politician. I'm afraid, as a child, it went right over my head and all the way home I kept asking my dad where the lion was. James Cagney, in the film, was the personification of the lion; lion being an analogy for a brave man who fought for the underdog within society and for what he thought was right.

There were other films that were aimed more at children but were also suitable viewing for adults that my mother and father took us to see. Disney's 1950 classic animated feature Pinocchio was one and a few years later there was Lady and the Tramp. Walt Disney also turned out a couple of educational nature feature films; firstly in 1954 came The Living Desert, followed in 1955 by its sequel, The Vanishing Prairie, both of which we were taken to see. Although the later film was viewed in the cinema at Blackley, before such visits to the cinema ceased altogether.

The Clayton Gang, a Move to Oldham & an Unkind Cut

Sometime in 1954, when things were getting a little crowded at Rosebank Road and Auntie Annie was about to get married it became time for Uncle Bob, Aunty Joan and Cousin Bobby to move out of granny Annie's house. Uncle Bob, now out of the army and working at Failsworth Hat Makers, put a relatively large deposit, thanks to his severance pay from the army, on a house in Chadderton near Oldham and within a few weeks they moved out of Newton Heath and into an end of terrace house with no bathroom and an outside toilet; a retrograde step in some ways but at least the house was their own, albeit on a small mortgage. They had returned to the days of the tin tub in front of the fire for bathing and also to placing a chamber pot under the bed. A chamber pot was known colloquially has a po, jerry or sometimes as a guzunder because it 'guz' under the bed.

I didn't see Cousin Bobby for a few weeks but when I did I had a little trouble understanding and following his speech; he had developed, over a short period, a very broad Oldham accent, saying things like: 'It's o'er thur, tha noors.' Which when translated meant 'It is over there, you know.' Or, 'Wurt's goorn?' which meant, 'where are you going?' But I soon learned to cope with Bobby's somewhat alien dialect. The Oldham people, known as Yonners to the Mancunians had an accent which seemed to me to be a hybrid dialect born of the illicit coupling of the Lancashire and Yorkshire accents. Their own town, if they were ever asked, is called Owd'am in their vernacular; to the uninitiated it is a somewhat strange, rolling accent. One weekend Bobby and I were going to the Greenfield area for the day, to climb Indian's Head and do a little hiking. Indian's Head is a rock formation, part of Wimberry stones located above Greenfield on the South side of the Chew Valley. On the day in question we had reached Oldham Town Centre and I asked one of the locals; a toothless old Yonner with a flat cap and ill fitting outer wear with a wescott (waistcoat) bearing a gold watch and chain and ambling along at a sedentary pace, aided by a rough cut walking cane and who appeared to be about ninety years old, 'Excuse me, sir, but could you tell us how to get to Greenfield?'

He replied, 'Tha guz tu't buzz stertion, o'er thur, wurt buzzes twizz, an' ye get on tu't number ten buzz an' that teks ye tuh Grinfeld.' Which when translated meant: You go over to the bus station, over there, where the buses turn around, and you get on the number ten bus and that takes you to Greenfield. Bobby, who by then, was like one of the natives, understood the old man quite easily and we followed his instructions and had a wonderful day out at Greenfield.

Before he departed Newton Heath for his new home in Chadderton Bobby was with me and our friends on the occasions when the Clayton gang ventured into Newton Heath. They came, with mischief in their minds, across Clayton Bridge level crossing and made their way to Christ the King School playing fields where they would vociferously shout out challenges to the youth of the Newton Heath district. When the gangs were at a distance of approximately twenty yards apart a stone throwing battle would ensue, those on home ground would have their snipers hidden behind buildings and trees to score coup from their places of safety. At other times the Newton Heath gang would make a foray into Clayton

Vale in a reciprocal battle. The gang members from either side were usually between twelve and fifteen years old but occasionally, when the older lads allowed it, younger kids would tag along. Those battles were not spur of the moment meetings but had been mooted up to a fortnight before the actual scrap. The jungle grapevine sent out rumours and messages and upon a said date, usually a Saturday, battle would be joined. Other skirmishes were by way of revenge to redeem some honour from a prior beating.

Now and again Bobby, me and our friends tagged along with the Newton Heath gang; some of us were armed with home made wooden catapults which were placed in our back pockets, like Dennis the Menace from the Beano comic. Those Y shaped pieces of wood were sawn from the limbs of trees in Tetlow's woods and depending on the type and gauge of elastic fitted, could sling a small stone thirty to fifty yards. We pre teen youngsters stayed at the rear and fired our catapults over the heads of the leaders.

On one occasion the Clayton gang arrived unexpectedly on Christ the King playing fields. Bobby and I and the Rogerson brothers were playing by the side of the prefab. There was no gang from Newton Heath present and so, when there was no response to their shouted challenge, the small gang from Clayton started to throw stones, randomly at first and then specifically at Bobby and I. We ran to the coal shed to take refuge. Hearing the noise from the stone throwers my mother came out to remonstrate with them. As she strode through the garden gate a stone whistled passed her face, missing her by inches. It careered onwards and through the kitchen window smashing the glass into a thousand shards and coming to rest upon the kitchen floor. The noise of the breaking glass and the sight of an obviously very irate adult, albeit a woman, caused the Clayton gang to drop their missiles and turn tail and run, laughing as they fled the scene. My father upon returning home from his work, at dinnertime, on that said Saturday measured up the size of glass needed and went out to purchase the necessary piece to fit the window frame. Glazing being part of a plumber's job in those days my father had all the tools and equipment necessary to re-glaze the frame and within an hour of his returning from work the job was completed. If my father had reported it to the council and waited for them to come and do the repair we would have had to wait until the following Monday.

Those battles were usually brought to an end by the local adults who would chase the opposing gang of youths away. Sometimes windows would be smashed and minor injuries sustained by the opposing factions. How there were never any serious injuries during those territorial battles beggars belief. The gangs of both sides were made up solely of males and the amount of youths in the gangs differed greatly each time they ventured forth, sometimes as few as half a dozen and up to fifteen. What that territorial rivalry was borne of I know not but it existed before I was born and was still going on when I left Newton Heath for pastures new.

At the top of Scotland Hall road was an area we called 'The Hollers,' (Hollows), and this was where the railway line separated Newton Heath from Clayton and was another entry into Clayton Vale where pitched, stone throwing battles would take place, although we had to scale a fence and cross the railroad track to get there. It seems that stone throwing battles have a history in the North of England and especially Manchester and Salford which started in the nineteenth century with a violent youth culture known as the Scuttlers. The Scuttlers wore their own distinct mode of garb and wore their hair in a distinctive style, as distinctive as it was different to the Teddy-boys of later years. The Scuttler's stone throwing battles were all based on territorial rivalry and when it came to fighting at close quarters they used their wide belts fitted with heavy buckles as weapons. It was common for the Ancoats and Collyhurst Scuttlers to venture into Salford to do battle with the Greengate Scuttlers and vice versa.

During the more pleasant days of summer, in the evenings or at week-ends, one pastime that my friends and I plus Cousin Bobby enjoyed was visiting what we called the clay hills. Those friends and classmates included Ray Wood, Colin Campbell and Stuart Seal amongst others. The clay hills were located next to the Leeds, Manchester rail line at the junction of Ten Acres Lane, Bank Bridge Road and Riverpark road and opposite Philip's Park Cemetery and behind the Co-op butter works where, much later, I worked as a class one driver for the Co-op transportation and delivery sector. It was an open space, close to the aqueduct which carried the railway line that separated Clayton from Newton Heath. It was made up of hills of clay covered in grass with a couple of small ponds and it was a place where we could find grass snakes and the occasional adder amongst other fauna. It was also the place where The Riverpark meat market and abattoir would later be built and where I would work in the late 60's for Barratt Bros Meat haulage.

Nearby and through the boundary fence of the railway land and across the railway bridge, was a signal box and my friends and I took great delight in illegally climbing the fence and trespassing on the railway property and throwing stones at the box to arouse the signalman's temper. The signalman would come to the door of his box and shout at us and wave his fist but a shower of stones, plucked from the ballast between the tracks, soon had him retreating to safety. We knew full well that he couldn't leave his post and so we were quite safe as we antagonised him. If he had been able to leave his post we would have made good our escape before he had made it down the steps, of which there were many. The signalman, in sheer desperation, would phone for the transport police, but we would be well gone by the time they turned up. We used to stand trackside to watch the steam engines passing; waving at the driver and fireman of both goods and passenger trains.

After Bobby's departure from Rosebank Road and after Aunty Annie's wedding to Harry Cowan, it seems that there was not enough cash going into the house and so my grandmother took in a lodger. The terms of Grandma's tenancy did not allow for the practise of sub-letting but unbeknownst to the landlord it was common practise to do so in those days of penury. The lodger was a young, attractive female named May. She was from out of town and about nineteen years of age and she had secured employment, in the evenings and on Saturday afternoon, at the Magnet cinema as an usherette and ice cream lady. At my grannies house she was allocated the tiny box room to sleep in but lived and dined with the family. When she could she would get us into the picture-house free of charge and managed, now and again, to get for us, free ice creams, although upon reflection I believe she may have paid for the ices out of her own money. Sadly, for us kids she neither lasted long at my grandmother's or at the Magnet before she went her own way. Perhaps she had been making eyes at recently married Aunty Annie's husband Harry and because of that, had been given her marching orders by my grandmother or maybe she had found a better job elsewhere or maybe she had become homesick and moved back to whence she had come.

Meanwhile at Bobby's new address in Chadderton his mother discovered, by what means I know not, that Bobby had something wrong with his external waterworks. He had great difficulty in drawing back his foreskin; in fact, he could not draw it back at all. Like me, Bobby was born a Christian and there was no religious requirement after birth to have the foreskin surgically removed. In Bobby's case it had obviously become a question of hygiene as he could not wash beneath the appendage and so he was referred to a specialist in things of a sexual and reproductive nature and upon receiving his appointment he was taken to the Royal Jewish Hospital where they were conversant with such things.

Some joker in the hospital, upon finding out what Bobby was in for told him that the implement used to carry out the operation had wooden handles that were fashioned from the wood of the juniper shrub. Think about it...... Juniper, ju-nipper, jew-nipper. No? Bobby never got it either, nor me at the time. Bobby was allocated a bed and his mum was told that he would stay until the following day to acclimatise himself to his surroundings and the next day he would, at the age of nine, be circumcised. Now, unlike a new born baby, who has no recollection of the event or the ensuing pain, Bobby carried the stigma of late circumcision with him for a long time. It was the immediate effects, however, that caused Bobby a lot of misery. He was in hospital for a week after the operation to remove the over tight, superfluous flesh, during which time his member was bandaged for cleanliness and protection, but after a week the dressing was removed and he was discharged and sent home and that was when his problems began.

When in bed at home the glans of his penis, (commonly known as the copper's helmet or in his case the Bobby's helmet), which was then ultra sensitive, tended to rub on his pyjamas and cause him a lot of pain. It also caused an erection which he could not get rid of until sleep overtook him. During the day time when he was walking around his glans rubbed against his underwear causing the same problem. Bobby was walking around in constant pain with a permanent hard on. His mother made him wear girl's knickers which, unlike Y fronts, had no outlet for his penis and it was an attempt by his mum to try to hold his rampant organ down. He had also taken on an unusual gait; he walked like a saddle sore cowboy, keeping his legs as far apart as his locomotion would allow, in an attempt to minimise the amount of friction between his clothes and his dangly bits. His private parts became an embarrassment to Bobby and he was kept away from school until the healing process was complete and until his mode of perambulation had returned to normal and no further, unexpected erections popped up.

Whit Walks, Teddy Boys and the Fairground

I remember Whitsuntide in 1955, before we moved to Blackley. We would gather to watch the Whit week walks, all dressed up in our new clothes, specially purchased, on the never-never, for the occasion. Church of England walks took place on Whit Monday whilst the Roman Catholics walked on the Friday. It seemed a good idea to keep the Proddy Dogs and the Cat Licks apart. Before we went to watch the Whit Week Walks we would go around to all the neighbours, resplendent in our finery, to show off our new clothes. Most of the neighbours would give us pennies and then our relatives would give us more cash. When we finally reached Oldham Road crowds lined the pavement four and five deep to watch the 'scholars,' as the young marchers were called by the older generation as they marched in the parades. Children were hoisted onto their father's shoulders to see the marches. Everybody was dressed in their best or new clobber.

Whitsuntide was the one time in the year when all the members of the Hampson family and its offshoots came from near and far to gather outside the Duke of York public house on the corner of Church Street and Oldham Road to see their brothers and sisters, nephews and nieces and to have a few drinks and watch the walks. Those Aunties and uncles that had gotten married either prior to or during World War II and had moved away from Newton Heath had the once a year opportunity, at Whitsuntide, to all get together as a family.

Aunty Hetty had married an Irish bricklayer named Peter Flanagan and they had moved to Moss Side. Uncle George had married a lady called Elsie Cammock and they had moved to the new council estate at Wythenshawe, Woodhouse Park to be exact. Close to them had moved my aunty Elsie and her husband Harry Gibbons who lived in a council flat close to Ringway Airport, now Manchester International Airport. Uncle John Hampson wed a lady called Betty Coyne and lived in Miles Plattting before moving to the more salubrious area of Bramhall. Both aunty Beatty and Uncle Fred and Uncle Walter and his spouse, Aunty Elsie moved to Blackley as did we. Aunty Joan and Uncle Bob moved to Chadderton, leaving Aunty Annie with her mother, my Gran, at Rosebank Road. Although the family had become somewhat fractured, Whitsuntide was the time all the relatives met up in Newton Heath, including all my numerous cousins.

While the adult relatives were enjoying their beer from the Duke of York the youngsters who had plenty of money that they had been given for looking so nice in their new clothes were despatched to Joe Hall's Temperance bar across the road. There, they could indulge themselves on Vimto and sweets without their parent's supervision. After our visit to Joe Hall's we would wander back to the Duke of York where, now and again our parents would buy us a bottle of lemonade and a packet of crisps and we would sit on the steps of the pub and devour them, only moving when an adult entered or left the pub.

Just prior to that time a new phenomenon was born in Britain, that new phenomenon was the Teddy-boy. With his flat top, south bank or Tony Curtis style haircut with massive quiff held in place by copious lashings of Brylcreem, his fingertip length drape jacket and drainpipe trousers and his thick crepe soled, brothel creeper shoes plus his love for rock 'n' roll music and his supposed penchant for violence, he was all the things that parents did not want their sons to become. The average age of the Teddy-Boys was between fifteen and nineteen; between eighteen and nineteen years of age they would have become liable for National Service and would have been inducted into the armed forces. Upon coming out of the army they would have matured into something other than Teddy-Boys, although not all ex squaddies hung up their drapes for good.

The term Teddy-boy was first coined in an article in the Daily Express in 1953 to describe the youth of the day who dressed in Edwardian style garb. The Teddy-boy was peculiar to post war Britain; America had its motor bike gangs as personified by Marlon Brando in the 1953 film The Wild One and we in Great Britain had the Teddy-boy. The Teddy-boy was noted for his outrageous and flamboyant mode of attire. He wore brightly coloured jackets and fluorescent socks and sported a well coiffured hairstyle, whereas American bikers wore blue jeans, white T shirts and black leather jackets. The rockers of the 60's adopted the same attire as the American bikers in their war with the mods. The Ted's were the first real youth culture in Britain since the Scuttlers and the first youths with money to spare in post war Britain.

On that day in 1955, the year that Bill Haley's Rock Around the Clock first topped the pop charts, although Shake Rattle & Roll had been a top ten entry in 1954, as we watched the 'scholars' march, a Teddy-boy, dressed in a hound's tooth patterned, Edwardian style suit with velvet collar and cuffs and with all the accoutrements such as a Slim Jim tie, loud waistcoat and thick crepe soled shoes, and a pint pot of mild beer in his hand sauntered up and stood next to me to watch the passing parade.

My father, who, as a tradesman plumber, was probably paid a basic wage for forty five hours of about £9.00 or £10.00 per week at that time, although more could be earned by way of overtime, turned to my uncle John and said 'Would you look at that suit? It must have cost a bloody score o' pounds.' (£20.00), 'I'd like to know where these youngsters get their bloody money from.'

The Teddy-boy turned to my father and smiled, whilst holding his tipped cigarette between his teeth and said 'Twenny five pounds actually,' and after seeing what he wanted to see he turned around and walked off to join a couple of other youths dressed in similar attire. A few years later I would adopt the Edwardian style of dress but by then it was the closing years of the Teddy-boy era.

Near the top of Orford Road, before it came to the junction with Briscoe Lane and to the side and rear of the tripe works that was situated there, was, as I remember it, some spare, rough ground where, annually or sometimes two and three times a year, especially on bank holidays, the fairground would set up. There were a number of fairground owners in the North of England, but the one that sticks out in my mind was Silcock's Fairground Amusements of Warrington. Silcock's were and still are typical travelling Fairground people, taking in such fairs as the Nottingham Goose Fair and the Daisy Nook Easter Fair and many more in the North West.

The tripe works, I think, belonged to UCP (United Cattle Products), who had tripe shops and UCP Cafes all over Lancashire. As I remember it had no residential properties adjoining it, although there were prefabs opposite. To one side was the graveyard, to the other side and to the rear was empty ground. This was, no doubt, because of the terrible stench that issued from the place as they boiled and prepared bits of dead animal for whatever uses it had. Besides the tripe, which was cow's or sheep's stomach prepared for human consumption, the tripe works prepared pigs trotters, cowheel, black puddings and other bits of offal which were the bovine, ovine or porcine delicacies of the day. They also prepared tripe that was used in the production of animal foods for dogs and cats.

I remember as a child having to pass the tripe works on the way to school. My sister and I and my mother used to hold handkerchiefs to our faces to try to quell the smell. I remember my mother and sister putting lavender water on their hankies but I refused it. It depended on which way the wind was blowing how far before and how far after passing the place one had to put the hankies to ones noses. How the workers at the tripe works put up with the smell I do not know, perhaps they just got used to it. The people that lived in the prefabs opposite must have suffered badly as the stench must have permeated the very structures in which they lived, or perhaps, they too just got used to it.

Because of the suggested roughness of fairground people and their transient lifestyle; most people called them gypsies and because of our lack of years we were only allowed to go to the fairground on our own during the daytime, during school holidays and at week-ends. In the evenings, supposedly for safety purposes, our parents took us. It was in the evening time, around the big rides such as the Waltzer, the Ferris Wheel and the Dodgem cars, that Teddy-boys would congregate and lean against the barriers with their girl friends and pals listening to the loud rock 'n' roll and other music of the day being pumped out by the massive speakers of the rides. The girls all wore their hair in a ponytail style and they dressed in flared skirts and blouses or pedal pusher pants and tight sweaters.

The lads that worked on the Waltzer, most of them Teddy-boys themselves, spun the cars that contained only girls, making the young ladies scream hysterically as the centrifugal force pushed them back into the seats and caused their ponytails to lash around and their flared skirts to blow up to reveal a glimpse of their bare thighs, knickers, stocking tops, and suspender belts. The lasses blushed as, with much difficulty and futility, they tried to hold their skirts and petticoats down with one hand as they tried to hold on to the restraining bar with the other as they whirled around faster and faster and the centrifugal force pressed them into the backs of the seats as they screamed louder and louder. On the dodgems the fare collectors stood on the rear of the bumper cars, holding on to the conductor bar as they collected the fares. They would reach over the occupants of the cars to seize the steering wheels of those containing only girls and force them to crash into other cars, once again resulting in shrill, ear piercing screams from the giggling girls.

There was, at times, some friction caused because the girls seemed to be drawn to the fairground workers and those same lads would go out of their way to chat up the smiling females which, occasionally, erupted into bouts of fisticuffs between the fairground workers and the local youths. Now and again I would notice one of the working youths wander off with the girl of his choice into a quiet corner or between the caravans and generators. What they got up to I could only guess at, but I had heard of it referred to as a perk of the job.

There was the acrid smell of diesel mingled with the sweet aroma of candy floss and toffee apples and the thump, thump, thump of the big diesel engined generators. There was the sound of metal on metal as the running gear of the machines and rides turned and the cogs meshed and steel wheels ran on steel tracks. There was the smell of hot grease from over worked machinery and finally there was the smell of hamburgers and hot dogs and onions wafting through the evening air. Raucous crowds of people, both young and old jostled each other as they moved around the crowded fairground in a hubbub of noise. There was an atmosphere of happiness, jollity and glee as the older lads and men made determined efforts to show their skill, strength and accuracy on the coconut shies and punch balls as they endeavoured to impress their lady friends. There was also the 'Test Your Strength' machine where youths and their elders queued up to swing a huge mallet at a plunger that would send a marker up a small tower with a bell at the top. The tower was graded and the higher the marker went, the stronger the mallet swinger was. It was a rare event for someone to send the marker zooming to the top to ring the bell and win a prize.

The latter day sharpshooters and general gunslingers tried in vain to cut the strings that held the prizes or knock down the aluminium figures on the shooting gallery with underpowered air rifles whose sights were very probably mis-aligned. Three shots a tanner (2 ½ p), said the sign, It should have said, 'you might as well close your eyes for all the chance you have.' Youngsters tried their luck at darts on the Stick three Cards and win a prize, Hook a Duck, Hoop-la or they played the penny slot machines or the roll-a-penny stalls and rode the smaller, slower roundabouts.

The prizes given out at fairgrounds at the time were cheap tat. Boys would spend ten bob (50p) to win a kewpie doll worth a shilling (5p) for their girl friends. The most popular prizes, after the soft toys, were coconuts and gold fish and one could always pick out a winner. Youths would walk home juggling a couple of coconuts or they would puncture them to drink the coconut milk before smashing the outer shell and eating the soft, white flesh within. Others would have a plastic bag filled with water and containing a goldfish in one hand and a coconut in the other. They would be laughing and joking, oblivious to the fact that they had spent ten times what the prizes were worth. They were heroes in the eyes of their wide eyed girlfriends who held the teddy bears and kewpie dolls that had been won for them in one hand and hugged their boy friends with the other.

I was overawed by the loud music and the massive vehicles with their huge generators. Some of the vehicles were bonneted Scammell ballast Trucks once used for heavy haulage or for military service. At the time I did not know that they were called ballast trucks but I was captivated by their sheer size and the flamboyant, multi-coloured, sign written liveries of those coach painted lorries. The ballast boxes on those vehicles were now the homes of the generators powered by Gardner, Cummins and Leyland engines.

Old vehicles of other makes, mostly ex forces vehicles such as Foden, Leyland, Atkinson, Thorneycroft and ERF and even the American Diamond T were also employed, but the fairground people had a specific leaning towards vehicles powered by the Gardner engine which was renowned for its reliability. The Gardner was known as a gaffers motor; it was dependable though not fast, it was frugal compared to the Cummins engine of equal horse power. Those trucks, when moving from site to site, towed two or three trailers; they were equivalent in size to the Australian road trains, although the distances that they covered could not be compared.

The large fairground rides such as The Waltzer, the Dodgems and the Ferris Wheel were constructed so that they could be packed away, lock, stock and barrel, into an eight wheeler prime mover and an 'A' framed, two axle trailer or later in the days of articulation into a forty foot, semi trailer; a place for everything and everything in its place. There would be the prime mover hitched to whatever ride the owner had; that would be hitched to the living accommodation in the form of a tandem axle caravan and then sometimes, hitched behind that would be a toffee apple or candy floss stall or kiosk. I wondered, at the time, how on earth they managed to get those vehicles and trailers around the corners on those old narrow roads. It was from seeing those old fairground juggernauts that I got the love of heavy vehicles, that was to dominate my adult life.

So enthralled was I by the vehicles belonging to the showmen that on the day that the fair was leaving for pastures new, a Monday during the school holidays as it happened, I convinced Cousin Bobby and Tommy and Terry Rogerson that we should go and watch them stowing the rides away and getting ready to move on. We went to the Fairground site and spent most of the day watching the showmen as they stripped the machines down and stored them in the wagons and trailers. It was amazing to see the massive rides taken down, folded up and stacked away. There were numerous vehicular movements, hitching up and un-hitching, moving of trailers and caravans and the pushing and pulling of toffee apple and candy floss and do-nut stalls until they were all packed up and ready to go. We four then ran to Briscoe Lane to watch the convoy depart. All the traffic on Briscoe lane stopped to watch the parade of vehicles pass, as if they couldn't be more pleased to see the back of the itinerants. The fairground people left the spare ground that had housed them for the past week one behind the other, nose to tail like a long snake uncoiling and winding its way through the long grass to pastures new, leaving behind them piles of litter and the detritus of a week's fairground visit.

On that day Cousin Bobby and Terry Rogerson were childishly playing around, pushing and shoving, pulling and tugging each other, as children do, when Terry dashed into the road to evade Bobby. He ran into the path of the lead vehicle of the fairground convoy. The driver slammed on his brakes and hit the horn. Terry stopped in front of the vehicle that was bearing down on him. He was like a rabbit caught in the headlights of a car and he was struck by the massive vehicle leaving the site; a Foden if I recall correctly. The Highway Code was the furthest thing from Terry's mind as he playfully dodged Bobby and made that fateful run and although the vehicles in the convoy were travelling slowly he was quite badly injured and an ambulance was called for. It was the weight of the vehicle that was responsible for the injuries which Terry received rather than the speed of the vehicle that hit him. Terry was rendered unconscious and Bobby was traumatised and crying. The police arrived and statements were taken, mainly from adults who were present. They came around later to interview Bobby while he was with his parents.

The cream coloured ambulance arrived quickly, preceded by the clamour of its loud clanging bell and Terry was tended to on the spot before being placed on a stretcher and taken to Booth Hall Children's Hospital in Blackley, Manchester. He lost a lot of the muscle and tissue from one arm which had been crushed and badly mangled by the fairground vehicle and his arm was never the same. He was still attending the hospital when I left Newton Heath and had as I remember, at least five operations on his mutilated and disfigured arm. Accusations of blame were thrown around, but I suppose Bobby and Terry were equally to blame. No blame could be attached to the driver of the fairground vehicle who was just going about his job when two children, oblivious to the danger, were fooling around in a dangerous environment, when one of them became a victim of circumstances.

Chapter 6

HOLIDAYS WITH THE FAMILY AND BELL'S PALSY

Holidays in the Fifties

Holidays in the 1950's were not like they are now. Different towns had different set holiday weeks, known in the North of England as Wakes Weeks, when factories would have a two weeks summer shutdown. Only the rich and famous travelled to the continent for their two weeks of sunshine; lesser mortals usually travelled to the nearest seaside town to their home town such as Blackpool and Southport if the city of Manchester or other Lancashire sites were their home towns. Londoners went to the South or East Coast to resorts such as Clacton or Southend on Sea or Eastbourne and Brighton. Those that lived in Yorkshire or Lincolnshire used the resorts along the east coast from Scarborough to Great Yarmouth and so on. Liverpudlians either holidayed at North Wales or took the ferry across the Mersey to New Brighton on the Wirral. The Wirral was jokingly referred to as the Scouse Riviera. New Brighton also had a tower based on the Eiffel tower. It was constructed in 1896 and was one hundred and three feet taller than Blackpool tower. It had its own winter gardens, fairground and ballroom. The tower was pulled down in the 1920's due to lack of maintenance and the surrounding buildings were destroyed by fire in the 1960's.

The Wirral was also the place where an industrialist from Bolton, named William Hesketh Lever, founded Lever Brothers Soap Factory. Lord Leverhulme, as he became known, was appalled by the slum conditions in which working class people had to live and so he had built, in 1888, a model village known as Port Sunlight to accommodate his workers. He also introduced a profit sharing scheme; he was a visionary and philanthropist who believed that a happy workforce was a productive workforce. Of course it was not all a philanthropic ideal, Lever knew that those people that lived in his model village could not skive off or throw a sickie without good reason and also they had to pay rent which went straight back to the Lever estate. Other model villages that sprung up at the time were The Bourneville Model village, built in 1879 by George Cadbury, of chocolate fame, for the workers at the Birmingham, Cadbury factory and the village at Saltaire, close to Bradford and on the banks of the River Aire built in1853 by Titus Salt to accommodate the workers from his woollen mill. Those model villages did not just serve as accommodation; they also included numerous social amenities such as shops, schools and surgeries. There were other model villages that sprung up near to the workplaces of coal miners and Railway workers to house the workers from those enterprises.

A foreign holiday to the working classes was a boat trip to the Isle of Man or Ireland or a trip up north of the border into Scotland. I felt as if I was going abroad when the family took the Royal Iris, Mersey Ferry from Liverpool to New Brighton.One was considered well travelled if one took the ferry from Weymouth to the Channel Islands or the ferry from Ullapool to the Inner or Outer Hebrides or from Aberdeen to the Shetland or Orkney Islands. A few brave families went on camping trips to the warmer climes of France, but not many working class families flew to theMediterranean resorts of coastal Spain or much less to Turkey or Greece. New World destinations and the Far East were unknown destinations for working class families. Conscripts into the armed forces could travel the world but usually into war zones like Suez, Palestine or Korea, where the chances of being killed far outweighed the attractions of the tourist resorts.

I recall holidaying as a family and usually with my mum's sister, my Aunty Beatty and her husband Uncle Fred and their two sons Freddy and Peter. Cousin Freddy was nearly three years my senior and Peter was one year older than me. They lived in a prefab in Blackley, opposite Booth Hall Children's Hospital, but because they were same sex children, with two years between them, they could share a bedroom which allowed them to stay in the prefab longer than our family could stay in the Prefab in Newton Heath. Although, after a few years those prefabs were served with compulsory purchase orders and all the residents had to be re-housed and the land upon which they had been built reverted back to Boggart Hole Clough, a Victorian public park from which the land had been borrowed.

Boggart Hole Clough is a one hundred and sixty four acre park in North Manchester, which was reputedly haunted by Boggarts. Boggarts are mischievous spirits found mainly in Lancashire and Yorkshire folklore. A Clough is a deep sided wooded valley of which a number can be found in Boggart Hole Clough. Known locally as 'The Clough,' the park has numerous leisure facilities including an athletics track, a café, a boating lake and angling pond. Fun runs are held there as are mountain bike days and there is an annual firework display on the nearest weekend to bonfire night. People go to the Clough for bird watching and to see other wild life such as rabbits, hares, squirrels, foxes amongst others. There are numerous types of trees in the park, most significantly, the Manchester Poplar. There are numerous fruit trees including apple, plum and cherry trees. Most of the fruit tees grow where the gardens of the prefabs were once situated.

When we went on our annual holiday we travelled to the chosen destination either by train or coach. I can remember travelling by train to Rhyl railway station in North Wales and then catching the local bus, weighed down by numerous suitcases, to a holiday camp in Gronant, where we stayed in little chalets. I do not remember the name of the camp in Gronant. It could have been Butlin's or Pontin's or a Haven camp, but what I do remember, upon reflection, is that the camp was exactly like the camp depicted years later in the TV show Hi-De-Hi, where families stayed in very basic chalet accommodations and where the communal dining room of the camp doubled as the function and entertainment room where shows were held and alcoholic beverages were served to the holidaymakers. The staff dressed in a uniform of white shirts or blouses, blazers with the camp's motif embroidered on the breast pocket and grey flannel trousers or skirts. The uniforms allowed the staff to stand out from the holidaymakers. They performed on stage, acted as waiters and babysitters and represented the camp in a whole host of functions and helpful tasks.

The British Holiday Camp as we know it was the brainchild of William 'Billy' Butlin who opened his first such camp on the bracing Lincolnshire seafront at Ingoldmells near Skegness in 1936. The camp was opened by celebrity aeronaut Amy Johnson. It was a place built for fun and leisure, with entertainments throughout the day and evening. Accommodation was in the purpose built but Spartan pre-fabricated chalets made for families. Everything about Butlin's Holiday Camp was family and fun oriented and that first camp became the template for all his other camps and of those of his followers and copiers such as Fred Pontin. The camps had their own launderettes, showers, swimming pools, Post offices and churches and communal dining rooms.

Billy Butlin was born in Cape Town, S. Africa in 1899. The family moved to Canada where Billy served in the army and then, after the First World War they settled in England where Billy earned a living working on the funfairs until he could afford his own hoop-la stall, then two, and then more. He opened his own funfair parks in various locations and as his empire grew the plan for his first holiday camp was born. Billy Butlin opened eight more holiday camps after Skegness and these were at Ayr in Scotand, Bognor, Barry Island in South Wales, Clacton, Filey, Mosney in County Meath in Ireland, Minehead and Pwllheli in South Wales and Mid Wales respectively, plus hotels at Blackpool and other seaside resorts. Sadly, there are only three Butlin's holiday camps left; these are at Skegness, Minehead and Bognor. Minehead and Bognor have hotels incorporated into their camps. The sites are now owned by Bourne Leisure which operates other leisure brands in the UK including Warner and Haven. Billy Butlin was knighted in 1964 and became Sir William Butlin. The camps' resident staff and entertainers were called Redcoats after the colour of their uniforms and some of those that started as Redcoats are now everyday names in the entertainment world like Des O'Connor, Jimmy Tarbuck, Dave Allen and Glenda Jackson. Billy Butlin died on 12th of June 1980, of a stomach illness following a number of heart attacks.

I also remember travelling to Towyn near Rhyl by coach. The coaches known by the old fashioned name of charabancs and commonly abbreviated to charas and pronounced 'sharrers' were boarded at Dean's Charabanc Garage in Newton Heath. I mostly remember the charas as being of the bonneted or half cab design with luggage racks along the interior sides of the coach above the seats. The racks were similar in construction to those on the trains of the day. The coaches were Crossley's, Bedford's or Leyland's and were based on truck chassis'. Families, including ours, went on day trips to the seaside on Dean's charas because it was cheaper than railway travel and almost as fast. The duke of York public house sometimes organised morning drives, on which we went with our parents.

The coach or coaches if more than one was needed would pick up all the travellers along with numerous crates of beer, outside the pub, take us all on a mystery tour, well, it was certainly a mystery to me, and return to the pub in the early evening. The return journey was punctuated by numerous toilet stops and when the coach was in motion everybody would be singing the popular tunes of the day. Most of the men were close to drunkenness, but still held bottles to their lips between verses. Some of the ladies weren't exactly sober either.

The summers of my childhood, as I remember them, were warmer and longer than those of today, much as the winters were colder and whiter. I remember swimming in the sea in my trunks and sunbathing on the sandy beaches of the resorts that we visited and I also recall that the coastal railway had to be crossed to access the beach from most of the North Wales Holiday Camps. My father said something to my uncle Fred that I didn't understand at the time and what he said was that he believed that Liverpool was the capital of North Wales. I came to know what he meant when I realised, later, that North Wales was the preferred holiday spot for Scousers and there were more Scouse accents to be heard than there were Welsh.

I must have been what can only be described as, completely stupid in my innocence and ignorance, as a young child. I was naïve to the point of distraction as will be demonstrated by the next recollection. If we didn't go away for a week's holiday by the seaside we would go on day's outings to places that were only a bus ride or two away. One such day out was to Lyme Park in Cheshire. Lyme Park is situated just off the A6 at Disley between Buxton and Manchester. It consists of a large mansion house surrounded by formal gardens. It has its own herds of red and fallow deer and some Highland Cattle and a large lake. Lyme Park now belongs to the National Trust to whom it was bequeathed, in 1946, by the Legh family who had owned the house and lands since 1388. There is an entrance fee to the grounds and the hall.

There was, when I was a child, a small road train with three or four carriages that used to transport visitors to various parts of the park at about five mph. On that day, long ago, when I visited Lyme Park with my sister and parents, with us was my Auntie Beattie and Uncle Fred and their two sons, Freddy and Peter. We clambered into the rearmost carriage and seated ourselves as comfortably as possible on the flat wooden seats. After we had travelled a couple of hundred yards young Fred stood up and jumped from the carriage and ran along behind it holding on to a grab rail at the back.

When, after being shouted at by his dad, he jumped back into the carriage, I thought to myself 'I'm gonna do that,' and before anybody could stop me I attempted the same mischief that Freddy had executed. I jumped from the carriage and as I hit the floor running, I stumbled and tripped over my own feet and rolled head over heels before coming to a halt in the middle of the tarmac. I raised myself to my hands and knees to see the road train pulling further away. I then saw my father leap from the moving vehicle and run towards me. Upon reaching me he helped me up, checked me over and then gave me the most severe ticking off. We then had to walk about half a mile to the next place on the agenda where we met up with the rest of the family. I distinctly remember a grinning Freddy, finding great amusement in my mishap.

A few weeks later and back in home territory on a miserable, windy and rainy day at the beginning of Autumn I was on a bus with the same family members on a journey to Aunty Beatty's prefab. As we were nearing our bus stop, just outside Booth Hall Children's Hospital, opposite which were the prefabs where Aunty Beattie and Uncle Fred lived, Cousin Freddy decked off the bus while it was still in motion, even though there was a large and visible sign forbidding it. The buses in those days had an open back end with a platform, the platform was fitted with chromium plated handles for passengers to hold on to and all buses had a conductor to collect fares and issue tickets. Seeing Freddy perform such a daring stunt, I said to no one in particular 'I can do that,' and I decked off the bus just as Freddy had done but with a somewhat different result. I once again, *'a la'* Lyme Park, stumbled and tripped over my own feet. The forward momentum that I picked up from jumping from a moving vehicle caused me to tumble forward and to roll along the road to come to rest, face down in the rubbish and water filled gutter.

The first person to reach me and come to my aid was Cousin Freddy, who helped me to my feet. My clothes were soaked and filthy and stuck to my jacket and trousers were the leaves from the sycamores and oaks that hung over the hospital's wall. There was a right angled rip in my new long trousers around the knee area exposing my abraded kneecap. By the time I had been helped to a standing position my father had arrived. If looks could have killed I would have withered and turned to dust at that very moment. He checked me over and patted me down as he had done at Lyme Park and once again berated me vehemently for being so 'bloody stupid.'

My clothes were stained and dripping due to my head over heels tumble and roll in the gutter, my hands and face were filthy and I had suffered gravel rash to my knees, but other than that I was undamaged. Uncle Fred, upon seeing that I was not seriously hurt said, 'Well, if something had gone really wrong we are outside local children's hospital and that would be the right place, it seems.' It appears that some youngsters, me in particular, just don't learn and with the number of mishaps that I experienced it is a wonder I ever reached the age to be able to drive Heavy Goods Vehicles.

The Greek Wedding in London

It was in 1955, during the school's six weeks summer holiday that invitations to a wedding turned up at the prefab. The wedding was that of my cousin Beryl, the daughter of my dad's sister Louisa and her husband William Bellini. Beryl was to marry a Greek lad named Georgiou Kyriakou and the wedding was to be a formal affair with all the ladies wearing evening dresses and all the men to wear dress suits and bow ties for the reception. We were to stay at Aunt Lou's house on Stoke Newington Common in North London for a week. Stoke Newington Common as mentioned earlier was just off the A10, Cambridge Road. The house was a large, Victorian, three storeys high, town house with a small pent-house built on the roof.

We travelled down to London, for the second time in four years, by steam train, in the middle of the week. As I remember it was the same train 'The Mancunian,' that carried us south. Once again the station was filled with the smoky exhalations of steam trains and again people appeared ghost like from the haze generated from those massive machines. On that second trip I was not so quick to stick my head out of the window. Upon arriving at Euston Station we once again caught a connecting local train to Stoke Newington station where Uncle Bill picked us up and ferried us to the common. I recognised the area and the house immediately and Aunt Lou made a terrific fuss over Val and me. There were a lot of people in Aunt Lou's house, some related, some not; we were introduced to everybody. After all the kisses from the distaff side, I went off and washed my face.

My memories of the wedding are somewhat scratchy but I do remember the newly married couple dancing around a big room, at the reception and everybody going up to them and pinning bank notes to them as they danced. Their clothes were completely covered in notes of all denominations from ten shilling notes to £5 notes and numerous denominations of Drachmas. I remember older swarthy looking people speaking a language that was totally incomprehensible to me. Men in traditional Greek clothing performed the Greek Circle Dance and as it continued the Bride and Groom joined in followed by numerous guests. At the reception candy covered almonds known as Koufeta were distributed as favours. After the meal, plates were smashed as a symbol of good luck.

My cousin Billy, Beryl's brother was dressed in his Royal blue Teddy-boy suit and singing the lyrics of Bill Haley's Rockin' Through the Rye.' He was with some of his mates, also Teddy-boys and he shuffled over to the Greek musicians who were dressed in traditional Greek attire and playing their traditional songs. Billy wanted to hear the latest Rock'n'roll tunes, so he threw a ten bob note, (50p) into the bowl which sat before the musicians for gratuities and said 'Play something a bit lively, mate. Will ya?' The lead musician looked down disparagingly at the ten bob note and then looked Billy up and down in an appraising manner and responded with a thick accent, 'Later sonny……. much, much later.'

That trip South was only the second time I had ever been to London and it was a wonderful time. We saw all the sites including Buckingham Palace, The Imperial War Museum, and The British Museum. We visited The Houses of Parliament and gazed upon the clock tower that contains Big Ben. We went to Hyde Park and strolled along the Serpentine and went for a look around the West End shops. We paid a visit to Madame Tussaud's Waxworks; we visited the Tower of London and gazed upon its many exhibits including the Crown Jewels and we saw Tower Bridge, but for me the highlight was feeding monkey nuts to the flock of pigeons in Trafalgar Square, as we had done on our first trip to the capital. They were the same pigeons that were responsible for giving Lord Nelson and Landseer's lions a white coat of avian manure and it brought back fond memories of Grandma Nellie. We took a boat trip along the River Thames and strolled along the embankment. My father pointed out the obelisk known as Cleopatra's needle. We saw much more on that second trip, but all too soon the time to make the return journey home to Manchester came around and once again, like the previous return journey four years earlier, we ended up on a train that seemed to stop at every station.

Grandma Nellie had passed away a year earlier. My father and Mother had gone to London to attend the funeral but had come home immediately after the service. Val and I had stayed with Grandma Annie until they got back. Nellie's husband, Benny had also passed on a few years earlier than Nellie, but not being directly related and because my father could not afford the train fare for the trip down to London on that occasion, my parents did not attend his funeral.

Facial Paralysis

It appears that I was a sickly child and as well as the numerous accidents that I experienced I also suffered from numerous illnesses and maladies. I can remember the horror on my mum's face when I developed a certain disease, if disease is the right word for the affliction that I suffered. It was on a Saturday morning when I joined the rest of the family sat around the dining table at breakfast-time. My mother looked at me with utter panic in her eyes, 'Laurie, what's up with your face?' she asked. I had no idea that there was anything wrong with my face, although I had been a little off colour the preceding day, but when I had retired the previous night my face was normal. I went to look in the mirror and was horrified by the sight that stared back at me. My lower left eyelid and eyebrow seemed to be drooping downwards and I found that I had difficulty closing the affected eye. My mouth had moved quite a distance from its original starting point and it is a mystery to me that I had not noticed it as I tried to shovel food into my cheek, which was almost where my mouth should have been. Facially I resembled Charles Laughton in his role as Quasimodo, Victor Hugo's deformed, Parisian campanologist.

Apparently I had suffered some type of facial paralysis and one side of my face had dropped. On the other side my mouth had moved sideways and upwards towards my right cheek. Being a Saturday, my parents could not get hold of the family doctor and so I was taken to Ancoat's hospital where I was diagnosed with Bell's palsy. Bell's palsy is paralysis of the facial muscles caused by a disorder of the facial nerves; it is thought to be caused by a viral infection. The virus that seems most likely is the Herpes Simplex virus, the same virus responsible for cold sores and it can, if not treated, become permanent. The disorder is named after the Scottish physiologist, Charles Bell (1774- 1842), who first described the condition and at the time it was considered to be a mild form of poliomyelitis.

I have no idea how they would treat such a disorder in these days of medical advancement but back in the 1950's the answer was to administer anti-viral drugs and use a stainless steel appliance that, in my case, hooked behind my left ear and came across my cheek where the other end hooked into the side of my mouth in an attempt to pull my oral cavity back to its original position. The strange implement had a piece of rubber around it where it fitted into my mouth and another piece where it hooked behind my ear. Despite the rubber sleeves, which were supposed to make the contrivance more comfortable to wear, it was painful, uncomfortable, embarrassing and downright ugly. Of course I had to remove the implement when eating or drinking. People, especially other children, who can be so cruel, found great amusement at my attempts at sipping from a cup. As I held the mug or beaker to my mouth to imbibe my liquid refreshment my drooping bottom lip could not hold the fluid in and I dribbled like a baby. Be it a hot infusion like tea or a cold drink such as milk or juice the contents of my mouth escaped and came running over my lips, down my chin and dribbled onto my clothes. I had the same problem when eating solid food, though to a lesser degree, even so, my mother made me use a baby's cup and wear a bib or tied a tea towel around my neck and down over my chest when eating meals at home.

That twisted, metal, instrument of torture, which was worthy of Tomas de Torquemada, the Spanish Inquisitor General (1420 – 1498), had to be worn for about two months and because of it I became an object of ridicule at school. Other kids would ask 'Why are you talking out of the side of your mouth?' or they would shout 'Hey Driver! You've got a face like the Hunchback of Notre Dame,' or 'Is your face melting?' Eating school dinners became a complete embarrassment to me as I dribbled food and drink down the front of my shirt and thus became the object of further taunts and jibes. I would remove the item of pain and torture in the hope that the taunts would cease but the slurs and insults would continue because of my lop-sided facial appearance.

Alternatively, I would forego my dinner and take a walk outside the school grounds to escape the taunts; Cousin Bobby would walk with me on those occasions and we would walk to our Grandmothers, who only lived a few minutes walk from Briscoe Lane and stay there until it was time to return to school. Gran would make us a sandwich on those occasions. After religiously swallowing the anti-viral drugs and enduring the pain inducing tool of torment and after several adjustments as it slowly corrected the problem over the weeks, the doctors told my mother that I need no longer take the drugs or wear the hated, stainless steel contrivance any more; I was cured, my mouth was back where it belonged, somewhere centrally above my chin and below my nose. I could close my eye properly again and my eyebrow was back where it should be. It seems that I was somewhat unique in contracting Bell's palsy at such an early age as it rarely attacks anyone below the age of fifteen and more usually it affects middle aged people. Although I still suffer from a lopsided smile, I am not alone as most people that suffered from Bell's palsy are affected by that residual problem.

Chapter 7

A Move to Blackley,
A Dirty Old Man, some
Scrumping and Riding Shotgun.

After the Christmas Party

Prior to the last Christmas before our family moved from Newton Heath to Blackley, Briscoe lane Primary School had an Xmas party, as they did each year before the school closed for the Yuletide holidays. Being that time of year dusk fell around 4 o'clock pm and that morning my mother had told me to make my way to my Grandma's house after the party, because my dad was working overtime. Gran's house was only about four hundred yards from Briscoe Lane school gates. My sister, Valerie was, at that time, attending Brookdale Park Secondary School and so I had to make the trip to Grandma's on my own. When the party finished at just after 3.30 pm all memories of what my mother had told me had gone from my mind and when I reached the school gates it was already starting to darken and instead of making my way to Grandma's I turned left and headed for home. When I approached the prefab twilight was darkening the sky further and the moon was out. I walked through the gate and down the path to the front door and pushed it, it did not open and so I went around the rear of the building and tried the back door. That too was locked so I peeped through the kitchen window; everything was in darkness and there was no sign of movement. I returned to the front of the prefab and peeped through the front window, it was just the same, dark and still. In the gloom I could make out the shape of the television sitting on its table in the corner with a lamp sitting on top of it, both were unlit. The street lamps had come on shedding a meagre luminescence around each lamppost. It was then that my mother's talk to me that morning came back to me, 'Laurie, your dad's working overtime tonight so after your party at school, make your way to Granny's house and wait there for Valerie and me to pick you up.'

I looked around me; all the other prefabs, of which there were five in Elbain Avenue, were in darkness. If I walked to Grandma's the long, safe and well lit way round, i.e. Through the prefab estate, up Orford Road, past the tripe works back to Briscoe Lane and down Scotland Hall Road it would take me too long and I might miss my mother and sister or cause a panic as to my whereabouts. I had to make my way to Grandma's on my own and in the dark. I became worried and panic set in. I started to cry and my nose started to run. I stood there for a few minutes and composed myself. I pulled the sleeve of my coat across my face to wipe away the tears and snot and decided that I would have to start on the ten minute journey to Gran's house by way of the unlit Taylor's Lane. My throat was constricted as I made my way onto the unlit pathway which was in darkness except for the weak light emitted by a full moon, I could scarcely breathe I was so scared. The moon threw a weak light that cast tenuous shadows from the trees in Tetlow's woods onto Taylor's Lane. The branches and twigs of the trees were like withered and twisted arms terminating in creaking, grasping talons swaying in the breeze as they reached out as if to seize me. I started to walk a little faster, then faster still and then I broke into a run. My heart pounded in the cavity of my chest and in my haste I tripped over a protruding stone and stumbled forward to land sprawled flat out, face down on the stony path. As I lay there my imagination ran riot and my mind conjured up all types of ghouls and spectres coming for me from the shadows of the woods, made even more sinister by the light of the moon and the evening breeze moving the barely discernable shadows across the ground and across my prostrate form. I tentatively rose to my feet and glanced around me. Scudding clouds obliterated the moon's light for a few seconds and when the clouds had passed and a little light returned I was still alone on the dark lane. I realised that I had travelled more than halfway down Taylor's Lane and that I was close to the junction with Orford Road and........ the old graveyard. I wished for more light because the full moon added eeriness and when the moon was full was the time when the werewolves and zombies were abroad. In the dim light of the moon, through the perimeter fence of the cemetery, I could see the ancient, misshapen and broken tombstones leaning at crazy angles and overgrown with weeds which were swaying eerily back and forth with the light wind which whistled and moaned lowly between the gravestones and vaults. The whole ghastly and ghostly scenario was enveloped in a thin, grey, graveyard mist from which my over active and fertile imagination created weird and spooky apparitions of flittering ghosts and wandering skeletons and I ran as fast as I could, the remaining distance, around the bend and onto Seabrook road where the street lighting lit up the roadway and where people were walking about on their way to Sarson's grocery shop or to their homes. The relief that I felt could not be described, my heart returned to a more normal rhythm and my breathing became less laboured. Within five minutes I was at Grandma's where I told her that I was a bit late because the party had run a little over time. Not long after my arrival at Grandma's my mum and my sister arrived and we all walked home together, that time I had no fear of walking up Taylor's Lane with my mum and elder sister, besides it was only five o'clock in the evening and I realised how foolish and childish I had been.

In the Cab of a Pantechnicon

About Eighteen months after Bobby's move to Oldham it was deemed necessary that my family move out of the prefab because of mine and Valerie's ages; she had just turned eleven and I was nine years of age and we were sharing the same bedroom and according to the council, the prefabs were coming to the end of their useful life. The prefabs, when they were built, were only supposed to have a ten year life span. I was nine years old when we left our prefab, but upon visiting the area ten years later it and the others around it were still being used.

Those humble, pre-fabricated abodes gave useful service to young families for twenty five years or more and in some areas they still stand to this day. My father had applied for a council house with three bedrooms and was offered one in the borough of Higher Blackley about three miles from Newton Heath. The house that we were offered was a new build property on an estate that was built on what used to be Blackley tip. We had to bid farewell to all our friends and neighbours to go and live on a council rubbish dump.

The move to Blackley was executed by the use of a pantechnicon removal lorry, unlike the hand cart used to move us into the prefab the vehicle was a custom built, 1951 'O' type, bonneted Bedford, probably with Bedford's own petrol engine or a Perkin's Diesel. My ears, at that time, had not become attuned to the different sounds of petrol and diesel engines. The vehicle had a Luton over the cab. A Luton is the continuation of the vehicles bodywork over the cab to allow for more loading space. To me, the vehicle appeared massive, similar to the prime movers of the fairground people. It probably had a gross weight of fourteen tons which gave plenty of space for our meagre belongings. The tail board was huge and when lowered it was used as a ramp into the back of the load area.

Once the removal men had loaded all our worldly possessions from the prefab into the lorry, the rear doors were closed and the tailboard lifted up and locked into place, I was told that I could sit in the cab for the journey to Blackley. I was in that cab before the driver. It was such a thrill for me to be sat in one of the passenger seats of a truck. There was no requirement for seat belts in those days. The truck was fitted with a double passenger seat to accommodate the two porters that loaded and unloaded the cargo, but on that instance and to allow me to travel up front, one of the porters had opted to travel in the back of the truck. The driver turned the ignition key and pressed a dash mounted starter button, the engine fired into life. He engaged the first gear, checked his mirrors, released the handbrake and pulled away, I watched with admiration as the driver changed gears, double de-clutching and virtually standing up as he wrestled with the huge steering wheel to manoeuvre the laden truck down narrow streets and around tight corners and even then I thought 'What a life, to be able to drive one of these big trucks.' There was no power steering and neither were the trucks of the day fitted with synchromesh gearboxes; it was all brute strength and skilful driving. As I enjoyed the thrill of being transported in the cab of the vehicle my father was travelling in the load area with all our chattels and worldly possessions and with the second porter to keep him company. Each item of furniture in the back of the truck was covered with a blanket and securely bound to the anchor points along the interior of the truck. The loaders had left two armchairs at the rear so that my father and the porter could travel in relative comfort. They were, like the rest of the cargo, secured to the walls of the van to stop any movement. Luckily there were lights in the load area for making the loading easier and that made it much more comfortable for my father and the porter travelling in the rear. My sister and mother followed along by courtesy of public transport.

Our new council house at 105, Plant Hill Road, Higher Blackley, Manchester, was everything my parents expected it to be. It had the requisite three bedrooms and all mod cons. The fireplace in the living room was classed as an all night burner that burned smokeless fuel. The living room itself was the full length of the house and had windows looking onto the front garden as well as the back. There was a spacious kitchen and a utility room. We had brought most of our old furniture from the prefab and although it was serviceable it would not be long before certain items would need replacing.

Two new Schools in a Short Time

New schools had to be found in Blackley for Val and me and opposite our new, council house there was a new Secondary Modern School being built. That was OK for our kid; she had started at Brookdale Park Secondary Modern in Newton Heath and temporarily moved to St Mary's in Moston until Plant Hill Secondary Modern opened in Blackley.

I was still a primary school pupil and so I was enrolled into Crab Lane Primary School; the worst six months of my life. Prior to starting at Crab Lane and because I had been deemed a clever little sod at Briscoe Lane, although I was totally lacking in worldly wisdom, I was given an exam to sit. The examination, I found out later, consisted of papers from the previous years eleven plus examination. I managed to achieve the standard that was desired of me and was put into a class of children a year my senior. I was taunted and tormented, accused of being a boffin and a bighead. I was pushed around and to some small degree bullied by my peers, but that was not the worst of what I had to endure.

One of the teachers there, a Mr Tarver, took an instant dislike to me. Tarver was probably in his late twenties and was obviously into body building; he rolled his shirt sleeves up high to display his biceps. He taught English and took gardening. I was made to look small in front of the class by Tarver who set me tasks that he knew were beyond me. If, in his mind, I had misbehaved, he would slipper me in front of the class. The tears that I shed, caused by Tarver, only brought ridicule from my peers. If it had been childish bullying I may have stood a chance. I, at least, could have fought back. What chance did I stand against a body-building, cruel and vindictive teacher?

The treatment that I received from that man had a detrimental effect on me and an adverse effect on my school work; on school days I would develop terrible, phantom stomach aches which would reduce me to tears and I would not go to school; consequently my learning was affected. I was put back to the year that I should have been in but Tarver taught that year as well so there was no escape. I was taken to see the family doctor who could find nothing physically wrong with me; he asked if there was anything untoward which was bothering me and if I was being bullied at school, to which I responded in the negative. Thankfully, the doctor saw beyond my negative responses and in a talk with my parents, suggested a change of schools.

Victoria Avenue Primary School was closer than Crab Lane to my home and my parents went through all the correct channels and eventually the Head Mistress called my parents and me for an interview. After discussing the pros and cons with the Head Mistress, when everything that I had endured spilled out, I was offered a place at that school in a class with people of my own age. I was put in a class where the form mistress was a Miss Hesford, a middle aged lady who took me under her wing and nurtured what latent talents I had left; my grades improved, I made new friends and I became a much happier child who wondered why he had not been sent to that school in the first place.

During the time I was at Crab Lane Primary and Victoria Avenue Primary schools between 1955 and 57 there was a craze amongst young boys to collect model racing cars made by the Dinky company and to race them down small hills in competition, the Marques collected included BRM, Maserati, Ferrari, Jaguar and many more The boys racing those cars pretended that they were the racing drivers of the day such as Jack Brabham, Juan Fangio, Mike Hawthorn and Stirling Moss. One young lad always wanted to be Tazio Nuvolari. I had never heard of Nuvolari at the time. He had died of a stroke in1953 and the lad that wanted to emulate him must have heard of him from his dad. I was somewhat precluded from that pastime because my interest lay in collecting models of the commercial trucks of the day such as Scammell, AEC, Guy, Thorneycroft etc; and I was forbidden to race big trucks against Dinky racing cars. That, at Crab Lane, was another way that I was ostracised from taking part in the play time activities.

During the time I was at Victoria Avenue, commercial television was introduced to an unsuspecting public in this fair land of ours. It was the first time that we had had more than one channel to watch; the BBC had competition. It was also the first time that we Brits had seen our television programs interrupted by the latest advertisements for Gibb's SR Toothpaste or hear a singing voice telling us that *'You'll Wonder Where the Yellow Went, When You Brush Your Teeth with Pepsodent.'* It was also the first time that we had read the legend on the screen stating 'End of Part One.' Some of the earlier adverts were better than the programmes that they interrupted; not so nowadays, I'm afraid, both the quality of the adverts and the programs have gotten worse. At the advent of commercial television, I think that our television was converted to receive the new channel, whether this was by way of a set top box I cannot remember.

One of the pupils in the class was a lad named David Ritchie, a nice enough lad but a bit of a tearaway. He was made to sit at the front of the class so the teachers could keep an eye on him. Even in those far gone days David used to carry a small sheath knife; for the sharpening of pencils, cutting initials into desk tops and for bravado. One day, shortly after the advent of the new commercial station, and while the teacher had her back to the class, as she wrote on the blackboard, David held up the knife to her back, and quickly brought it down in a stabbing motion and then put it into his desk and said dramatically 'End of Part One.' The teacher quickly spun around on her heels to be greeted by a sea of smirking but otherwise innocent, young faces.

The brief time I spent at Victoria Avenue Primary School must rate as the happiest of my school days. It was hard work and at the last exam I came second in the class, being beaten, by the narrowest of margins, to the first and top of the class position by one John Tuke. On my school report where all my grades were A's and A+'s, Miss Hesford wrote something that became an embarrassment to me every time my mother or father showed the report to relatives or friends. The sentence that she wrote in her neat, copperplate handwriting, so legible and precise that not a word could be misconstrued or misinterpreted was: *Laurie is a hard working and studious pupil whose work never ceases to satisfy, he is always polite; a pleasant and obliging child and I wish him all the best for the future.* Then the embarrassing bit; *I WILL MISS THOSE TWINKLING BLUE EYES NEXT TERM.*

By that time we had settled into our new house and all the schooling arrangements were satisfactory, things were looking up and money was not as tight as it had been in the preceding years, so my father decided that my mother should have a new fangled twin tub, top loader washing machine. There were, at the time, a band of door to door salesmen going around selling anything from the Encyclopaedia Britannica to vacuum cleaners and washing machines and it was from one of those travelling salesmen that dad bought, on hire purchase, a Rolls Rapide, Twin tub, Washing machine. The Rolls Rapide which cost thirty nine guineas, (£41. 95p) paid for at six shillings and eight pence, (38p) per week with added interest, was manufactured on an assembly line in the Rolls Razor Factory in Cricklewood, which was owned by an entrepreneur by the name of John Bloom. It took a couple of weeks for the washing machine to be delivered, but my mother was overjoyed upon its arrival. Around about the same time my father thought that it was about time we upgraded our fourteen inch television. The thing to do in those days was to rent a set from shops such as Fred Dawes' rentals. So he and my mother went round to the local Fred Dawes' shop and started to look at the new television sets with built in commercial television; no more set top box for us. They decided on a model with a twenty one inch screen, to me it was like being at the picture show. When BBC2 started to be broadcast in 1964, we once again had a set top box to receive the new station but when colour television was broadcast in 1967, my father demanded, from Fred Dawes' a new television capable of receiving the colour transmissions, or he would take his custom elsewhere. We got our new television, another twenty one inch model, and that set was delivered the following week. The first colour TV broadcast began in 1967 on BBC 2 and on BBC1 and ITV in 1969.

Around the start of the1960's my father started to think that a fitted carpet was needed in the living room instead of two large rugs and an expanse of bare floor that we had put up with for the prior five years. It was during that period that advertisements on the new commercial television started to show adverts for Cyril Lord Carpets whose slogan was *'This is a luxury you can afford----- By Cyril Lord.'* So father called in a Cyril Lord representative to measure up and within a fortnight we had a luxurious deep pile, royal blue, wall to wall carpet with thick, springy underlay, once again paid for on the never, never. Before we became the recipients of a luxurious fitted carpet the floor cleaning had been done by way of a mop and broom and a manually operated push along Ewbank carpet sweeper. All we needed then was a new fangled electric vacuum cleaner and once again a knock on the front door brought a door to door salesman to our domain. When the front door was answered, the rep stood there with a smile on his face and a cylinder vacuum cleaner under his arm and the hose and attachments at his feet on the doorstep. He introduced himself and led into his sales pitch. He was invited in to give a demonstration of his cleaning apparatus. He spread dust and muck, from a container and picked up an ashtray from the table and emptied it over our new, luxurious fitted carpet. My mother's face was a picture as he spread his muck on the new, deep pile carpet; her mouth was agape until the salesman assured her that everything would be all right. The rep then plugged the cleaner into an available socket and pressed the on-off switch on his machine; there was a brilliant flash, a small bang and smoke started to rise from the rear end of the vacuum cleaner and then....... nothing, the motor had died. The vendor of that fine cleaning machine stood there, his face flushed to a beetroot red and he stammered as his salesman's spiel abandoned him; he apologised emphatically, 'I'm t-t-terribly s-s-sorry. It's just a m-minor set back; I think the f-f-fuse has blown. I'll g-go and get another m-m machine from my van.'

'Well I hope the other machine fares better than this one,' said my father.

'Oh, it will,' said the rep, recovering his confidence 'This is just an old demonstration model and I'm afraid it has seen better days.' And with that he went to his vehicle and returned with a box which contained a brand new, shiny machine with which he finished his demonstration. The new vacuum cleaner sucked up the ash and fag ends and the dust and grime that the salesman had spread so liberally upon our new fitted carpet, with ease. Both mum and dad were suitably impressed and after a bit of bartering whereby the salesman offered a considerable discount and an extended warranty for the trouble caused my father purchased the said machine. He paid a deposit and settled the remainder of the bill the next week. We had years of service from that Electrolux, cylindrical vacuum cleaner.

Scrumping for Apples and Trouble with the Police

The move to Blackley happened when I was nine years old going on ten and still a child, prone to follow childish pursuits. One of those pursuits ended up with me and some newly made friends from Victoria Avenue Primary School, being taken home in a Black Maria by the local constabulary. The reason for this was because we had found a house on

Hill Lane that had a mature apple tree in the front garden and it was the time of year when it was in fruit. The gang of youths that included me gathered across the street from the house with the apple tree, we were carrying out a reconnaissance exercise. We moved a few yards up the street and then a few yards down the other way trying to ascertain whether there was anybody in the house. In our naivety we failed to realise that we were acting suspiciously and in a shady and devious manner. After our reconnoitring was completed and we had ascertained that nobody moved about in the house, we moved, as one, towards the apple tree.

I clambered onto the garden wall and was balanced there, precariously, on the coping stones, stretching to reach for the lower branches that bore the elusive fruit, when a police van approached. I turned around to see what was happening and promptly lost my balance. My feet slipped from the top of the half round coping stones and I fell backwards, arms outstretched into a fruit bearing, blackberry, bramble bush in the garden. A couple of the lads tried to make good their escape but were apprehended. A neighbour had seen us skulking around and acting warily and with hesitation and had phoned the police. The officers, after pulling on their leather gloves, experienced some difficulty as they extricated me, badly scratched, torn and stained with blackberry juice from the brambles. They then took the names and addresses of all involved and put us into the rear of the Paddy Wagon and took us home one by one.

The route that the driver took meant that I was the last one to be taken home and when the Black Maria pulled up outside our house, one of the policemen opened up the back, gripped me by the sleeve of my coat, walked me up the path to the front door and knocked. My father answered the door to be confronted by the Bobby holding his son, the very dangerous criminal and apple thief, by the arm.

My dad invited the copper in and once in the sitting room he asked 'Right Officer, what's this all about?'

The police constable replied 'We received a complaint that a number of youths were loitering with intent on Hill Lane and your son was amongst them, we have already taken the others home and had a word with their parents.'

My Father turned to me and asked, 'Well, what have you got to say for yourself?'

I replied, 'We was on'y scrumping, dad, we was after the apples.'

The policeman spoke up saying, 'They have all told the same story and frankly I believe them, but the tree that they were trying to take the apples from contained cooking apples which don't make for very good eating, so I'll leave it to you, Mr Driver, to chastise and punish your son.'

My father looked at me and shook his head; he replied to the policeman, 'Oh, don't you worry I'll chastise him alright.' When the officer had finished and my dad had seen him to the door, he walked back into the living room and gave me a sharp clip round the earhole and said, 'Next time you go scrumping, go for eating apples not cookers, you daft little bugger.'

Rusty Nails and Penicillin

Not long after the move to Blackley, my sister and I were playing, in our still uncultivated rear garden. We were with the children of the family next door at 103 Plant Hill Road, we lived at 105. Those children were Colin and Elaine Jones. During our play, I happened to stand, accidently, on a small piece of wood which had a rusty nail protruding from it. The rusty nail penetrated the sole of one of my plimsolls and went into the underside of my left foot and stuck there. I yelled in pain and started to hop around the garden on my uninjured foot as I held my injured foot with my right hand. It was obvious that I was about to take a tumble, which I did, adding embarrassment to injury. The others, not surprisingly, burst into laughter at my antics. After picking myself up I sat on the back step and gingerly pulled the wood away from the underside of my footwear and the nail came with it. I then removed my shoe and sock to ascertain how much damage the nail had caused. There was a small amount of blood and a small perforation mark where the nail had entered the ball of my foot. The site of the perforation throbbed a little and it hurt, but I wasn't going to be accused of being a sissy so I went indoors and took a band-aid from the medical box, rubbed a little antiseptic ointment on the injury, covered the puncture mark with the plaster, replaced my footwear and returned outside where I continued to play. The day passed and I completely forgot about the injury to my foot until bedtime when the injured spot started to itch. I checked it out before I went to bed. It had turned a little red and throbbed a little more, so I had a bath, applied some Fuller's Earth Cream to the injured area and retired to my bed. Fuller's Earth Cream or powder was considered a universal panacea at the time and was used for cuts, spots and pimples, nappy rash etc; and as a poultice to draw pus and poison from wounds and boils.

The following morning I awoke after tossing and turning through a fitful night's sleep, my foot had become swollen; the arch of my foot had almost disappeared into the oedema. The skin was taut and shiny like an over inflated balloon and rounded like a cantaloupe. Redness around the injury sent out tentacles of red lines akin to small veins that looked like the roadways on an Ordnance Survey map. The throbbing continued unabated; In-between each pulsation their came a burning, stabbing sensation. I placed my foot to the linoleum of my bedroom floor; the pressure sent further paroxysms of excruciating pain up my left leg. With some difficulty I limped downstairs where my mother was working in the kitchen. She noticed my limp and enquired as to what had occurred. I showed her my injured foot; there was a sharp intake of breath and I told her of my little accident the day before.

After I had explained what had happened she told me what an idiot I was and then the maternal sympathy came to the fore, 'you poor little thing. Let mummy take a look.' And with that she took control of everything. Firstly she bathed the injury and spread some salve over it, she then bandaged my foot and declared that a visit to Booth Hall Children's Hospital, in Blackley, was required. So, off we went to Booth Hall with me limping, one foot with a shoe on and the injured foot with a slipper which had been cut with scissors to get it over my swollen extremity and the bandages and me moaning as I followed my mother, who had become my nurse and carer.

We entered the hospital building to be greeted by that smell that all hospitals used to have. It was the smell of ether, anaesthetics and cleanliness. Once we had registered, we were shown to a waiting room where we sat until, after a lengthy passage of time, my name was called. My mother and I went into an examination room to be greeted by a doctor, who, after viewing and then prodding and poking my swollen extremity, took a few seconds to think and said something about anti-biotics and injections. A hypodermic syringe was taken from its sterile wrapping and filled with a colourless liquid and then the injection was administered. Immediately I became dizzy; I started to sweat and I felt clammy, my vision became blurred and my breathing became laboured as I wheezed and struggled for breath. Nausea and light-headedness overcame me and I swayed back and forth. I reached out for something to support me; missed what I had reached for and so clutched at the doctor's white coat and slid to the floor in a swoon, where I lay in a heap at the man's feet, unconscious.

Once again penicillin had been wrongly administered. My mother, after such a long passage of time, had either forgotten or not thought to tell the doctor of my allergy and the doctor had been remiss in not enquiring as to any allergies I might have had prior to giving the injection. Once again medical staff consulted with one another in an effort to find a drug to counteract the effects of the penicillin.

In the meantime I had been placed on a couch in the consulting room, where I regained my senses. After a few minutes a pretty, young nurse, who smelled of all things nice, gave me some tablets to take orally and a further injection was given. There were more sharp intakes of breath from several medical staff as they waited, in anticipation, for the result of the second injection. After a lie down and a hot drink I slowly recovered and was able to stand. My powers of locomotion returned and I was released into the care of my mother and taken home with a course of oral, anti-biotics to take for a fortnight. I was kept off school for a week until the swelling had subsided and my limp had disappeared and I could walk normally. It seems that, in some cases, penicillin is not the universal panacea it is proclaimed to be.

An Accident on Bonfire Night
& The ABC Minors

On our first Bonfire Night in Blackley, which was also my father's birthday celebration, we had a relatively small bonfire in the back garden. The neighbours from either side came. They were the Jones's and the Paul's. Cousin's Peter, Freddy and Walter and Irene and their parents came. Also invited were the Tyror's from Jurby Avenue and a few others. The Tyror's back garden was adjacent to ours and Young John Tyror was a pal of mine. John's dad brought to the site, what could only be described as industrial fireworks, the type used for professional displays. When they were set off those fireworks lit up the sky and described fantastic patterns in multi coloured sparks high up in the heavens. The rockets travelled further than the usual smaller types and let out numerous displays of vari-hued patterns.

While the adults enjoyed bottles of beer the younger element ate treacle toffee, potatoes roasted in the glowing embers around the fire and a gingerbread and treacle cake known as parkin, all washed down with lemonade or ginger beer. Cousin Walter after watching Mister Tyror's fantastic fireworks display decided that he too could capture the people's imagination. He found my father's industrial, leather gauntlets, picked up a rocket, lit it and let it go from his hand He did the same thing with a number of rockets before turning his attention to the Roman Candles which he also let off from his gauntleted hands. Walter did, at least, have the sense not to point the fireworks at anybody, but it wasn't long before his father, seeing the possibility of a serious accident came behind him and gave him clip behind the ear, which caused Walter to skulk off and sulk.

Being a bit of a show off I thought that I would like to do something equally outrageous and so I picked up a Catherine Wheel, unwound it and lit it. As it burnt and spluttered, throwing out sparks in all directions, I whirled it around describing patterns in the air and I held it aloft allowing the brightly coloured sparks to fall. Holding it aloft allowed the remaining gunpowder to fall and gather at the base where I held it. As it burned lower and I was about to discard it, there was an almighty bang and a brilliant flash followed by a shrill scream as my right hand took the brunt of the heat and the blast of the explosion. Once again, my youthful exuberance and utter stupidity had come to the fore and I was blubbering like a baby as I shook my hand up and down in a futile effort to ease the pain.

My father came running over to his injured and tearful son. He took me inside to ascertain the extent of the damage to my arms appendage. The skin had not been broken and so my father ushered me to the kitchen sink where he turned on the cold water tap and made me stand there for twenty minutes or more with my hand under the running cold water. His quick thinking saved me a lot of problems; the blistering that came up was nowhere near as extensive as it might have been, due to his actions. I was then taken, in a neighbour's car, to Booth Hall Hospital where my wounds were dressed, once again, with, what seemed to be, the same gauze, which was impregnated with the efficacious, stinking yellow balm that had been applied all those years before when I burned my leg. My father was very angry and he verbally lambasted me for ruining both his birthday celebrations and the general Bonfire Night celebrations. There was, though, something good that came out of my trauma, at school I was unable to write due to my heavily bandaged hand and because of the injury I escaped most of the homework.

After moving to Blackley, the evening trips to the pictures, once a week with the rest of the family became fewer and finally ceased all together. The Saturday, children's matinee started at 10am. The venue, in Blackley, when we did go, was the ABC Avenue cinema on the corner of Victoria Avenue East and Manchester New Road. We joined the cinema club and became ABC Minors but I cannot recall any advantages of being a member.

When I reached the age of ten I was considered old enough to visit the cinema without parental company, so long as I went with my sister or a friend or two. I remember going to see Disney's Davy Crockett and its sequel Davy Crockett and the River Pirates and Old Yeller, based on a book by Fred Gipson which is the heart rending story of a family dog in the old West, all three of those films starred Fess Parker and I also remember going to see Moby Dick starring Gregory Peck as Captain Ahab and Richard Basehart as Ishmael, on their quest for the great, white whale. Children's styles, games and toys were ever evolving and at that time all the young boys wore Davy Crockett hats and the girls spun their hula hoops around their waists. It seems that girls were more adept with the hula hoop than their male counterparts; the yo-yo was another popular craze during the fifties.

Would You Like a Sweetie & Bacon's and Bacon Butties

Cousin Bobby and I kept in close contact and would spend alternate week-ends at each other's houses. We were both bought bicycles by our parents and being summertime and being off school, we would cycle back and forth to each other's house and ride off on days out, although we didn't go everywhere on our bikes. At ten years of age we were considered old enough to go to town, on the bus, on our own. Things were a lot more innocent in those days, or so it was thought.

After a trip into Manchester town centre on a Saturday morning, Bobby and I were walking towards Stevenson's Square, which was, at the time, a bus terminus. We had been warned not to use the subterranean public conveniences in the square or those in Piccadilly Gardens for that matter, because they were the haunts of 'strange and nasty people.' On the day in question we were going to catch the number 98 bus service, out of Stevenson Square, towards Oldham which would take us and deposit us not far from Bob's house in Chadderton.

The pair of us was perambulating down one of the little used, narrow side streets; I believe it was Little Lever Street, which led to the square when a scruffy, wizened old man with wild, wispy hair spilling from underneath an old, battered and stained trilby hat and wearing a tatty, frayed and ragged raincoat over voluminous, badly stained trousers ambled towards us. He had in one hand a walking stick and with the other he held out to me, what appeared to be, a bag of toffees and he said, 'Ee'yar, lickle boy. Would you like a sweetie?' Foolishly I put my hand out and the man, dropping the bag, quickly grabbed my wrist and started to pull me along towards a side entry. The bag, of course, was empty. Bobby quickly ran in front of the old man and kicked him as hard as he could in the shins; the old geezer yelped in pain and loosed his grip on my wrist as he bent to rub his shins. Bobby grabbed hold of my arm and pulled me away from the dirty old man and said, 'Quick! Let's go!' We ran off, looking back to see the dirty old bugger shaking his walking stick in the air at us. That was second time Bobby had saved me. We ran into Stevenson's Square where there were numerous people milling around, shopping and waiting for buses. We joined the queue for the No 98 and boarded when it arrived; we never told anyone about the old 'strange and nasty person' that had accosted us, even though there was a police station around the corner on Newton Street. I only hope that because of our failure to report the incident that no other child suffered at the hands of that perverted old man.

In Blackley village there was a haulage company called Bacon's Tippers. Jimmy Bacon and his brother ran a small fleet of tipper trucks on local work. The wagons used by Bacon's were mostly early Bedford ten tonners and from being eleven years old I used to go down to Bacon's yard and watch the drivers reversing into the yard. I talked to the drivers as they fuelled their vehicles and also to the mechanics and even to the Bacon brothers. After a while, one of the drivers asked me if I would like to go on a run with him on Saturday morning, I jumped at the chance. There was a lot of demolition going on around Manchester at the time; it was the start of the slum clearance that went on for a decade and more. The drivers were paid by the load; the more loads they did, the more they earned. The interior of the trucks seemed as if they had never been cleaned, they were full of dirt and dust from building sites and land fill sites. The exterior of the trucks fared no better; there were dents and bumps all over them. The tipper bodies had a particularly hard time of it with the buckets of loading machines banging on their sides and pressing down on the load to make it safer so that stray bricks would not come flying off the load and into the roadway. Bits of debris did come off the loads at times but I do not remember any of Bacon's drivers being prosecuted for an unsafe load although they should have had a fly sheet over the load for absolute safety; but of course that would have caused the drivers to lose time and therefore money. Tippers have a hard life compared to long haul vehicles or those that deliver food or furniture and so their life span is relatively shorter.

Bacon's had contracts to transport hardcore from the demolition sites to new build sites or road construction sites. Saturday mornings travelling around as the shotgun rider in Bacon's trucks became a regular occurrence that I looked forward to. I worked with various drivers and I used to jump out of the cab at the tipping site and release the tailboard before tipping and lock it up after the load was shed. It was during those days that I was introduced to the greasy spoon transport cafes of the day, where I would have a bacon butty and a large mug of tea paid for by the driver who would tuck into the Full Monty, which I considered, at the time, to be enough to feed Goliath.

Upon returning home, about dinner time, covered in the grime from the building sites, I would tell my dad of the adventures of the day. He used to say 'I don't know where you get all this love of commercial vehicles from; you must have petrol or diesel in your veins. I cannot remember anyone else in the family, be it on your mum's side or mine who was a driver or that had the slightest interest in driving or transport.' There was if the opportunities were there, a tendency for males to learn a trade. In those long ago days, professional drivers were viewed as nothing more than labourers. With the advent, in 1969/70, of the vocational driving license things improved for the driver but, alas, to some sections of the community, he is still viewed as the lowest of the low, within the working fraternity.

I did find out later, however, that my Grandfather George Hampson was a carter by profession in his earlier years, in Hulme. He was once the proud owner of a horse and four wheeled open cart with which he practiced general carting which included contracts for taking bales of cotton to the mills and finished goods for delivery elsewhere, both for the domestic market and for export which meant that he would have worked for the railway companies as a subcontractor and also he would have delivered to Manchester Docks. He also tendered for any other transport work that he could undertake. He plied his trade as a carter between the wars as an independent trader. All inland transport was nationalised after the Second World War and independent hauliers did not start to surface again until1951.

Chapter 8

THE 11+ AND AN INTRODUCTION TO PLANT HILL SCHOOL AND A LITTLE MORE TROUBLE WITH THE LAW.

The Alpha Stream at Plant Hill School

The final test and educational hurdle at Victoria Avenue Junior School that the pupils had to face was the eleven plus examination; I studied hard and crammed relentlessly and I and a couple of others from the same class, Alan Pawson and, Roderick Diggle, Graham Boothby and John Tuke passed the said exam. John Tuke went to a Technical college and Pawson, Diggle, Boothby and I were put into the Alpha or Grammar stream at the local secondary modern, which just happened to be Plant Hill Secondary where my sister Valerie went and which was situated right opposite the house where we lived on Plant Hill Road.

On the induction day to Plant Hill School, which I think was the 8th of September 1957, the new intake were herded into the assembly hall. All the new starters were around the same age; into their twelfth year of existence. We stood or sat on the floor awaiting the arrival of our new headmaster, a Mr Blomeley. We did not have long to wait when a sight that very few present had seen, in reality, appeared before us; Mr Blomeley strode onto the stage dressed in full gown with a mortar board cap perched upon his head. Most of us in the hall that day had only seen the cap and gown on television or in films and his appearance commanded immediate attention and respect which was manifested by sharp intakes of breath followed by a deathly silence and then, a few seconds later, by loud applause.

That headmaster, who, in his black cap and gown, looked to us as if he should have been addressing a new intake of university students, rather than the rag, tag collection of ex-primary school kids, started his welcoming speech. He went on to relate what was and what wasn't allowed and of the type of behaviour expected of us; the rules on the school uniform, which were then compulsory and the general rules of the school, which all in all was a code of conduct for all Plant Hill Comprehensive School scholars. Plant Hill was one of the first Comprehensive schools in Manchester.

The allocation of each student to his or her class was next to follow. Our new headmaster did this from a list that he held in his hands. After he had read out approximately thirty names he said 'Those are the students for Form H. Your form master will lead and you will follow to your class.' With that statement a teacher stepped forward and marched his students to their classroom. This procedure went on from H to G and G to F, right through to Form A until there were only about thirty five students left.

Pawson, Diggle, Boothby and I were among those that remained; we looked at each other in bemusement. Chattering began in earnest amongst those that were left when, at last, Mr Blomeley resumed his allocation duties 'Quiet Please! You pupils that are left are in the Alpha or Grammar Stream of this school, this is the education stream for those that have passed or are borderline passes of the eleven plus examination. You will be taught a similar curriculum to those that have received scholarships and others that are at the local Grammar School. Like all the other students of this school I wish you every success for the future and I will leave you in the capable hands of your form teacher who will escort you to your classroom.' And with that he marched purposely off the stage, his black gown flowing behind him like that of the Caped Crusader from Gotham City. Our new form master then marched us to our form room.

For that first year, our form classroom was on the top floor of the school, the classroom had a normal entrance at the front but at the back was a double door that led onto a roof that was level with the floor of the classroom, bar for an insert to stop the ingress of rainwater. The roof formed a bridge to another part of the school and situated on that roof were a number of bee hives. The school, via its gardening classes, produced its own honey which was sold on parent's evenings and other social occasions, to boost school funds.

Plant Hill, at the time, taught approximately one thousand pupils and was an inter-denominational school and upon being allocated my desk in class I found myself sat next to a catholic boy named Peter Shanley. Also in the class were the Ely twins, Eric and Graham, a couple of Jewish lads from Cheetham whose father owned a tailor's shop in that mainly Jewish area of Manchester and there was Cameron Menzies who was a Scottish Presbyterian. There were children of various religions spread throughout the school.Plant Hill was also the first school in the Manchester area to have its own swimming baths within its complex.

At the top of the short drive from the main entrance to the school was a covered square approximately sixty feet by sixty feet which was always in shadow and therefore rather dark and gloomy; it was known, by the pupils, as the covered space place. At one end of the covered space place was the boiler room where the caretaker hung out, opposite on the other side was a door which served as an emergency exit for the gymnasium, the other two sides had partially open walls which one could walk through and which led to other parts of the school. It was a place where the older boys and girls met up for snogging sessions and a quick fumble while the younger lads sneaked a peep at what was going on. It wasn't long before the younger lads decided to find out what this fumbling was all about and we would then coerce young girls into the cloakrooms or under the stairs where numerous male hands would be plunged down the blouses of the young nymphettes. We soon found out which girls were willing participants and which weren't.

During the first year at Plant Hill I met some very good friends. Ronnie Rhodes, who lived about three quarters of a mile from where I lived, was a particular good friend. I had met Ronnie at Crab Lane Primary School which he lived close to; he was one of the very few that I had befriended at that school. We renewed our friendship and became true and steadfast pals. That friendship lasted until we were both forty years old when Ronnie, for reasons unknown to those around him, took his own life.

There was Dave Leigh who was also a good friend who later joined the army and then moved to Chorley. Graham Boothby, whose family owned a sweet and grocery shop on Victoria Avenue at the top of Plant Hill Road, was another good friend. There was Philip Lloyd who hailed from Droylsden where his mother and father owned a grocery shop. Phil played the trumpet and the cornet. After gaining a degree in maths and then attending Teacher Training College he emigrated from England to

New Zealand where he took up the post of Head of Mathematics at a girl's school. He also became a member of and played trumpet for the New Zealand Simfonia Orchestra and took time out from his teaching career to tour with the orchestra nationally and internationally. He has recorded a number of cd's with the orchestra.

There was something of an affinity between Philip and me borne from the fact that we shared the same birth date. Ken Barnes who had come from Dommett Street School in Blackley Village was another friend I met at Plant Hill. I still see Ken occasionally; he is a Labour councillor on the local council. There were plenty more, some good friends and others close acquaintances and yet others with whom I was not overly friendly.

We still had twice yearly exams and although I had been close to the top of the class at primary school the Alpha Stream was a different kettle of fish. There was no single subject of science such as the lower forms had. The Alpha stream's sciences were split into three different subjects; Physics, Chemistry and Biology. We had different branches of mathematics to study such as arithmetic, geometry, trigonometry and much more that the lower forms didn't. Each workshop lesson such as metalwork and woodwork had separate lessons dealing with the theoretical side of those subjects plus there were other subjects from the Grammar School curriculum. There were clever kids from other districts of Manchester and although I was not totally out of my depth, my finishing position within the first year examination was around the middle of the class. Those that did less well and came within the last four or five were removed from the Alpha Stream and replaced with those from Form A that had done exceptionally well.

Hell Drivers and a Broken
Arm and a Bent Nose

While I was in my twelfth year of being, a film came to the Avenue picture house that I just had to see. The problem was that it bore an 'A' certificate, which meant I could not get in to see it unless accompanied by an adult. The ruse which was used to get around this was to wait for an adult and ask him or her if they would take you in.

Ronnie Rhodes and myself waited until we saw what seemed to us a likely and amenable young man and his girlfriend approaching the entrance to the cinema, we approached the couple and Ronnie asked the male of the pair 'Excuse me, mister, but if we give you the entrance fee would you take us in?' At first the man said no, but his girlfriend intervened 'Aw, come on, take the lads in. There's no harm done.' The young man, easily swayed by his girlfriend's pouting pleas, said 'O.K, but once we're in I don't want you two sat anywhere near us. Right?' we agreed and with that we gave up our money and followed the couple in. Once inside, the courting couple went to accommodate seats on the back row while Ronnie and I found seats elsewhere.

That film that I was so desperate to see was: Hell Drivers, starring Patrick McGoohan, Sean Connery, Stanley Baker, Herbert Lom, with Jill Ireland and a host of other stars. The film was about the cut throat business of haulage and the underhand methods used by both drivers and management. It was about tipper trucks in that instance and to me the stars of the film were the Kew Dodge trucks, built with the same cab as the Leyland Comet and known as the Parrot Nose because of the shape of the bonnet.

The film was a thrill a minute, roller coaster ride of truck driving, albeit to give the sensation of fast moving vehicles, the film was speeded up when the action required it. I loved the life that the film portrayed: the happy go lucky attitude of the people in that profession. I admired the truck drivers in the film, albeit they were only actors, because they exuded an air of roughness and toughness, which nowadays would be called machismo.

I had friends other than those from school and one day as I was riding my bicycle down Plant Hill Road towards my home I saw a couple of mates talking outside the public phone box on the corner of Longton Road, not more than one hundred and fifty yards from my home. One lad was called Alan and the other Stuart and I rode over to chat with them. As we were chatting three more lads that I did not know came over to join the company. Alan and Stuart knew all three and I found out later that one of them was called Jimmy McDonough and that he was quite a bit older than me. He was a bully and a trouble causer who had two elder brothers that would beat up anybody that bested Jimmy in a fair fight, not that he had many fair fights because he always picked his mark and caught his adversaries unawares as he did in my case.

I was stood astride my bike with one leg either side of the crossbar, with my hands resting on the handlebars, when, for no apparent reason, McDonough started to walk around me and my bike. He was like a panther stalking its prey, slow and warily determined, his eyes never leaving me. As he went around the rear of my bike I turned my head the opposite way to catch him coming around my other side, when suddenly he swung his arm out purposely, so that his forearm smashed into my face, specifically my nose. He then calmly walked away from me and my bike and carried on conversing with the others as if nothing untoward had happened. The unexpected blow knocked me and my bike to the ground and my nose started to spurt blood profusely. The lad named Alan came over to where I had fallen and helped me to my feet and picked up my bike. He then, in no uncertain terms, told me to get on my bike and go because, 'That Jimmy McDonough is a bit of a nutter and he'll start on you again. Now Go!' I did not need telling twice, I jumped on my bike and rode away, pedalling as fast as I could in the direction of home.

As I rode around the bend at Plant Hill Park a stray dog ran through the park gates, into the road and into my path. I tried to swerve to avoid the animal but, because I only held onto the handlebars with one hand as I tried to staunch the flow of blood with the other, I ran into the canine jaywalker and went sailing over the handlebars to come crashing down onto the tarmac with my left arm underneath me. After picking myself up I discovered that my left arm had been rendered useless, I could barely move it and it hurt like hell. I managed, with great difficulty, to pick up my bike and push it the short distance home where I propped it up outside the front of the house before entering. Upon seeing me, with blood dripping from my nose and staining the front of my shirt a bright red, my mother enquired as to my welfare as she ushered me into the kitchen to stem the flow of blood. I told her what had happened, being careful, due to acute embarrassment, to leave out the episode with Jimmy McDonough. I told her that the bleeding nose was a direct result of my falling from my bike and that I thought I had broken my arm and perhaps my nose. My mother fashioned a sling from one of her headscarves and put it around my neck to support my injured arm. My father, upon hearing the conversation came into the kitchen. He looked at me and with the knowing look of an ex boxer said 'That ain't the result of you coming off your bike, is it? Come on now, Laurie tell the truth, someone has punched you in the nose, ain't they?'

'It wasn't my fault, dad, honest, it was a big lad. He just come up and hit me for nowt while I was stood with my bike.'

'A big lad, eh? Older than you is he?'

'Yeah, I think he's about fifteen.'

'Right, where did this happen?'

'Just by the phone box at Longton Road.'

'O.K., let's go an' have a look at this hero and teach him a lesson shall we?' and with that he steered me through the house and out on the street and towards the phone box. As we approached, the group of lads were still there and Jimmy McDonough had his back to us. My father asked me which one had hit me and I pointed him out. Dad went up to him and tapped him on the shoulder. McDonough turned around, spotted me in my blood stained shirt and my father, he put two and two together and the colour drained from his face. The other lads all took a couple of paces back and my father spoke directly to Jimmy McDonough, 'What's your name, son?'

The reply was, 'I'm James McDonough. Why?'

Without answering McDonough's question my father carried on 'How old are you, son?'

'I'm fifteen.'

'Fifteen, eh? You'll be a man soon enough and working for a living. What would a near grown man want to be punching an eleven year old boy in the nose for nothing for?'

'Hi-hi-hi-he started it, hi-hi-he was t-t-taking the piss.' stuttered McDonough.

After McDonough's quaking response my dad turned to Alan and Stuart and said, 'Is that right? Did Laurie say anything to this guy? Did he taunt him or make fun of him?'

'No.' replied Alan, 'McDonough just went up to him while Laurie was stood there with his bike between his legs, minding his own business and he just hit him, while Laurie wasn't looking either.'

Like a lightning bolt my father's left arm shot out and he gripped the front of McDonough's shirt and hoisted him off the ground. He pushed him towards and held him up against the telephone kiosk and said, 'Right, let's see what kinda man you are now, ya little turd.'

I looked at McDonough's face. His eyes were glistening with moisture and had welled up; then the dam broke and his tears overflowed his lower eyelids and coursed down his ashen cheeks and he said in a quivering voice that was almost a whisper and full of fear, 'I-i-if you hit me, mister, I'll b-b-bring m-m-mi dad and m-m-mi bruvvers to sort you out.'

My Father laughed and said, 'In my experience son, cowards and bullies beget cowards and bullies so you bring your dad and your brothers and tell them to bring your uncles because if they're out like you they'll be a bunch of shithouses,' and with that he bunched his right hand into a fist and drew his arm back as if to punch McDonough. McDonough closed his eyes and squirmed as my father let his punch fly, at the same instant my father released his grip on McDonough who fell to the floor in a quivering, trembling heap as my dad's fist flew over his head. Then, there came the fetid smell, McDonough, in abject fear, had voided his bowels. Alan and Stuart and even McDonough's compatriots who were stood at a distance and ready to take flight, were pointing down at the sobbing and frightened youth on the floor and they were laughing. McDonough picked himself up, glanced at my father and then at the others that stood there, then he turned tail and ran down Longton Road away from his tormentors, his blue, Wrangler jeans displaying a large damp patch to the rear. His two mates ran after him. They were laughing loudly. Whenever mine and McDonough's paths crossed, after that day, he gave me a wide berth and even crossed the road to avoid me. I knew that my father, who had never struck me in anger, would not strike McDonough but he surely put the fear of God into him. After that short but decisive encounter, my dad put his arm around my shoulder and said 'Right, son, there endeth the lesson, now let's get you to hospital and have that arm looked at.'

In the excitement and with the adrenalin rush I had forgotten all about the pain that I was in.

Once again, I was taken to Booth Hall Children's Hospital where, by now they were compiling a rather thick medical dossier on me. After a short wait I was taken into radiography where my arm was subjected to Mr Roentgen's X-rays. After the snapshots of my injured arm were completed I took them, in a large brown envelope, to the orthopaedic section of the hospital where the X-ray photographs were clipped to a light box and studied by the orthopaedic doctor who, after a few minutes cogitation and consideration informed my father and me that I had sustained a Greenstick fracture of the left arm to the bone called the radius. A greenstick fracture is so called because the fracture is incomplete and splintered and resembles a broken green twig. I was then directed to the plaster room where my arm was first wrapped in cotton wool. The plaster of Paris bandages were then soaked and wrapped spirally around my arm from my elbow to my wrist and between my thumb and forefinger. I then had to wait until the plaster had set before I was allowed to go home. My arm would remain in plaster for three months. Whilst in the orthopaedic department my nose was examined. It wasn't broken but it was found to have a deviated septum, courtesy of Jimmy McDonough, who I now know, was a coward, bully and a thug who took great delight in humiliating kids that were younger and smaller than he was.

Six-Five Special, Oh Boy!
& Boy Meets Girl

At the beginning of 1957 not long after my eleventh birthday on Saturday the 23rd of February, a new programme came on the BBC television. That show was the brainchild of producer Jack Goode and was called 'Six-Five Special,' it was the first rock 'n' roll show to be shown on British Television and just the show the teenagers of the day and myself had been waiting for. It derived its name from the time it aired; five past six in the evening. The first show was compered by DJ Pete Murray and the following shows by ex boxer Freddie Mills. The stars of the show were Don Lang and his Frantic Five, Tommy Steele, Lonnie Donegan, Terry Dene, The John Barry Seven, Wee Willie Harris and Jim Dale and others. Because of BBC strictures and the fact that Jack Goode did not see eye to eye with the BBC hierarchy, the show descended into farce. The rock 'n' roll element, which had brought the programme to the forefront of television entertainment, was almost lost with the programme relying on such middle of the road headliners as Denis Lotis, Dickie Valentine and Michael Holliday. Jack Goode Subsequently joined ABC and was given free rein which led to the programme he had always wanted to make; Oh Boy! The show was broadcast live from London's Hackney Empire. The comperes were Tony Hall and Jim Henney. It was Oh Boy! that finally finished Six-Five Special off; the BBC show could not compete with the new ATV show and was quickly withdrawn.

Oh Boy's first major discovery was Harry Roger Webb better known as Cliff Richard. Other notable acts on Oh Boy! were Marty Wilde, Billy Fury, Lord Rockingham's Eleven, The Vernon Girls, Cuddly Dudley, Vince Eager, Dickie Pride and The Dallas Boys. OH Boy! started in October 1958, although there was a trial run in June 1958 and it ran for a year until September 1959 when it was replaced by Boy Meets Girl which was again produced by Jack Goode who also presented the programme with the occasional help of Marty Wilde. Between them they introduced such stars as Terry Dene, Joe Brown, Adam Faith and Cliff Richard and the great American Rock 'n' Rollers, Eddie Cochran and Freddy Cannon. Those were the shows that people of my age and teenagers watched on a Saturday evening.

An Illegal Shooting

It was while I was in the second year at Plant Hill that I had my second brush with the law. It came about because my father bought me, as a birthday present, a Diana, model sixteen, air rifle with a calibre of .177. At first I used it quite responsibly for target practise, improving my skill using both waisted pellets and darts, it came about that I had a couple of mates round one Saturday evening in the summertime, those mates were Francis (Franny) Butterworth and Wilf Doyle. Franny lived across the road in a bungalow on Plant Hill School property; he was the son of the school caretaker. Wilfred Michael Doyle lived just around the corner in Jurby Avenue in a block of three storey flats, he answered to either Wilf or Mike.

On the Saturday evening in question, my sister Val was going out with our cousin Irene and would be staying the night at Irene's house. My mum and dad were going out for the evening to the ICI Club; a recreation club for the employees of ICI and their families and friends and which was owned and run by my father's place of work, the Imperial Chemical Industries whose site took up several acres of land in Blackley and where my father had found employment as a maintenance plumber before we moved from Newton Heath. My Uncle Fred and my Uncle Walter also worked for the ICI, Walter as a pipefitter and Fred as a process worker in the dye sheds. My parents went out that Saturday evening at about 8.30pm leaving me with orders to behave and to be in bed for 11pm, which left Franny, Wilf and me to carry on with our target practise in the back garden.

About fifty yards distant from the back garden were a block of flats of the same design of those where Wilf lived. It had reached 10.30pm and darkness was descending and Wilf was about to take a shot at the paper target when he saw a figure appear at the window of one of the flats. He turned round to me and Franny with a daft grin on his face and said, 'Should I?'

Franny and I looked at each other and I said, yeah, why not?'

With that Wilfred lifted the rifle to his shoulder, sighted and pulled the trigger; we heard the pellet strike the glass and we all ran to hide behind my dad's garage. The guy from the flat opened his window and shouted, 'I know who you are, you little bastards and I'm gonna get the police on you.'

With that threat Wilf re-loaded, poked the rifle round the garage and took another pot-shot at the man.

After that incident we retired into the house to watch the television and after about twenty minutes there was a knock on the door. I took a peep through the curtains and saw two burly Bobbies stood at the front door. We didn't believe he would, but our victim had actually called the police and there they stood, at the door looking every bit the figures of authority that they were. I turned to Franny and Wilf and said in a low voice, 'It's the police, turn the tele off and keep quiet.'

The knocking was repeated but much louder; then silence.

I peeped cautiously through a chink in the curtains and saw the coppers talking to our next door neighbour, Mr Jones. I said to the other two prime suspects, 'Come on, let's go upstairs.' We had just reached my bedroom door when the knocking was repeated and after a few seconds Mr Jones', who had been recruited, by the police, as a mediator, spoke to us through the letterbox, 'Laurie, we know that you're in there. These nice policemen just want to ask you a few questions, so come on and open the door, you're not in any trouble.' We remained silent. Franny and Wilf; both Catholics, had their eyes closed and their hands clasped in front of their faces and their lips moved in silent prayer; that's how serious they thought our predicament was.

Mumbled voices could be heard from outside but we could not make out what was being said. After a few more minutes we heard the doors of a vehicle being slammed shut and then the vehicle was started up, peering through the window from the darkness of the bedroom I saw the police van being driven away. Mr Jones had returned to the safety of his home, just in case the cornered, gun-totin' desperado's decided to shoot their way out.

In fear, we waited a few minutes more when Franny said, 'they've gone, I'm gonna make a break for it.'

Although there was no one to hear us, we crept, ever so quietly downstairs where Franny opened the door slightly, stuck his head out and looked up and down the road, it was clear and he stated, 'I'm outa here.'

He opened the door fully and made a dash for home. He made it to the bungalow and waved from his front door. I closed the door and Wilf and I went back upstairs.

It was not much longer when I heard the key in the front door, still clothed, I dived under the bedclothes and Wilf scrambled under the bed. My mother came upstairs and opened my bedroom door to see, what appeared to her to be, a peacefully sleeping son and so she returned downstairs. After a short space of time I heard a knock on the front door. Various thoughts went through my head. Had the police returned with a warrant for my arrest? Would I spend a night in the cells? What about Wilf beneath my bed. I heard the front door being opened and then I heard a very distraught Mrs Doyle, Wilf's mother, enquiring as to the whereabouts of her wayward son. She knew that he had been with me earlier. I heard footsteps on the stairs, my bedroom door opened, the light was switched on and my mother started to gently shake me to awaken me from my pretend sleep. I moaned, yawned, rubbed my eyes and sat up. 'What is it mum? What's up?'

Luckily for me, she did not notice that I still wore the same striped shirt that I had worn through the day, she must have taken it for my pyjama top. She looked at me sternly and asked, 'Laurie, where's Wilfred Doyle? His mother is downstairs and she's very upset. Do you know where Wilf is?'

In my response I was totally untruthful, 'He left just after you and dad went out and I haven't seen him since. I thought he had gone home.'

'Are you sure?' mum asked.

'Course I am.' I replied.

'O.K' she said I'll go and tell Mrs Doyle. Now you go back to sleep, I hope young Wilfred turns up and he's OK, good night son.' She must have suspected something because as she reached the door to my bedroom she bent down and looked under my bed but Wilf had scrunched himself up into the furthest, darkest corner and my mother failed to spot him. Wilf's mother had to then report her son as missing so there were two police enquiries being conducted that were directly linked. I then went to sleep leaving Wilf to sleep as best he could on the floor under the bed. Wilf lived with his mother; his father was absent, for what reason I don't know. He was an only child to a single mum.

The next morning at approximately 8 o'clock am, there was a loud rat-a- tat, tat on the front door. My father who was none too pleased about having his Sunday morning lie in disturbed, especially after a few pints the night before, went down and opened the door to be greeted by two P. C.'s from Plant Hill Police station, he invited them in and after listening to the tales of indiscriminate shooting and of the missing youth he stormed upstairs and into my bedroom. Something had aroused his suspicions. Had Wilf shuffled or made a noise? Did he breathe too loudly? I don't know what it was but my father gripped the underside of my bed and pulled it away from the wall, as I was still recumbent in it, to find young Mr Doyle squashed into the corner, quaking with fear. I was told to get dressed and Wilf and I were marched downstairs to face the wrath of the law.

After a good talking to by the police, we stood before them shamefaced. They really had a go at Wilf for causing his mother so much distress. I glanced at Wilf and saw tears rolling down his cheeks. 'Oh', said one of the boys in blue, 'The fellow that you shot at told us that there were three of you involved. Who was the other lad?'

Here my father interjected, 'That other boy was Francis Butterworth and he lives in the bungalow, in the school grounds, across the road.'

I was glad that my father had named Francis as the third lad because that meant that Wilf and I had not grassed him up or told on him, an act which would have broken all the rules and codes of friendship. The Bobbies apologised to my dad for disturbing him so early on a Sunday morning and the last words they said before leaving and taking Wilf with them to return him to his mother were 'There will, of course, be prosecutions.'

We all had to attend the local police station with our parents to be formally charged. I cannot remember the full charges but it was something like criminal damage, discharging a weapon within fifty yards of the public highway and wilfully causing another person to be shot. In actuality the air rifle was not that powerful. Over the distance it could not have broken a pane of glass and if the victim had been injured by a pellet it would have been when he opened his window and Wilf took a second shot at him, even so it would have barely bruised him. I am not trying to make excuses; we three were totally stupid and irresponsible and we deserved to be prosecuted.

A few weeks later we each received our summonses to attend the Juvenile Court on Minshull Street in Manchester Town Centre. For the court appearance our respective parents dressed us up in our best suits with neckties and freshly laundered white shirts after making us take a bath and wash our hair. I had adopted a flat top hairstyle with a quiff in the Teddy-boy style, but for my court appearance my mum cut my quiff away until I had a nice, neat, short crew cut. The other two accused appeared in court with their hair cut short with side partings and slicked down with Brylcreem. It was all done to make us look as if 'butter wouldn't melt in our mouths' and to portray us as pictures of innocence to the magistrates.

The chief magistrate on the panel read out the charges and asked us how we were to plead. We had been caught bang to rights and so the only plea we could offer was one of guilty. The two outer magistrates leant inwards towards the man in the middle. They talked and discussed at length what should be done with these young malcontents and juvenile delinquents that stood before them, they talked very lowly sometimes nodding their heads and sometimes shaking them and occasionally they would glance up at us. They suddenly finished their conversation and resumed their original positions.

The chap in the middle, who it seemed, was the foreman of the panel, was a slim person dressed in a dark pinstripe suit; he had a very shiny bald head with an inch width of hair above his ears and widening around the back of his head as it descended into the nape of his neck. His glossy pate reflected the high, fluorescent, courtroom lights giving his head the appearance of a very bright, white, dome. He had a very prominent, long, sharp nose along which he could not help but look down on people with his beady, peering eyes which stared through spectacles that were poised half way down his long angular nose. Below his nose he sported a very thin pencil line moustache, below which were pale, thin lips. Sat, one on either side of him, were two elderly, smartly dressed women, one had a bouffant type hairstyle with a blue rinse to cover the grey whilst the other had her wiry, grey hair pulled back very severely and tied in a bun. The plump lady with the bouffant had a pleasant and friendly appearance and she wore just the right amount of make up. She frequently smiled at us, her pink lips parting slightly to show straight, white teeth; she was the archetypal, doting grandmother figure dressed in a light grey business suit with a skirt. The woman with the drawn back bun in her hair was a stick thin battleaxe with a rock solid, stern countenance that looked as if it would crack if she might condescend to smile. The harridan had the puckered lips of someone who had been sucking on a lemon. Her harsh, Draconian and pedagogic bearing was more than a little frightening, like a strict, female martinet. She seemed to be the archetypal, dedicated, spinster frump and misanthropist. She was dressed in a dark trouser suit which was almost mannish.

After their long discussion the male of the three addressed us, the accused and our parents, He rambled on about taking responsibility for our actions and he accused my father of being 'irresponsible for purchasing such a dangerous plaything as the air rifle for an immature child such as your son.'

My father's face reddened somewhat, at the magistrates remarks. Reddened somewhat is a bit of an understatement, his face turned redder than a London bus, more red than a post office pillar box or a ripe tomato.

167

I believe that if he had been anywhere else but in court, for which he had the utmost respect, he would not have been spoken to in such a manner without defending himself. As it was he stood there, embarrassed, and took it.

I know that air rifles can be dangerous in the wrong hands, but the magistrate talked as if we had been wielding a twelve bore, sawn off shotgun or a Winchester repeating carbine. He told us that we were lucky that we were not in court charged with graver crimes and how we had cost the council a lot of money for the search for a youth who wasn't actually missing at all; about wasted manpower and the upset and distress we had caused other people. After about twenty minutes of demeaning, discrediting and humiliating us he told us that we would be fined the sum of twelve shillings, (60p) each. We were then dismissed from the courtroom and directed to the counter where fines were paid.

As we made our way to the payment counter Mrs Doyle tugged on my dad's arm and said, 'Excuse me, Mr Driver, but I ain't got two ha'pennies to rub together, I'm skint 'cept for our bus fares home. Could you possibly lend me the twelve shillings until I get the maintenance cheque, for Wilfred?'

My dad looked at the destitute woman and said, 'Yeah, I'll pay the fine for you, pay me back when you're able.'

He paid the fines but I believe that he never saw that twelve shillings again, perhaps, in some small way he felt responsible for her because of my stupid actions. He may never have got the money off Wilf's mum but he made me pay back every penny of my fine, by instalments, out of my weekly spending allowance, until it was paid off.

After the shooting incident I gained a little notoriety at school. Other kids asked what it was like to be arrested and taken before the beak. I revelled in my new found infamy and the story grew with each telling. News travelled fast via the grapevine and because of a little passage in the local newspaper I became known to the parents of my peers. I became the local juvenile delinquent, the leader of a law-breaking gang and a child who the parents of other children did not want their own offspring associating with.

It transpired that one evening the father of a classmate of mine called Dave Leigh, came to call on my father. I was sat watching the television with the rest of the family, I was not planning any shootings or robberies or any other misdemeanour. There was a rat-a-tat tat upon the front door and my father rose from his chair to answer the call. As he opened the door the person there started to rant and rave so vehemently that he was almost incoherent. My father said 'Whoa! Slow down! What's this all about?'

'I'll tell you what this is all about.' He said, 'It's about your son Laurie. He's always getting into trouble and causing problems. Why, he's even been to court for his crimes, he is a known criminal. He's a bad influence on my son David and I don't want him near my son. I forbid your lad to fraternise with mine. Is that clear?' ranted Mr Leigh.

'Ill tell you what's clear to me,' said my dad, 'and that is that you are jumped up little pipsqueak who has come around here to denigrate my son when you do not know any of the facts.'

With that my father took a step forward which took him out of the house and on to the footpath, at the same time Mr Leigh took a faltering step backwards and my father continued, 'You arrogant little bastard, my son is a good lad who has made a mistake for which he has paid ......'

'He's a trouble causer.' interrupted Mr Leigh.

'A trouble causer is he? Why you cocky little sod,' said my dad as he bunched his fist and took another step forward, 'I ought to knock your bloody head off.' But by that time he was talking to himself because Dave Leigh's dad had made a hasty retreat which would have put Roger Bannister to shame and from a safe distance he shouted 'Keep him away from my son, that's all.'

My dad ignored Mr Leigh's parting remark.

After Mr Leigh's hasty departure my father came back into the house and into the living room from where we had been watching through the window and from where we had heard everything and he said, 'Well you all heard that little altercation, and you, Laurie, must keep away from David. I know he's a good mate an' all that but you heard what his father said.'

I knew that there was little or no point in arguing with my dad so I nodded my agreement. The problem was, how to stop two kids from the same class at school from fraternising, it was impossible, and because we had the same circle of friends we still met up out of school; we just didn't tell our parents and we remained firm friends throughout our youth and into adulthood.

Dave left home shortly after leaving school and rented a flat on Hermitage Road in Crumpsall with another friend named Ronnie Allen who wasn't getting on with his parents in their family home. It seems to me that even if I was a bad influence, things could not have been perfect at home for Dave or he would not have been in such a hurry to flee the nest. He later joined the army and upon serving his allocated time and leaving the armed forces he set up his own carpet and furniture cleaning business in Chorley to where he had moved and where he lives, with his family, to this day.

AVRO's Burns Down &
Good Times at Belle Vue

Approximately two miles from where I lived in Blackley was AVRO's aviation factory, on Greengate, Chadderton. The factory was named after its founder Alliot Verdon Roe, the first man in England to make a powered flight. That first flight was at Brooklands Racetrack at Weybridge, Surrey in 1908 when his flimsy machine flew for approximately seventy five yards. A.V. Roe was a pioneer amongst British aviators. The first AVRO factory was built in Newton Heath but in 1938 with the clouds of war darkening the skies it was decided to erect a custom built factory on Greengate, Chadderton. The factory became one of the biggest employers in the area. The Lancaster bomber was produced at AVRO at Greengate as was the Vulcan and many more war time and peace time aeroplanes. AVRO had a second factory in the North at Woodford Aerodrome in Cheshire and a factory in Lincolnshire. Avro's was later taken over by British Aerospace.

During 1959 & 1960 AVRO's factory at Greengate, Chadderton was hit by a series of fires in various parts of the factory. The worst, which devoured a large part of the production plant and numerous offices, occurred on October 3, 1959. I remember looking out from our house on Plant Hill Road to see the whole sky lit up, with an eerie red and orange glow, by the massive conflagration. The evening gloom had turned to a rosy brightness because the flames were so huge and powerful.

A lot of the local youths, myself included, got on their bicycles and rode down Victoria Avenue East to view the fire at a closer proximity. We soon ran into a road block, the police had stopped anyone getting within a couple of hundred yards in all directions, all the major roads were closed and numerous small streets were no go areas. Many houses were evacuated. The fire brigade was out in force, there were numerous tenders and from where we had been stopped we could see the ladders, high in the air with the heroic firemen, silhouetted against the red sky, directing gushers of water into the blaze. Finally the blaze was brought under control and in time the plant and offices were rebuilt, but the event was talked about at school and elsewhere for months.

When Cousin Bobby reached the age of twelve he had a sudden attack of the maturities; he decided that Bobby was an immature, infantile and childish title. From that day on he would be known as Bob. If anybody addressed him as Bobby he would inform them that that appellation was no longer to be used and his moniker from then on would be Bob or Robert and not Bobby. Everybody that was acquainted with Bob agreed and settled for the diminutive of Bob rather than the rather formal Robert. The same thing had occurred with Cousin Freddy a couple of years earlier when he decided to become Fred instead of Freddy for pretty much the same reasons, although he hated his full title of Frederick.

When Bob and I were between twelve and fourteen years of age we used to watch wrestling on the television on Saturday afternoons. That was until we discovered that we could watch the real thing at King's Hall in the Belle Vue complex on Hyde Road, in Gorton, on Saturday evenings.

Belle Vue was a multi entertainment facility that was opened by John Jennison in June 1836. It was originally opened as an area of zoological gardens with numerous exotic animals and plants. There were lions and tigers, a monkey house, giraffes and many more animals from around the world. One of the main attractions in the 1950's was a hybrid cross between a male Tiger and a lioness, known as a Tigon. There was an Indian Elephant named Maharaja that earned its keep by allowing, at a fee, children and adults to ride upon its back. The elephant, which came from a Scottish zoo, was also used to perform heavy duty labour. There was a Reptile House and a large aviary. I remember there being on show, a skull of a Hippopotamus, which had been killed in a fight with its mother whose lower tusk had penetrated the younger animal's skull, thereby killing it. It is said that there are more human deaths in Africa credited to the Hippopotamus than there are to lions. Belle Vue complex, at its best, covered one hundred and sixty five acres and over two million people visited it annually.

The Jennison family finally relinquished control of Belle Vue in 1925 and it was then under the charge of Gerald Isles. Over the years the complex grew; a funfair was added which had all the rides considered necessary. The Bobs was a roller coaster constructed from timber and I swear that the whole structure shook as the cars traversed its ups and downs and curves and switchbacks on steel rails. There were water flumes, a haunted house, The Ghost Train, carousels, a hall of mirrors and much more.

Belle Vue had its own dance band and such famous singers of the day like Dickie Valentine and Alma Cogan performed there. There was a greyhound racing track and a speedway track where the Belle Vue Aces outrode most of the opposition. Pete Craven is the name I remember best from the Aces team. Fireworks displays were held there and Belle Vue had its own circus. Boxing matches and title fights were held in King's Hall which also hosted, on most Saturday evenings, the wrestling bouts that Bob and I went to see.

When Bob and I were going to see the wrestling at King's Hall, Belle Vue on a Saturday evening we would get ready after dinner and make our way to the Belle Vue complex where we would buy our entrance tickets to the zoological gardens and our tickets to the wrestling. We would then enjoy an afternoon on the rides and in the zoo before going into King's Hall to watch the wrestling bouts. The wrestlers at Belle Vue were a colourful lot and one of my favourites was Billy Two Rivers. Billy was a Canadian Native Indian of the Mohawk tribe. He was born in 1935 and took up wrestling at sixteen years of age. In his prime he stood six feet tall and weighed in at two hundred pounds. He travelled the world as a wrestler and performed often at Belle Vue in the 60's. His gimmick was to enter the ring wearing warpaint and a full Indian war bonnet which when removed revealed a Mohawk hairstyle. I remember that his favourite move was to do a war dance around his opponent, whooping wildly, he would then suddenly throw out his arm and give his opponent a tomahawk chop across the throat. Mister Two Rivers retired from wrestling in 1976 and later at forty three years of age he entered politics on behalf of his people on the Canadian Kahnawake reservation.

'Dirty' Dominic Pye, who wrestled regularly at King's Hall, was the son of Jack Pye, one of wrestling's greatest post war exponents. Jack was known as the uncrowned king of the mat. Vic and Bert Royal also fought a lot at Belle Vue sometimes on their own but more often than not, as a tag team sometimes billed as the Faulkner Brothers and other times as the Royal Brothers. I am sure that I also saw Jackie Pallo and Mick McManus at Belle Vue amongst many more wrestlers of the day. Wrestling has always been a contentious sport with some people believing it not to be a sport at all and that it was and is all staged and I must admit that some of the forearm smashes, if they had truly connected when dished out by those wrestlers would have felled an elephant. I once read somewhere that some professional wrestlers were members of the actors union Equity; says it all I suppose.

Belle Vue entertained generation after generation of families with its many attractions. I remember going to the Christmas Circus with the company that my father worked for at the time (I.C.I.). There were numerous animal acts, elephants, liberty horses and then a cage would be erected and the big cats would be led into the ring to perform. The highlight of the Big Cats Show was when the Lion Tamer put his head in the lion's mouth. I am sure that I was not alone in hoping that the lion would snap its jaws shut at that precise moment. The big felines were controlled by the tamer with a whip and a chair and there is no doubting the bravery of that man, as there is no doubting the cruelty to the animals. There were clowns; the white clown with his white face and white, sequined suit was known as a Pierrot and the tramps, with their red noses, brightly coloured hair, baggy trousers, and big feet were his underlings. All those acts were introduced and controlled by the Ringmaster who if I remember rightly was George Lockhart who had come from the Tower Circus at Blackpool. He was resplendent in his black top hat, white gloves and red tailed coat. George Lockhart died in 1972 aged ninety.

Latterly Belle Vue was taken over by Trust House Forte and shortly after in late 1977, the zoo closed for the final time and the amusement park closed in 1980. All that is left of this once wonderful complex is the Greyhound Racing Track which is given over, when needed to the Belle Vue Aces to show their riding skills on the Speedway track.

Chapter 9

A Trip to France, Sexual Awakening,
and Rock 'n' Roll.

It was while I was in the second year that a trip to France was arranged for the second year classes that were learning French as a second language. The cost of the trip was seventeen guineas (£17. 17s or £17.85p), plus some spending money and about half of the pupils of the Alpha Stream went on that educational voyage, including myself. It was an equal distribution of boys and girls that took the opportunity to the visit our continental peers in France, the home of Brigitte Bardot, Maurice Chevalier, Charles de Gaulle and the Horse burger.

The adventure started with all of the travellers meeting at the school where a coach awaited us to take us down to the south coast port of Newhaven where we boarded a ferry for the French port of Dieppe. It took the coach driver most of the day to drive to Newhaven and the ferry that we had to board was a night time sailing. Four teachers accompanied the students on the trip which was of a fortnight's duration.

After docking at Dieppe and clearing customs, the coach took us to the coastal town of Fecamp, in Normandy, where we stayed in an establishment that was separated into two dormitories, one for *Les jeune homme* and one for *Les jeune fille*. The teachers had their own separate, *chambres simple*, but rumours abounded amongst the pupils, borne out of the flirtatious manner of the tutors in question, that a certain couple of the teachers, whose partners were back in England, were sleeping together.

The establishment had *un salle a manger* and separate *salle des bain*. I suppose it was the French equivalent to a youth hostel. Each day we went on excursions which were supposed to be educational and by which we could enhance our knowledge of the *Langage Francais*. I cannot remember the itinerary but we visited some interesting places including Le Havre where we visited the church of Notre Dame; not to be confused with the Notre Dame de Paris. We visited Bayeux where we saw the famous tapestry and cathedral. We also saw lace making and porcelain production. The *Tappisserie de Bayeux* is not, in actuality, a tapestry but an embroidered cloth twenty inches wide by two hundred and thirty feet long, which purports to explain the events leading up to the 1066 invasion of England by the Normans led by William the Conqueror and of the events of the invasion itself. It depicts King Harold Godwinson's death by an arrow in the eye and the defeat of the Anglo-Saxon English; it also depicts Halley's Comet which was supposed to serve as an omen of Harold's defeat.

Rouen, which we were informed, was the capital of Normandy was another of the towns that we visited. We paid a visit to the Abbey in Fecamp where the Benedictine order of monks first made the nectar like liqueur named after them. Benedictine is an herbal beverage liqueur containing twenty seven plants and spices. It was first distilled in 1510 at the Benedictine *Abbaye* in Fecamp, from a recipe developed by a monk named Dom Bernardo Vincelli. It is a powerful drink being 43% alcohol, (86%) proof.

The beaches of Normandy where we were shown around and went into the German fortifications known as pill boxes were also visited and even thirteen years after the cessation of the hostilities of WWII, we found spent cartridges and cartridge cases. The allied cemeteries also on the agenda; numerous white gravestones laid out symmetrically on lawns that were more manicured than mown. Many and varied *Chateaux* and churches were visited and lots of little villages and towns whose names now escape me.

After the trip to the Benedictine *Monastere*, where we were allowed to taste the equivalent of a thimble full of the sweet tasting liqueur, some of the boys and girls had a collection and managed, without the teachers knowledge, to buy a couple of large bottles from a local wine shop or *Debit de boissons*, in Fecamp and after evening dinner, those that had contributed to the collection met up in the grounds of the hostel to sample the delightful drink.

The bottles were passed around between the pupils like winos would pass the bottle around a bombsite brazier. It wasn't long before the girls started giggling uncontrollably, a couple of the lads started brawling. One lad, named Roger, walked into a tree and knocked himself out. Boys started chasing girls trying to kiss them and get a quick feel. There was shouting and screaming which reached the ears of the teachers. All four teachers marched out to where the noise emanated to find a group of pissed up teenagers who had never experienced alcohol before and therefore could not handle it. Some were staggering about, others lay where they had fallen and at least one was spewing up in the flowerbeds. The 2 large bottles which once contained the Benedictine by this time, of course, were laying on the ground, empty, devoid of the sweet, nectar like, intoxicating liqueur.

The teachers rounded us up and we were sent to our respective dormitories. The male teachers took the boys and the female teachers escorted the girls. We were threatened that our parents would be told of our drunken escapades and we were sent to bed immediately, it was only 8pm. Next morning there were some who were unable to face breakfast, others were vomiting until mid morning. Teachers passed around headache tablets and there were numerous vows of 'Never again,' followed by a lecture on the evils of drink. Those that did not take part in the evening of drunken debauchery took the Mickey out of those of us that did and taunted us about being sent to bed early and the resulting hangovers the following morning.

Some of the things that we innocents abroad encountered were a shock to our naive, *Anglais* sensibilities; the *pissoir* (Gentleman's public toilets) took some getting used to. Males using the *pissoir* to urinate were on open view to passers by. They, *las toilette,* were constructed so as to leave little to the imagination. It didn't bother the French but it was something of a culture shock to us innocents abroad. Most of us were to shy to use them and so we crossed our legs and struggled with full bladders until we could use indoor *toilettes*.

Les Francais have always had a broader outlook than the somewhat reserved *Anglais* people when it comes to being libertarian and open and one day the teachers and pupils were sat outside a typical continental street cafe; the pupils were enjoying the *cafe au lait, alfresco* and *au soleil,* whilst the teachers sipped their *vin blanc, ou, vin rouge* when a young and very beautiful woman with a babe in arms came along and sat quite close to us. Upon sitting down and placing her order with *le garcon,* she opened her blouse and flopped out one of her swollen mammaries and offered the nipple up to the mouth of *l'enfant* and sat there quite content as the baby suckled. The young males in our group, including me, had never before seen a complete stranger flop out her breast and feed her infant child and we gazed in open mouthed awe at the scene before us, Teachers quickly moved amongst us saying 'Don't stare! Look the other way!' they, it seemed, were more embarrassed than we pupils were.

All too soon the day arrived for us to return to Blighty. The coach transported us to the port where we were shunted through the nothing to declare section of *Les Douane,* before boarding the ferry for a night time sailing from Dieppe to Newhaven where the long trip from the South coast to Manchester would begin. Parents would meet their offspring at the school gates and take them home. Because I lived across the road from Plant Hill School, I only had to cross the road after getting off the coach and I was home. The trip to France was enjoyed by everyone that went but I don't think that any one of us came back with a greater knowledge of the French language than when we left. Fortunately the threat to enlighten our parents about the drunken evening in Fecamp was just that, a threat and no more was heard about it.

While I was in France my parents and my sister took a short break to London where they stayed with my father's sister, my Aunt Lou and her husband, my uncle Bill Bellini. Valerie was taken to see all the tourist attractions in the Big Smoke, through the day and taken to the pictures on some evenings. She was taken to see The Sweet Smell of Success, starring Tony Curtis and the musical South Pacific among others. The latter part of the week was spent at the Bellini's holiday home on the Isle of Sheppey. My sister and parents probably had a better or equally as good a time as I had in France.

Most of the pupils, male and female, that went to France on that school trip brought some illicit contraband or mementos back with them. Some brought cigarettes and some brought wine. My little piece of illicit contraband was a flick knife. Why I bought it I don't know but I had it hidden in the lining of my jacket as we passed through customs. That, as it happened, wasn't necessary as the customs officers, probably perceiving us to be a group of innocents school childeren, just chalked a big letter X on all of our cases and waved us through. Once I had gotten the smuggled weapon home I hid it away from prying eyes by secreting it under my mattress, not realising that mothers when they changed the bed clothes also turned the mattress.

A couple of days after the return from France, I was going out to one of my friends one evening and I thought I would take my new switchblade to show to him. I slid my hand under the mattress and to my surprise I could not feel the cold steel of my knife, I groped further under the mattress but still no knife. I panicked and lifted the mattress up; there was no sign of the blade, where could it be? It couldn't just disappear into thin air or dissolve into the mattress. I was mystified and at a loss as to the flick knife's whereabouts. I wondered if I had left it in the pocket of my jacket or another coat and so I gave up looking and went downstairs to check my other garments. I walked into the kitchen and there was my mother with her back to me, at the draining board, peeling potatoes. She slowly turned around to confront me and that was when I saw that the implement with which she was peeling the spuds was none other than my flick knife. Nothing was said but the knife was never seen again from that day onwards.

The Early 60's

I was in the third year at Plant Hill School at the advent of the 1960's, the decade that seems to be remembered by everyone, whether they were there or not. There are things that people do not remember and some of those and other salient landmarks of the first three years of the 60's I will relate here. It was on the 3rd of February 1960 that Harold Macmillan made his '*Winds of Change,*' speech in the Houses of Parliament in Cape Town. It was the first sign that Britain had accepted that the days of Empire were over and it dramatically speeded up the process of African independence. On the 21st of March, anti apartheid protesters were arrested outside South Africa House in Westminster. The 18th of April saw a large CND demonstration in Trafalgar Square. Princess Margaret married Anthony Armstrong-Jones in Westminster Abbey on the 6th of May. On the 18th May 1960, Real Madrid won the European Cup for the fifth time, defeating Eintracht Frankfurt 7 – 3 at Hampden Park Glasgow. Cyprus gained its independence on the 16th of August as did Nigeria on 1st of October. The 19th September saw the first traffic wardens deployed on the streets of London and on the 2nd November 1960, Penguin books were acquitted of obscenity for publishing D.H. Lawrence's '*Lady Chatterley's Lover*'. In December 1960, Coronation Street burst onto our television screens. The angry young men were still turning out their kitchen sink dramas in1960 with Stan Barstow's *'A Kind of Loving'* and David Storey's *'This Sporting Life'*.Robert Bolt's *'A Man for all Season's'* was also published that year, which was also the year that John F. Kennedy won the US presidential elections against vice president Richard Nixon, by a narrow margin, he was sworn in on 20th of January 1961. During the Second year of the 60's, on the 17th of May, 1961 South Africa announced that it would become a republic outside the Commonwealth. Between June and September Kuwait ceased to be a British Protectorate. The 2nd July 1961 brought the death of Ernest Hemingway by gunshot wounds, he committed suicide. During September, many hundreds of demonstrators were arrested in CND protests including its President Bertrand Russell. On 10th October 1961 a volcanic eruption forced the evacuation of the entire population of Tristan da Cunha (pop 275) to England. On the 10th November 1961, Catch 22 by Joseph Heller was published and during the year, Muriel Spark's *'The Prime of Miss Jean Brodie'*, was also published. In August 1962 Jamaica, Trinidad and Tobago became independent and Uganda gained its independence on the 9th of October. The 4th October saw the release of the Beatle's first single, Love Me Do, and between 22nd and 28th of October, the world held its breath as it was brought to the brink of nuclear war during the Cuban missile crisis. Tanganyika became an independent country on the 9th of September. During 1962 Anthony Burgess's controversial novel *'A Clockwork Orange'*, was published, later to become an even more controversial film and the first James Bond film, *'Dr No'*, starring Sean Connery and featuring Ursula Andress emerging from the sea in that unforgettable white Bikini, was released.

Sexual Precocity

By the time we were in the third year of the alpha stream we had discovered a girl of easy virtue. She was in the same year but from form E or F, her name was Linda Wood and it was common knowledge that Linda would. She was sexually precocious and she had lost her virginity to a local lad of sixteen years when she was only thirteen, albeit almost fourteen and once she had tasted the forbidden pleasure of sexual intercourse she wanted more. At the time she would not have anything to do with the lads from the same year or younger, other than to let us have a feel of her breasts and that was usually when three or four of us trapped her in the cloakroom. The few fifteen and sixteen year old boys that had experienced sex at Plant

Hill, whilst Linda was a student, lost their virginity to her. Cruelly, she was nick named 'Scrubber Woody.'

She wasn't the prettiest girl at the school; she wore national health, pink, wire framed glasses and had a glide in one eye, she came from a poor family and wore threadbare clothing, even the school logo was hand embroidered onto the pocket of her blazer by her mother and her white socks and blouses had took on a grey cast from over washing, but from the age of thirteen years she had the most magnificent pair of knockers. One lad, a mate of mine, who was fifteen at the time and was a year my senior and studied in the year above me and when Linda was fourteen, told me, as he told anyone who wanted to listen, of his initiation to sex via Linda Wood in these, somewhat, cleaned up and sanitised terms: 'I went on the Pike Fold fields with her yesterday dinner time, we were in the long grass in a little nook and I had her tits out havin' a good feel. I had a right hard on and I started to rub her pubes when I felt her hand rubbin' me up, down there. It was the first time I'd ever had a girl's hand on it. She asked me if I'd ever done it, you know, gone all the way. I said I hadn't done it yet, when she asked me if I wanted to do it with her, you know, have a shag? I replied that I would but that I didn't know what to do and I was a complete beginner. Then she told me not to worry because she'd done it loadsa times and I wouldn't be the first lad that she'd had to show the way. Then she undid my flies and fumbled about until she had my penis out. Then she stopped and told me to wait while she took off her draws. She then lay on her back and told me to get between her legs, which I did.

Then she grabbed hold of my privates with one hand and she then guided the end of it into her vagina and then she let go and moved her other hand and she told me to push my penis up her. I pushed it into her and then withdrew partially and then pushed it up again, her legs came up around my back and she started thrusting back at me, going like a rabbit. We went faster and faster but within a minute I ejaculated. I've never experienced anything like it, it was unbelievable, bloody fantastic an' if she'll let me, I'm gonna have her again.'

I listened with my mouth wide open. 'Was it really that good?' I asked.

'Well, Laurie, I'll tell you what, masturbation is definitely secondary to full sex; even when you cum your donk the sensation is so much more thrilling than jerking off.'

Linda Wood's dad didn't work although her mother did. Her father always had enough money to go to the pub every lunch time so another, older, mate of mine called Jack went with her to her house some dinnertimes and had it off with her on the settee while her dad was getting pissed up in The Lion and Lamb public house. Those that I know who had sex with Linda had said they always rode bareback; no condoms. One of the older lads said that wearing a condom was like having sex in a Pac-a-mac. The pac-a-mac was a fold away disposable raincoat with a hood attached that was popular at the time.

It was my misfortune to be one of the unlucky ones who never had sex with Linda while she was at school, although one morning at break time, when I had just turned fifteen, she came up behind me while I was chatting with some pals, She put her hand between my legs and started to squeeze my testicles. I turned round and she released my genitals and slowly ran off, stopped, turned around and cocked her head to one side in a gesturing, come hither pose and with that come and get me look in her eyes. She did the same thing the next day but I was a bit scared and never chased after her, so I missed my chance of losing my virginity early and probably, by all accounts, of getting the best experience of my early teens. My mates urged me on by saying that I would be the first lad from our year to have sex with her but I used the excuse that I didn't fancy her, in truth, I was too young and too scared of making a fool of myself as I had no experience of the distaff side other than a quick grope under the stairs or in the cloakrooms.

Linda carried on doing what she did best and as far as I know, while at school, she never caught any social disease or fell pregnant, unlike her younger sister who was rumoured to have caught gonorrhoea while she was still at school. Linda wasn't the only schoolgirl at Plant Hill that was said to be having full sex, although none started quite as young as Linda and her sister, most waited until they were fifteen or sixteen and were courting regular boyfriends, although one or two others did put it around a bit and that was in the early sixties. Those girls and the boys they went with were experiencing free love a couple of years before the free love, hippy set of the mid to late sixties. I must say that the vast majority of girls, by far, probably left school with their virginity intact.

It wasn't until Linda had left school and started work and I was sixteen years old and still studying in the fifth year when we met around a bonfire, in the darkness of the night of November fifth. The bonfire was on a common; a plot of uncultivated, overgrown, little used land up a passageway, to the rear of the houses on Mirfield Road and Plant Hill Road. The entrance to the plot of land was via an unpaved pathway at the junction of the two roads. The bonfire itself was situated centrally in what was about a ½ acre of land that contained a number of bushes and trees around its perimeter.

I was stood alone at the time, about twenty feet away from the pile of wood that would later be lit and old three piece suites that would serve as extra fuel for the bonfire but would initially be sat on to watch the fire and the fireworks. It was only those old three piece suites that were stuffed with horse hair that were safe to burn on the bonfire. The more modern suites, even in the 50's, were unsafe to burn because of the chemicals used in the manufacture of the foam filling but, nevertheless, they were burnt. It was only because they were lit outside in the open air and any prevailing wind dispersed the poisonous fumes, that people did not become intoxicated by the toxic gases from those old foam filled three piece suites. It is the fumes from such furniture that has been responsible for numerous deaths in household conflagrations over the years. There were only a couple of people about waiting for the fire to be lit as I waited for my mates to show up. As I waited Linda entered the common and came over and started talking with me, then she gripped my hand and said 'Come on, follow me before any adults show up.' She then started to walk towards a stand of trees and bushes at a far corner of the patch of land. I followed her like a little puppy dog into the bushes where she turned towards me and started to kiss me. My hands went straight to her breasts and her hand started pulling the zip of my jeans down.

I said 'Look Linda, I'm a complete novice; I'm ignorant, innocent, totally inexperienced; I've never been with a girl in this way before.'

She replied, just as she had told my mate a year or so earlier, 'Don't you worry; you're not the first lad that I've had to show the way,' and with that she leaned back against a tree trunk with her hips thrust forward. It seemed that Linda took great delight in introducing lads to the act of sex. The earth around the tree had become banked up and the roots were exposed and when Linda backed up to the tree she was raised to my height and our eyes were on the same level.

With a lot of amateurish fumbling from me and a little annoyance at my lack of knowledge from her, I lost my virginity to Linda that evening. I remember, without going into too much detail, going about the act much too fast and eager because she said 'Bloody 'ell, Laurie, slow down a bit, it's not a bloody race.' For me, it was a hurried but enjoyable affair; I was worried that someone would catch us in a compromising position, doing what we shouldn't be doing. Linda, though, wasn't quite so happy and she said, 'Bloody 'ell, Laurie, yuh should a' pulled it out. I don't want a bloody baby, yuh know.'

When the clandestine coupling was over, she took some tissues from her coat pocket. She handed me a couple and she wiped herself, she then discarded the tissues in the bushes. I cleaned myself up as best I could and we adjusted our clothing. The wanton and free loving girl then asked me if I had enjoyed the experience, to which I replied in the affirmative. She then complimented me on my initiation into the world of sex, saying, 'Well, Laurie, that wa'n't bad for yer first time but yuh'll 'ave to learn to pull it out before yuh finish.' We then peeped out from the place of our furtive mating in the bushes to make sure that there was nobody within the immediate vicinity. We then ventured out from different parts of the bushes into what was, by then, a quite crowded common. The bonfire had been lit and so we joined the other revellers around the fire as they celebrated the failure of the gunpowder plot in 1605, when a group of Catholic men led by Robert Catesby and including Guido Fawkes placed a number of barrels of gunpowder in the basement of the Houses of Parliament in an attempt to kill the anti Catholic King, James 1st and the kings leaders. An effigy of Guy Fawkes, not Catesby, is burned because he was the plotter left in the basement to light the fuse and thus was the first of the gang to be arrested.

My first sexual encounter was every bit as good as I hoped it would be albeit not very long and I think I might have preferred it to have been a more civilised and formal affair in bed with a naked female rather than being a stand up, knee trembler, outside on a cold November night. Although the excitement of that first sexual encounter was magnified by the fact that there were people nearby, enjoying themselves in other ways and I was committing that act in close proximity to those people.

As we walked towards the fire I saw some of my mates stood around the burning mass and so we went over to join them. Linda then noticed another bunch of four lads that she knew, so she said her good byes and went to join them. I watched them laughing and joking before they went, with Linda, into another dark corner of the common, where they could not be seen and no doubt they all had a good grope and feel of Linda's breasts. My mates cajoled and wheedled until I told them of my experience minutes before. They all whooped and slapped me on the back in congratulations. Questions came thick and fast, querying what it was like to have sex and was Linda any good; well with her wide experience she certainly was. Later, as I walked home on my own, I looked around me to see that there was nobody about and I jumped up and clicked my heels together as I punched the air shouting 'I did it, I did it!'

That November night was the one and only time that I had sex with Linda and I wasn't to see her for another four years when she boarded a bus that I was already on. I nodded to her but I don't think she recognised me because she walked right past me without any acknowledgement. She was dressed in the hippy attire of the day and she had a young, snotty nosed toddler in tow, which was obviously her own. It seems that someone else had not pulled out on time. As I see it, nobody at school ever made a sexual conquest of Linda but she made numerous sexual conquests of many teenage boys.

Rock 'n' Roll

Sex wasn't the only subject that pre-occupied the minds of adolescent lads at the time although, I must admit, it was a major theme and source of temptation. There were other things occurred prior to the sexual initiation described above. My main distraction was music and I had built up a love all things rock 'n' roll. I had listened to rock 'n' roll music since I was ten years of age and appreciated it as it grew in popularity. It became my favourite type of music sometime in 1958 when my father bought a brand new, state of the art, radiogram.

That radiogram had a hydraulic type ram under the lid that ensured that it came down slowly, so that it could not slam and thus jolt and scratch the fragile, vinyl records that may have been playing. In the centre of the turntable was a spindle that could be loaded with up to eight records at a time. Besides the automatic play one could play single discs or place a larger spindle over the single play spindle to play ex juke box records. The delivery man that came to deliver and set up the new machine also brought a few records, some were of the brittle 78 rpm shellac type and some were of the 45 rpm flexible vinyl type, some with centres and some without. Those records were brought along to demonstrate the capabilities of the new radiogram. During the change over from 78 to 45rpm the same record could be purchased on either format and some 78's were manufactured using the new vinyl of which the 45's were made.

Once he had the machine set up he placed one of the ten inch, 78rpm records onto the turntable, he then lifted the arm containing the stylus and gently lowered it onto the start of the disc and it started to play a wonderful sound which issued forth from the twin speakers. The record that he played was a fast rock 'n' roll song entitled 'Bony Moronie,' and sung by Larry Williams, a rock'n'roll pianist and once it had played he turned it over to play the B side; 'You Bug Me Baby,' another out and out rocker. He then played one of the other records that he had brought for demonstration purposes, that disc, which was on one of the new 45rpm, seven inch, vinyl discs, was called 'Fabulous' and the 'B' side was entitled 'Just Lookin' and was sung by Charlie Gracie, one of the early American rock 'n' roll artistes.He then loaded the centre spindle with eight 45rpm singles and demonstrated the automatic facility. He played discs featuring Little Richard, Frankie Lymon & the Teenagers, Elvis Presley, The Platters, Bill Haley and his Comets, Jerry Lee Lewis, The Crickets and many more. The delivery man left but before departing he told me that I could have the demonstration records that he had brought so that I could start my own collection of rock 'n' roll records. My father wasn't impressed by my taste in music. He regularly stated 'I don't know what you see in that rubbish, you can't understand a word they sing.' And this from an English speaking cockney who listened to opera sung in Italian.

Rock'n'roll as defined by Webster's Dictionary is as follows:- *A style of popular music of Afro-American origin, characterized by an insistent, heavily accented syncopated rhythm and the obsessive repetition of short musical phrases, tending to build up tension in an audience and induce a state of group frenzy when played very loud.* The Compact Oxford English Dictionary describes Rock'n'roll in a rather less descriptive way:- *A type of popular dance music originating in the 1950's, having a heavy beat and simple melodies.* Both are fair descriptions, but rock'n'roll was much more than that; it was start of a youth culture that had never been seen before. The teenagers had something of their own, something that they could relate to. It started with the American Rhythm & Blues music as sung by blues shouters such as Big Joe Turner, which in turn took in Doo-Wop music. It then branched into Country & Western as Western Swing and Rock-a-Billy and it grew. The music, which was seen as no more than a fad, has lasted into the 21st century.

In 1955, Sony had brought out the first affordable transistor radio and by the end of the decade and into the early sixties almost every pre pubescent child and teenager had received one of those tiny portable radios as a birthday or Christmas present. I had one and I used to listen to Luxembourg 208 on it. Luxembourg was the first commercial radio to be broadcast in Britain beating the pirate ships such as Radio Caroline by a decade. It launched the career of many famous DJ's including Emperor Rosco, Alan Freeman, Mike Reid, Paul Burnett and David 'Kid' Jensen. Radio Luxembourg was the station to tune into to listen to popular music and Rock 'n' Roll and American R&B music. It introduced me to a whole host of American performers that just didn't get airplay from the BBC. It also spawned a generation that took their transistor radios to bed to listen to the Top Twenty under the bedclothes.

For my fourteenth birthday, my parents bought me a Dansette record player for my bedroom, where I could play my Rock 'n' Roll music to my hearts delight. It was no ordinary record player for it had a two piece lid. That lid was detachable and contained a speaker in each half. Each speaker had a ten feet length of electrical flex attached which plugged into the rear of the record player. The speakers could then be positioned at opposite ends of the room and the sound could be heard from both speakers. It was not true stereo but it was as good as one could get at the time and it gave me years of enjoyment.

The Scourge of Acne

I believe that I was thirteen or fourteen years of age when acne struck and my face took on a life of its own; I had more spots than my sister's polka dot dress. I don't remember exactly when my battle with acne started but unlike most youths of my age who had the occasional, small outbreak of pustules, blackheads and spots I had massive outbreaks of boils and carbuncles. They were not just limited to my face either; my shoulders, back, chest and upper arms were also affected. I became somewhat withdrawn and, because of embarrassment I stopped going to the swimming baths with my friends. Others at school shunned me in case my problem was contagious and I became a bit of a pariah except to my close friends.

Every week I would visit my general practitioner in the hope that some universal panacea had been found to treat *Acne Vulgaris*. But alas, no such medication had been discovered. I tried numerous proprietary brands of skin care applications and various prescription drugs and ointments. I was referred to the Manchester Skin Hospital, which was then a specialist hospital situated on Quay Street in the city centre, where I was photographed, discussed, studied by dermatologists and toasted in front of sun-ray lamps to no effect. I was given special diets: no chocolate or nuts, plenty of green leafy vegetables, no fried food. I was given more wonder cures to try; they didn't work.

Later, in their television show, Peter cook and Dudley More performed a song entitled Spotty Muldoon and if any song was devised to ruin a young man's confidence, Spotty Muldoon was that song. I suffered taunts and name calling at school which caused me to retort in the only way I knew how, I fought my antagonists. To me, my countenance was such a mess that a few punches and lumps and bruises could not have made it any worse and so fisticuffs were resorted to. I won more than I lost and lo and behold, despite the craggy and inflamed visage, people started to respect me and the name calling ceased, girls started to talk to me again and even though I was to suffer active acne until I was fifty years old, life became more bearable.

I still bear the facial and body scars of that adolescent scourge and I still remember the taunts such as the recommendation that when I started to shave I would need to use a four wheel drive electric razor. In an attempt to reduce the scarring that blighted my body and my face the dermatologist at Manchester Skin Hospital recommended a course of derm-abrasion. Derm-abrasion is an operation whereby the skin is, literally, sandpapered off to remove the top and subsequent layers of dermis to attempt to lessen the noticeable appearance of scar tissue. In my twenties I underwent my first derm-abrasion operation. Prior to the operation I had my head shaved so that my hair would not get in the way. After the operation and because of the amount of swelling and the rawness of the abraded skin my head resembled a bright red, bowling ball.

When the skin had healed and settled down I could not see any great difference between the before and the after and so in my thirties I had my second derm-abrasion op. That second operation left me just as disillusioned as the first and when I saw the consultant dermatologist he told me something that I believe he should have disclosed before the operations. He told me, quote, 'Derm-abrasion is more subjective than objective.' unquote. This particular subject was not at all pleased with the results. What I really needed was something that was of an objective nature, something palpable that I could appreciate and that I could see the difference in.

By the time I was in my forties a new laser treatment was offered, which I took, in the vain hope that my scarred appearance would be improved. After the operations and laser treatment there was a small but quite insignificant improvement and the overall effect was minimal due to the deepness of the scarring and I was still being plagued by outbreaks of spots, boils, blackheads and the odd carbuncle.

It was a new and controversial drug that curtailed my acne; otherwise I would still be suffering to this day. The drug was called Roaccutane and the controversy attached to it stems from the fact that there had been a number of suicides of young people in America that were linked to the drug. I had read about this new cure on the internet and approached my doctor about prescribing it for me. My GP was, at first, reluctant to prescribe the drug, because of the controversy, but upon further research it was found that no person of mature years had suffered the disastrous side effects and so in 1996 I obtained what, to me, was a wonder cure, albeit a little too late in life.

Roaccutane works by drying out the skin oils internally, by working on the sebaceous glands. The active ingredient in Roaccutane (Isotretinoin) allows only the necessary amount of natural oils to be released, instead of the excessive amounts, which cause the pores to become blocked, which in turn cause acne. The Isotretinoin in Roaccutane thus stops spots, boils and blackheads from forming. How I wish it had been available when I was a teenager as I am sure it would have changed my whole outlook on life.

Cannonball and Rough Football

At the time that the acne attacked my teenage body and face, a programme started on the television that had me enthralled. Luckily it also had my father enthralled or I might never have seen it. It was a Canadian trucking series that went by the name of Cannonball. It was about the adventures of a Canadian trucker called Mike Malone played by Paul Birch and his co-driver Jerry Austin played by William Campbell. It was my introduction to the North American Trucking scene as the drivers drove through Canada and the States. It was also the first time that I had seen the big bonneted Yankee trucks.

The truck that Mike Malone drove was an articulated rig with a 1956, GMC950 Bull nosed tractor unit and although the trucks were small by today's standards it was still a worthwhile show and was the forerunner of American shows such as Movin' On.' with Claude Akins as Sonny Pruitt and his co-driver Will Chandler, played by Frank Converse. Movin' On was a more modern show shot in colour and the vehicle used was a 1974 conventional Kenworth 925; each show was an hour long. Cannonball consisted of shows that ran for thirty minutes and it was shot in black and white and was all the more atmospheric for it; the series ran for thirty nine shows and I didn't miss a one.

Not long after the Cannonball series finished there came on the television, a documentary about trucking in Australia. I am not sure whether it was on BBC or on the newly formed commercial station, then known as ATV. Once again I was glued to the television for the program. It showed trucks with two and three trailers crossing the Nullabor Plain running parallel to the Great Australian Bight in the antipodes. The vehicles that were used were American or Canadian and because of their length and the number of trailers involved, were known as road trains. British trucks such as Bedford's and Leyland's were popular in Australia but were used mainly on local distribution, it seems that the British Marques were just not up to the job of pulling up to three trailers across that vast land, with the exception of Scammell's, Leyland Hippo's, and Foden's and ERF's. To me, it was a great pleasure to watch those Kenworth's, Mack's, Western Star's and Peterbilt's hauling two or three trailers across the antipodean continent. They were phenomenally long and huge in every way. Even viewing it in black and white it enforced in me the desire to drive large, heavy goods vehicles.

I was not the sporting type whilst at school. I did not join, nor was I selected for any of the school teams, be it swimming, cricket, rugby or football, but I did enjoy a kick around in the playground at playtime. I remember that those kick-a-bouts weren't for the faint hearted. They were very tactile games with some very rough and tough contact and even rougher and tougher players. Around the perimeter fence of the playground there was a border of rough terrain which contained some large pieces of rubble. I remember one particular dinner time kick-a-bout when a lad called Dennis Wheeler was playing. Dennis was a good strong player, fast and skilful; he had been picked for the school football team. On that particular day in question someone kicked a high ball and someone shouted, 'On yer 'ead, Wheeler!'

Unfortunately some young hooligan had also thrown a large stone, plucked from somewhere near the perimeter fence, into the air. Wheeler turned around and glanced upwards to see the silhouette of something coming towards him. He jumped into the air and swung his head and made contact with the remnant of the brick. There was a resounding crack and Wheeler fell to the floor unconscious and with blood pouring from the wound on his head. The other players ran to his assistance; a teacher came to his aid and Wheeler opened his eyes and uttered the immortal words, 'Please sir, I fink I've broke me 'ead.' An ambulance had been called and Wheeler was ferried to hospital where a fractured skull was confirmed.

Dennis Wheeler was off school for over three months and he has an indentation at the front of his skull to this day. The young idiot that threw the offending object into the air owned up, under threat from witnesses, to his stupid act but alas, I cannot remember whether or not the punishment that he received fitted the moronic and imbecilic act of tomfoolery that had been committed.

Horror Films & Our First Car & a Trip to Devon

I am not sure whether it was during 1959 or 1960 when the Regal Cinema on Oxford Road in Manchester was showing either a season of Hammer Horror films or a season of Vincent Price films. Vincent price, of course acted in most of the Hammer House of Horror films along with Peter Cushing and Christopher Lee. The thing that caught the eyes of Cousin Bob and me, as we glanced through the entertainment section of the Manchester Evening News, was the showing of a horror film in glorious 3D and in full colour. The film was originally released in 1953, but was being re-shown during that Regal season. The title of the film was *House of Wax,* starring Vincent Price, Charles Bronson and Carolyn Jones.

Bob and I were only approximately fourteen years old and were not allowed entrance to see an X rated horror film; the minimum age being sixteen. We dressed in an attempt to look a little older. Bob was the same height and build as his father and so he wore his dad's gabardine Macintosh, belted round the waist and we joined the queue outside the picture house to see the three dimensional cinematic feast that awaited us. Neither of us smoked but as we approached the kiosk where the entrance fee was paid, we each lit up a Woodbine cigarette, which we had stolen from our parents, in another attempt to elevate our age. The cigarette immediately caused in me an attack of coughing which almost ended in a seizure as I went red and struggled to breathe. Bob, being a couple of months older than me pushed the money towards the attendant through a haze of blue cigarette smoke and said in a voice an octave lower than his natural voice, 'Two for the stalls, please.'

The attendant pulled the cash towards him and then gazed up and down at Bob and me in an appraising manner through the smoky mist and asked, 'Just how old are you two anyway?'

'Sixteen.' Bob Replied.

'Okay,' said the teller with a knowing smile pasted upon his face, 'In you go.' So in we went to enjoy our first horror film. The next week we were back at the Regal to see another Vincent Price horror film entitled *The Tingler,* which was in black and white with a sequence in shades of red and there were special effects to heighten the fear factor of the film. Those special effects consisted of random seats being fitted with machines that, at the requisite time would send a small electrical charge through the seats to give a tingling sensation and a contingent of the St John's Ambulance, or someone dressed to look like them, at the entrance. After having gained admittance to a city centre venue to see horror films we then tried other venues to see X rated films and we were never once turned away, be they horror films or sexy X's.

There were other picture houses in the city centre that Bob and I visited on occasions. They were picture houses that were open all day and were known as news theatres. Customers could enter those venues at any time during the day and not be disappointed because they would not walk in half way through a feature film. The Manchester News Theatre was situated on High Street and was a subterranean vault situated below street level. Generally, as I remember them, the news theatres would show Pathe News interspersed with cartoons and short films. Another news theatre was the Tatler Theatre, situated at the bottom of the approach to Oxford Road Railway Station and the corner of Whitworth Street West. The Tatler later became the Cornerhouse picture house dedicated to showing arty films but prior to that Bob and I spent many an hour there. We went to those venues because the entrance fee was low compared to standard picture houses and the entertainment was good.

I remember my father buying our first family car in 1960, that car was a 1953 Ford Anglia; model E494A, with an engine displacement of 933cc. It was a two door, vehicle with four seats and that model was nicknamed the Noddy car. Like most other cars of that vintage it was painted black. As that great motor engineer, Henry Ford reputedly said of his old Model T, 'You can have any colour you want, so long as it's black.' It was dad's pride and joy and we had it for a few years before he traded it in during 1964 for a 1959 more modern Ford Anglia with the 100e engine with a displacement of 1172cc.

My father decided that the older car would transport the family down to Dawlish on the Devon coast midway between the rivers Exe and Teign. My sister decided against the trip and stayed with our cousin Irene and her family, my mum's brother Walter and his wife Aunty Elsie and Irene's brother, Cousin Walt. In place of Valerie, we asked Cousin Bob if he wanted to make up the numbers and he jumped at the opportunity. None of us had been to Devon or that far south prior to that. Holidays before that momentous journey had been of a more local nature and it was years in the future before we would go abroad. Even my father, who was a Londoner by birth, had never travelled to the South coast, other than one trip to Brighton when, as a young man and a guest of Dr Barnardo's, he and a party of youths were taken for a short break to the seaside town.

For our holiday in Devon, my father worked out a southerly route, with the help of the Reader's Digest, Driver's Atlas of Britain, that would take us down mostly; little used 'A' roads and even lesser used 'B' roads. We packed the boot of the car with our luggage and all the holiday necessities plus a hamper with sandwiches, fruit and a vacuum flask of coffee to sate and slake our hunger and thirst on the long journey. It was a wonderful idea and a well worked out route that my father planned. It took in some wonderful scenery and pleasant countryside. The down side of the route was that it took us more than nine hours to get to our destination. It was the furthest my father had ever driven and upon arrival at our digs we all suffered cramps and aches and pains. The Ford Anglia of that particular model was not the most commodious of vehicles and even after numerous stops to stretch our legs and to top up the radiator, when we finally exited the car for the last time we were all bent double like incapacitated old people. If I had been bent any more I could have been rolled along like a hoop and stick.

The holiday in Devon was fantastic, the weather was scorching, like summers of yore used to be, when people didn't have to visit the Costas to get a suntan. Bob and I found plenty to do. In the evenings we visited the seaside fairground where we attempted to chat up the local talent. During the daytime and when we had spent our allowance we fished for crabs in the rock pools on the beach, we swam in the sea or we just strolled along the seashore as the small, residualwaves from the rollers lapped at our feet and at other times we played ball games on the sand, sometimes with newly made acquaintances, by ourselves or with my parents. We also explored the town of Dawlish and the surrounding area, but didn't find much to interest us there. Cousin Bob, like his father, was fair complexioned with straw coloured hair, unlike my mother and father and me who had dark hair and a darker shade of skin. Bob and I did quite a lot of sunbathing on the beach and by the end of the third day I had turned a nice shade of brown and some of my more prominent acne had dried up. Bob however had burnt himself badly, he had turned the bright red of a freshly boiled lobster and had trouble sitting comfortably and sleeping, he even found it difficult and painful to perambulate, come to think about it, he found it difficult to do anything other than swim in the sea which seemed to have a cooling and somewhat therapeutic affect on his cracked and blistered skin. My mother chastised him for being so foolish as to lie in the sun for such long periods even though he had used sun cream. I cannot remember the number of times I inadvertently put my arm around Bob's shoulder or pushed him playfully only to hear him curse and almost cry in pain. I was continually offering him my apologies.

Other than that, a wonderful time was had by all..............that was until the time came to depart. Then, faces were glum, hearts were sad, moods were dampened, for we all remembered, too readily, the protracted and tedious trip down into Devon and we were not looking forward to the trip back home. As luck would have it, my father, the map reader, scout and pioneer, had worked out a new and better route. He had studied the map book and gazetteer and discovered a fairly straightforward route home. He found his way onto the A38 and followed it up to Birmingham via Exeter, Bristol, Gloucester and Worcester. No motorways in those days, although the roads that we followed took an almost parallel route to that which the M5 follows now. From Birmingham he picked up the A34 which ran through Cannock, Stafford, Newcastle-under-Lyme, Congleton, and Wilmslow and so on, and much to our collective relief, to Manchester.

By the time we were ready to leave Dawlish, my mother took a look at Bob's blistered, cracked and sunburnt back, which was his worst affected area. His skin was raw and had started to itch relentlessly and to peel like the paper thin bark of a silver birch. His face had divested itself of its epidermis leaving his facial skin taut and crimson in colour as if he had a permanent blush; he found the trip home very difficult. He had actually drawn blood through the excessive rubbing and scratching. My mother tried to ease his pain and itching by the application of various salves and ointments, but to very little effect. My father had to stop the car numerous times, on the way home, to let Bob have some respite from the undulations and bumps in the road and for my mother to apply more soothing balm to his back and of course to top up the radiator and give the rest of us a break. Still, Bob squirmed, wriggled and writhed in pain all the way home even though he was given the front seat to allow him a little more room to stretch out and to squirm in his throes of agony.

Bob stayed at our family home on the evening we returned from Dawlish and my mother made him take a cool bath after which she plastered his back, shoulders and face with medicated balm. By the next morning the swelling of his face had subsided and the redness had turned to more of a pink. His back and shoulders were still raw but the pain had diminished considerably. By the time my father ran him home he was much more comfortable.

At the end of the holidays I returned to school and carried on with my studies and preparation for the next round of examinations. When the results for the end of year exams were issued, I was, once again, somewhere around the middle of the class.

Chapter 10

CYCLING EXCURSIONS AND
A TRIP TO THE EMERALD ISLE.

A Couple of Cycling Trips & the Black Bull

Cousin Bob, Ronnie Rhodes, Dave Leigh and I had become keen cyclists over the years and we had taken up cycling to places further afield. During the Easter holidays of 1960 we decided on a ride to Southport for the day. We set off at about 0700hrs and I think it took us about four and a half hours to get there. Upon arriving in the town we chained our bikes to a fence on the promenade and spent about an hour and half on the beach, where we consumed the sandwiches and water that we had prepared at home and which were tucked away in our saddle bags. After we had finished our repast and had rested and replenished our energy levels, we then visited the Pleasure Beach where we spent what spare cash we had on the biggest and fastest rides. A walk around Lord Street and the adjacent roads filled in the time before we used the public conveniences to freshen up and refill our water bottles. We returned to our bikes, unchained them and checked them over. It was found that my bike had a puncture to the rear wheel. Ronnie pointed it out and said, 'Hey Laurie, you've got a puncture, but don't worry it's only flat at the bottom.' We all helped in the mending of the punctured inner tube and within twenty minutes a repair was affected. We then mounted our bicycles and headed back to

Manchester, stopping for a look around Ormskirk before cycling along the A570 to pick up the A580 East Lancashire Road for the longest leg of the return journey, arriving home, exhausted and hungry, at about 2000hrs.

My bike, at the time, was a new, steel framed, BSA racing machine fitted with drop handlebars, Cyclo Benelux derailleur gears of which there were five on the back sprocket. It also had a second gear wheel on the front sprocket, commonly known as a double clanger which effectively doubled the number of gears available giving me access to ten gears in all. It is a moot point whether some of the gears on the double clanger directly equated to some of those on the back sprocket or the ratios were so close that it would make very little difference. Ronnie, who took every endeavour very seriously, had saved up for months and with further help from his father purchased a top of the market Claude Butler racing bike with lightweight alloy frame and wheels. It had the same number of gears as mine but his Derailleur set was made by Campagnolo and his bike was a lot smoother and faster. Cousin Bob had a Coventry Eagle, lightweight racer and Dave Leigh, like me, had a relatively cheap, but strictly functional bike, made for racing or touring. Both Bob's and Dave's bikes were fitted with Simplex derailleur gear sets.

Ronnie Rhodes had joined a cycling club in Prestwich, I think it was called the 'Prestwich Harriers and Cycling Club,' and he and I went on a ride that Ronnie had undertaken before with his club. This ride was from Manchester through the Peak District National Park via Glossop and the Snake pass (A57), over Ladybower reservoir to Bamford, returning via Hope and Castleton and then through the Vale of Edale to Chapel-èn- le-Frith. At Chapel-en-le-Frith we had to make a decision whether to ride along the A6 to New Mills and on to Stockport or down the A624 to Hayfield, back to Glossop and then home; we took the scenic route via Glossop. It was a hard, very tiring ride, up and down dale and as we were passing close by Mam Tor, in Derbyshire, which is sometimes called shivering mountain because of its frequent landslides, I actually nodded off on a downward stretch; yes, I fell asleep as I free-wheeled along the roadway on my bike.

During my short nap I veered off the road on to some loose shale and careered, at an angle of ninety degrees into a dry stone wall which was approximately three feet high. Just prior to impact, a hasty shout from Ronnie caused me to open my eyes and attempt to brake. I managed to slow down a little but not enough. The bike came to an immediate halt as the front wheel came into contact with the wall and the impact shook me into full wakefulness as I was catapulted, in what seemed to be slow motion, over the handlebars and over the wall and into a farmer's field. The field on the far side of the wall was about three feet lower than the road surface and there was a ditch excavated to a depth of a further three feet below the field's surface; the ditch was about three feet wide. As I came to earth, face downwards, on the far side of the moat like channel, I managed to avoid the numerous cow-pats that abounded, except for one. My left hand was completely immersed, up to my wrist in a foot wide dollop of cow dung; I was badly shaken but unhurt and I picked myself up and went over to the ditch which had a trickle of water at its base. I climbed down into the ditch and washed, as best as I could, the smelly, hay laced dung off my hand and wrist. I then dusted myself down and then clambered part way up the wall and poked my head over the top. The sight that greeted me was one of Ronnie Rhodes, who, at that point had alighted from his cycle and was pointing at me from a doubled up position as he shook with laughter at my mishap. His countenance then changed and took on a more serious aspect as he pointed beyond me and shouted, 'Hurry up, Laurie, climb over, quick!' Don't look back!' Well, what do you do when somebody tells you not to look back? I glanced backwards over my shoulder to see what Ronnie was pointing at, to behold a bloody, great, black bull charging towards me at great speed, cloven hooves thundering on the turf as they threw up large divots, eyes red with fury and vapour issuing from its flared nostrils. Well, I was over that wall in two seconds flat. The huge, black, snorting beast slid to a halt before it should fall into the ditch which ran along the wall, put there for just that purpose.

Ronnie, by now, was laughing again, but only intermittently and he came over and took my arm as I clambered onto the road side of the wall. Once I had reached the safety of the roadside I turned towards the field and leant on the drystone wall and stared in disbelief at the enraged, snorting, half ton of well muscled beast on the other side of the wall. A tremor ran through my body. The bull was pawing the ground with one of its hooves and tossing its head in rage. The massive, black head was topped with un-polled, razor sharp horns that were quite easily capable of the disembowelment of errant cyclists. After I had regained my composure and my breath, an inspection of my velocipede was conducted. The wheel was not buckled but the front forks had been pushed slightly backwards but the bike was still able to be ridden and so, after a brief rest and something to eat and drink we set off for home. I was somewhat bruised and rode a little slower than the norm, but I too was now laughing at my mishap and narrow escape. We finally made it home some time after darkness had fallen. The following week my bicycle had to be taken to a local bicycle repair shop to have a repair affected upon the forks. Luckily for me my father initially paid the cost of the repairs, but like the fine that I received after my court appearance, I had to pay him back out of my allowance. It appears that the bicycle repair shop had to order a new set of forks from the makers and they had to be sprayed in the original colour and then re-fitted to the bike and I was without my main mode of transport for over a month.

Bray, the Wicklow Mountains & The Fishing License

The following year, during the summer holidays, my Uncle Bob, Aunty Joan and young Bob were going on holiday to Ireland and as companionship for Bob junior I was invited. I remember travelling down to Holyhead, by way of the boat-train, where we boarded the ferry for Dun Laoghaire. Upon disembarking we caught a local train service down to Bray, Co Wicklow where we were booked into a guest house on a bed, breakfast and evening meal basis. As we made our way from the railway station to the digs, on foot, we noticed that there was the smell of ozone in the air as it blew off the Irish Sea. We found that the sea air was rather more bracing in the mornings, but in the afternoon and early evening it mellowed into a pleasant sea breeze. On the day that we arrived a pale yellow sun shone weakly from a hazy sky casting insubstantial, flimsy shadows before us; a few white clouds scudded across the otherwise grey sky, but the deceiving warmth from the sun soon had us sweating, as we laboured with our suitcases, to the guest house where we would be laying our heads and dining for the coming week.

Dun Laoghaire is approximately mid way between Dublin and Bray, maybe eight or nine miles to each place. Once we were ensconced in our digs and our rooms had been allocated and we had unpacked and put away our clothes in the closets provided, there was only time for our evening meal, a bit of TV and then to bed. The following day was to be a day of discovery for Bob and me. We explored the town of Bray with our guardians, looking in the shops and finding our way around. It was on that day that Uncle Bob bought Bob and I a wrist watch each. I was very grateful; I don't think that I had ever owned a watch before that.

The accommodation in which we stayed was a small cottage type, three bedroomed, guest house. One bedroom was used by the proprietors and the other two were the guest's rooms where Bobby and I and Aunty Joan and Uncle Bob slept; we were the only guests staying in the house at that time, although there was another couple staying in a converted outbuilding to the rear of the main house. The dining room was a large room where all the guests dined together at set times. There was no such thing as *en suite* bathrooms; the cottage had just one communal bathroom which contained a wash hand basin, a toilet, a bath and a separate shower cabinet. There was another toilet downstairs which was accompanied by a wash basin. Each guest bedroom though, had a washstand which had on its top surface a large water pitcher and a wash bowl, known as the jug and basin, along with soap placed on a saucer, on top of the washstand to allow guests to freshen up in their rooms. There was also tea and coffee making facilities, the anomaly being that one had to go down to the kitchen or to the bathroom to fill up the kettle before one could have a brew. The converted outbuilding had been fitted with its own toilet, washing and bathing facilities and consisted of two bedrooms and a dayroom.

Bray, a resort and market town standing on the River Dargle, has a small harbour and fine esplanade, it is at the foot of the Wicklow Mountains and there is one mountain quite close to where we were staying that had at its summit a stone cross. The mountain with the cross at its summit is Bray Head and it stands at two hundred and forty one metres, (790ft) the cross is actually made from concrete and was erected to commemorate the death of Jesus and the Christian Jubilee Year of 1950. The said mountain stands between Bray and Greystones.

The days in Ireland were balmy rather than burning, more soothing than sweltering and Bob and I decided that our first task, every day of our stay, was to climb to the summit of Bray Head as a form of exercise. Our first ascent was a little laborious, we were not used to that type of exercise and so we stopped a few times to rest our aching limbs. It got easier with each ascent. At the top there was a cool breeze, but we hardly noticed due to the exertions of the climb. We noticed that all around and even upon the cross people had carved their initials so Bob and I followed suit and carved our initials in the ground, in the shadow of the cross and filled the carvings in with small white pebbles. I'd like to think that those initials are still there, but over the passage of time and given the number of visitors that have made the ascent of Bray Head and trampled the ground around the cross, I believe that those initials will now be well gone.

On the second day Uncle Bob hired a reel and rod and, bought some bait, he then headed for the river to fish for trout. He hadn't done much game fishing before; he could cast a line but he was actually a novice. After about four hours standing on the banks of the river casting out he actually managed to catch two trout. It was as he landed the second fish that he heard a voice from the bridge above him. He turned to see a ruddy faced, overweight policeman. The rotund officer shouted 'Will ye wait dere? Oi'll be wantin' a word wit' yez!' With that question asked he started to make his way down, part walking, part climbing and part stumbling, to where uncle Bob was attempting the fine art of angling. 'Bejayz', dat was hard work struggling down dere.' said the constable, gasping for breath as the belt around his tunic struggled to hold in his ample girth. 'Now den, can oi see yer permit to fish, if ye please?'

'Permit?' said Uncle Bob 'What Permit? I haven't got a permit.'

'De permit ye need to fish dese beautiful, Oirish waters, laddie an' oi knew yeh don't have one cos oi'm de man dat issues 'em.'

'I'm ever so sorry.' Said uncle Bob, 'but nobody told me I needed a permit.'

'Ah, dat'll be Seamus down at de Tackle and Bait Shop; he's a bit of a divil, is Seamus, especially wit' incomers like yersel'; he doesn't tell people what dey need to know, ye know.'

'Well, what will I do now?' asked Uncle Bob.

'Weeeeeell, Oi could arrest yez and charge yez wit' poachin' and yeh would pay a big foine, but Oi'm a reas'nable sort o' fella and oi'm quoite partial to a bit o' trout moiself, now'. So, if oi confiscate one trout from yer, we'll call dat your foine an' we'll say no more about it. But will yeh be sure to get yersel' a permit any other toime yer wantin' to be fishin' around here. Now oi'll wish yeh top o' the day and good luck to yeh.'

With that the well rounded policeman, still wheezing as his tunic's buttons threatened to pop and fly and his face a purple hue, bent down with some difficulty and picked up the bigger of the two trout. He wrapped up the aquatic vertebrate in Uncle Bob's unread newspaper and then he struggled as he scrambled back up the hill to the roadway where he stopped and leant against the bridge, for support, until the wheezing and spluttering had stopped and he could breathe a little easier and his face had receded from deep puce to red. He tugged at the bottom of his tunic and then he turned and waved to uncle Bob, who waved back. The constable then waddled off down the road like a penguin with his next meal tucked underneath his arm. The second trout was taken back to the B&B where it was gutted, cleaned and cooked by the landlady of the digs and served up with boiled potatoes and green vegetables to Uncle Bob for his evening meal. During the meal, Uncle Bob related to everyone there the tale of the policeman, the missing permit, the unread newspaper and the trout.

Guinness, Medals & Fish & Chips

The following day we travelled to Dublin, the capital of the Republic of Ireland, where Uncle Bob who liked a drop of the black stuff took us to the Guinness brewery where we went on an escorted tour of that establishment. At the end of the tour there was a tasting whereby Aunty Joan had a glass or two of the Irish brew and Uncle Bob had a couple of pints and young Bob and I got bugger all. After the brewery tour we took a tour around the town. I remember that we strolled by the side of the Liffey and saw Dublin Castle. We then walked down O'Connell Street, where Nelson's Pillar rose into the air and then crossed the Liffey at O'Connell Bridge to see Trinity College, Christ Church and St Patrick's Cathedral. We had dinner in a small street café, paid for by Uncle Bob.

Nelson's Pillar, erected to commemorate Nelson's victory at Trafalgar in 1805 and was started with the laying of the foundation stone on 15th February 1808 and was finished long before the similar Nelson's column was erected in Trafalgar Square, London in 1849. The Pillar was one hundred and twenty one feet high topped by a thirteen feet tall statue, in Portland stone, of Lord Nelson by Cork sculptor Thomas Kirk. The Pillar had an internal spiral staircase and it was some ten metres shorter than the more famous Nelson's Column in London. The Nelson's Pillar in Dublin was destroyed on 8th March1966 by the IRA who planted a bomb that destroyed the upper half of the pillar, throwing the statue of Nelson into the street. The bottom half was blown up by the Irish Army Engineers. That planned demolition caused more damage on O'Connell Street than the original IRA's explosion.

Dublin has rich links with literature; Jonathon Swift (1667-1745), author of *Gulliver's Travels* was born in Hoe's Court and was dean of the cathedral for thirty two years. The writer and dramatist George Bernard Shaw (1856-1950), who wrote amongst other plays *Caesar and Cleopatra, Androcles and the Lion* and *Arms and the Man,* was born in Synge Street and writer Oliver Goldsmith (1728-74), author of *She Stoops to Conquer* and *The Vicar of Wakefield,* was a student at Trinity College. Oscar Wilde, (1854-1900), playwright, wit and author of *The Picture of Dorian Gray* and numerous plays and poems was born in Merrion Square and James Joyce (1882-1941), author of *Ulysses* and *The Dubliners,* was also born in the city. Known for his horror stories was Bram Stoker (1847-1912), author of numerous novels and short stories such as '*The Lady of the shroud,* and *The Lair of the White Worm*' but best remembered for his novel *Dracula.* Other famous Irish literary scholars include Samuel Beckett, Brendan Behan, Maeve Binchey, Seamus Heaney, Sean O'Casey, and William Butler Yeats.

One day of the Irish Holiday, after our morning's constitutional with the mountain, I remember Bob and I were playing on a local beach, skimming stones on the calm sea when we were approached by a young Irish lad of about our age. He picked up a flat pebble and skimmed it into the sea where it did far better than the stones Bob and I were skimming, 'Dat's de way yeh do it'. Says he and from there we struck up a conversation.

The youth walked with us to a local park where we sat on the grass. As the Irish lad sat and crossed his legs it became quite obvious that he had forgotten to button his flies. Bob looked at me and me at him; we both started to laugh. The young paddy asked 'What yez laughin' at?

Bob replied, 'You're losing your medals, mate.'

'Bejayzus an' begorrah!' Exclaimed paddy as his hands went to his coat pockets, 'Oi can't be losin' dem, now, can oi, moi ma'll kill mi for sure.'

Bob and I were dumbfounded, we looked at each other in complete bewilderment, we had no idea what the young Irish lad was talking about until he pulled from his pocket a small tobacco tin which he opened and showed to us the contents, which just happened to be his grandfather's WW1 medals with ribbons attached. Why the youth carried that little treasure chest of memorabilia around with him we never found out, but we then had to explain to him about his trousers being undone. He laughed about his lapse of memory and fastened his medals up and we spent a pleasant day with paddy before we said goodbye and went back to the B&B for our evening meal.

On another day, after we had completed our climb and descent of Bray head, we strolled into Greystones from the foot of Bray Head and along Greystones' northern beach and past the harbour. Greystones is approximately five miles from Bray and is so called because of the grey stones along the shore line; whether they are a special type of rock I know not but they look just like any other grey stones to me. It took us just under two hours to walk to Greystones. We enjoyed some time playing on the beach and looking in the little shops. From the harbour we could look back and see Bray Head and Sugarloaf Mountain and the peaks of the other Wicklow mountains, which were cloaked in a thin mist that hung over them like a diaphanous, shimmering, gossamer curtain. The mountains appeared to be floating in a sea of swaying vapour, with just their peaks protruding through the top.

At around mid day we enjoyed fish and chips in the salt laden air by the harbour as we gazed upon all manner of fishing vessels with buoys tied to them and which were filled with ropes and nets. The smell of fish mingled with the sea air produced a not unpleasant aroma. All too soon it came time to depart from Greystones and make our way back to our digs in Bray. As we walked away from the harbour town the air became heavy and the skies darkened ominously as big, heavy, and dark cumulo-nimbus clouds rolled in from the sea, the temperature dropped and it started to rain; slowly at first and then it increased in intensity and volume. There were deafening thunderclaps followed by magnificent flashes of lightning as God stamped around his heaven turning the lights on and off. The winds had gotten stronger and nearby trees were, it seemed, bending from the waist as their outer branches whipped the air, discarding their leaves and snapping the smaller branchlets and twigs. Roof gutters overflowed with the volume of water suddenly imposed upon them. Water from the downspouts splashed onto the pavement to join the already flooded walkway. The gutters in the roadway ran like torrents as the drains failed to accept the monumental flow. Bob and I looked back towards the harbour to see huge waves crashing against the sea wall and casting their spray, mingled with rain, across the promenade. People dashed for shelter and cafes and shops suddenly filled up with customers pretending to browse as they sought refuge from the tempest. Fishing boats in the water bobbed and pitched and rolled violently in the swirling turbulence that, minutes before had been as calm as a mill pond. Once we had left Greystones there was little in the way of shelter and our clothes became drenched and stuck to our bodies, like a second skin. As we walked into the wind, bent forwards at a forty five degree angle and chilled by its ferocity, rainwater coursed off our uncovered heads and down the inside of our collars and down our backs. Even as we leant forwards the water ran down our foreheads and noses and cascaded off the ends like miniature waterfalls and still, the lightning zig-zagged across the sky, coming to Earth in the distance to be followed by ear splitting claps of thunder. The Wicklow Mountains were, by then, quite indistinguishable from the clouds that surrounded and enclosed them. The tips of the few peaks that showed through the clouds seemed unattached to their bases as if they sailed in the misty vapour. By the time we reached our accommodation, footsore, weary, sodden and cold it was time for a warming and cleansing shower, an evening meal and an early night.

We were only a week in Ireland and a very pleasant week it was; it only rained the once, but oh, how it rained. The timepieces that Uncle Bob had bought young Bob and I on our arrival proved invaluable in getting us back to the digs each night in time for our evening meal, but the week passed all too quickly and before we knew it, it was time to pack our belongings and head up the coast, leaving the pleasant town and the people of Bray behind us, to travel to Dun Laoghaire, to catch the ferry to Holyhead where we would catch the boat-train back to Manchester.

The sailing to Holyhead was rough and choppy with high winds and much pitching and yawing and took about four and a half hours. Bobby and I were stood outside on the deck, by the ship's rail for most of the journey, braving the elements, dressed in disposable, plastic pac-a-macs. We saw numerous people stumble past us with their hands held to their mouths, their complexions grey; others were retching as they walked. A great number of sick bags were seen to be floating in the ferry's wake as passengers threw their breakfasts over the side. Strangely, none of our party was affected; it must have been the barley sugar sweets that Uncle Bob made us suck before boarding and whilst travelling. When we arrived at Holyhead and disembarked from the ferry it was still raining, though not as heavily. We saw the boat- train standing alongside the quayside platform awaiting our arrival and the arrival of our fellow travellers. It appeared like a long winding serpent with smoke and steam issuing from its head and we were its fodder. We made our way to the steamer and its train of carriages. To find a coach with an empty compartment we walked along the platform, looking into the carriages for almost the full length of the train before we found that which we sought.

We entered the empty compartment and we stowed our luggage on the overhead nets, we removed our wet outer garments and made ourselves comfortable as we settled into what was a pleasant journey back to Manchester. After a couple of hours or so of winding our way through the Welsh and English countryside we finally arrived at our destination and alighted from the train at Manchester Victoria station. It was then that we observed the hustle and bustle on the station and then again outside and we realised what a wonderful, idyllic life and what a wonderful, green and pleasant country the Irish have. The traffic in Manchester was three or four times the amount that was to be seen in rural Ireland; nobody in Manchester, be it people perambulating or people driving in cars, had any time for anyone else, they were like people on a mission that must not fail. People walked headlong, bumping into others with no apologies, keeping to an undrawn line from which they must not deviate unless forced to by someone more aggressive than themselves. The difference between the laid back, tranquil life in Ireland and the hectic life of Manchester could not be more pronounced. As we struggled along the platform with our cases I noticed my father stood beyond the ticket barrier, waving to us. He had come to pick us up and deliver us home. The Ford Anglia that my father owned and which was parked near the goods platform, in a restricted area, was not built to carry three adults and two youths. Uncle Bob sat in the front with my dad and the rest of us squashed into the rear. My father dropped Cousin Bobby and his parents off at their home in Chadderton and then on the journey to Blackley I sat in the front seat, regaling my father of my adventures in Ireland, which I repeated to my mother and Valerie when we arrived home.

My last two years at school were spent in preparation for our final exams. From the fourth year we picked what subjects we wanted and dropped those that we didn't. I dropped technical drawing for art and I also dropped physics because it is a mathematical science and I only kept mathematics because like the subject of English language it was a compulsory subject. Most of the other subjects I kept. Because some subjects were dropped students had, what were termed as, free periods. Those periods were supposed to be used for revision and learning, but a lot of students, me included at various times used them for bunking off.

Motor Cycles & Black Leather Jackets

Around that time, like most lads of a similar age, I took an interest in what my mother and father called death traps but which were usually known as motorcycles. My friend Ronnie Rhodes' dad was a keen motorcyclist and at the time he had an old Royal Enfield, 350cc bike, the model was The Bullet, which is still being produced in the Sub-Continent of India.

Ron Rhodes senior was about to by another bike; a triumph 500cc, pre unit, Tiger 100. His Enfield Bullet was not in running order and so he told Ron junior that if he could get it running he could have it, probably thinking that he had no chance of repairing the bike. Ronnie recruited me and a friend called Ted Kelly and we worked on that bike for six months. We had the workshop manual and borrowed Big Ron's tools, we bought very few parts and we eventually got the bike up and running but we were still too young to ride it on the roads. In fact we never rode it at all and when young Ron was old enough he traded it in for a later model 250cc Ariel four stroke bike.

Another friend, Keith Wilson, who was a little older than us and had a motorcycle license and rode dirt track bikes, made us a proposition. He knew someone who was selling a 1953, single cylinder, Panther 350cc, sloper for a few quid. A Panther sloper was a single cylinder bike on which the cylinder did not sit upright but sloped forward at about the same angle as the front down tube of the bike's frame. He suggested that if there were twelve of us willing to put up the princely sum of 10shillings (50p) each to buy the bike, he would keep the bike at his house and he would ride it to Pike Fold fields where each of the stakeholders could ride it to their hearts content. So that is exactly what we did. We clubbed in for petrol when it was needed; no one got a free ride. There was no paperwork with the bike; no registration document or log book, but that didn't bother us boys.

The Panther motor cycle was a bit grubby but it didn't have any oil leaks, the tyres were reasonable and the tank still had the word Panther sign written in gold on both sides of the tank. The knee pads on the tank were worn but in fair condition and the only part of the bike that did actually show any bad wear was the rider's single, tractor style seat which was torn. There were numerous small spots of rust at various points along the bikes frame and mudguards. The pillion pad, which was a padded block, upholstered in foam and leather and screwed to the rear mudguard, looked brand new; as if nobody had ever sat upon it. The brake shoes were worn but the brakes worked adequately and it was fitted with a swing arm and the front suspension was of the newer telescopic type; all in all we had purchased a bargain.

The Panther in all its various guises was, traditionally, a bike to be used as a combination, which is to say that most Panthers were made to accommodate sidecars. The bikes were fitted with Panther's own high torque, low revving engine which was ideal for pulling the extra weight of a sidecar. The 350cc Panther that we purchased however was ridden solo.

It wasn't fast, it would probably do no more than 50mph at full throttle but Keith said 'It may not be the fastest machine around but it'll climb a brick wall in first gear.' He wasn't far out either.

Most of us that put up the money had never actually ridden a motorcycle before and at the time, there was no helmet law and so none of us except Keith wore a helmet. None of us had insurance except perhaps Keith who may have been covered on his dirt bike insurance, although that was a moot point. We all did, however, possess that necessary article of clothing that most youths of the day wore; the black, leather jacket. Keith, true to his word, rode the bike onto Pike Fold fields whenever asked, but that was mainly at week ends.

The first time I threw my leg over the saddle of that black, iron steed will remain in my memory for ever; I shall never forget that experience. I felt like Marlon Brando with my white T shirt and black, studded leather jacket and blue denim jeans with turn ups. Keith was stood by the side of the machine giving me instructions, indicating at the various controls, 'That's the clutch, that's the brake and that's the accelerator and that's the gear shift. On the opposite side to the gear shift is the rear brake.' As I remember, the gear shift was one down and two up.

The bike had a valve lifter toggle on the handlebars for compression when kicking the bike into life. Starting the machine up was a work of art; the ignition was turned on, then the petrol valve was opened. The valves were lifted and the kick-start pushed up and down until the compression stroke was found. The kick-start was then thrust down with all the might one could muster. If the bike fired it emitted a low throaty roar as the twist throttle was opened. The bike would then settle into a nice tick over; 'a stroke every lamppost' as it was described. The initial roar was like that of the big cat the machine was named after as was the loud purring on tick over. If it did not fire up the procedure was repeated until it did. More than once, one of us youths was thrown on our backsides if the bike kicked back. Once the bike was started, Keith instructed me thus, 'Pull the clutch lever in, and now tap the gear lever down.' Then he asked, 'Are you ready?' to which I nodded in the affirmative. He then said, 'Gently, give 'er some revs and at the same time slowly release the clutch.'

I, in my eagerness, gave the accelerator a fistful and let the clutch go. The front wheel lifted momentarily, off the ground and then crashed back down to earth with a thump causing the telescopic suspension to bottom out. The suspension bounced back to its starting position as the bike shot forward and the momentum coupled with the flying start and my lack of experience caused me to lose my grip on the handlebars. I then accomplished something that a tumbling acrobat would have been proud to have achieved as I performed a perfectly executed backward roll over the pillion pad and rear mudguard to land on my arse in a deep pool of mud. The resulting splashdown spattered me all over in a semi-liquid brown slime. The bike continued forward under its own momentum, swerving crazily for about ten yards. It then toppled over onto its side with its rear wheel still spinning until the engine stalled. I saw people running towards me, I thought, to offer assistance, but they carried on running right past me to the bike. It seemed that the welfare of the bike was of more importance than the welfare of the mud bespattered rider. My once white T shirt, my blue, denim jeans and my black leather jacket were begrimed and filthy, along with my hands and face, with mud and I now looked more like one of the Clay People from the adventures of Flash Gordon than the iconic Marlon Brando. In retrospect and considering my previous record of riding two wheeled conveyances, it seems that my attempt at riding a two wheeled vehicle, powered by an internal combustion engine, was doomed to failure from the start.

That was not the only time I came off the bike, nor was I the only one to have such a mishap. Most of us, if not all, came off more than once until we were almost capable of riding in a competent manner. By the time we could all ride safely, the bike, unfortunately, after the rough handling it had undergone from a dozen novices, finally gave up the ghost and was abandoned on some spare land nearby, where, within a week it was picked up by the council refuse collectors and disposed of. We had all had our ten shillings worth of fun and enjoyment from the once trusty steed.

For the final years at school the class that I was in had an English teacher by the name of Mr Kennedy. Kennedy took the class for both English Language and English Literature, he had taught at numerous establishments, one of those being a reformatory for young offenders. Because of his background he would not stand any tomfoolery in his classes, any insubordination was immediately addressed, to the detriment of the subordinate; he was a hard taskmaster was Kennedy. I was fortunate, or maybe unfortunate depending upon one's point of view, because he singled me out as the one in the class he thought was most likely to succeed at both of the English subjects; he had high hopes for me and pushed me to the limits. I did not mind because I enjoyed English Language and English Literature. I was an avid reader and willing student, but I believe that I never lived up to Mr Kennedy's expectations of me.

Each pupil went to see the Careers Officer, whose job it was to steer us in the right direction as far as employment was concerned, based on out academic achievements and our leanings towards certain subjects. At the time my father wanted me to be an electrician or to go into engineering but my preferred choice of career was in the printing trade and it was in that trade that I hoped to secure a position. There were no high falutin' reasons for my choice other than the fact that I had heard that the remuneration was high once one had served one's time as an apprentice and it was a relatively clean job with normal working hours. Shift work could be introduced at age eighteen but I could live with that. My ambition was to join one of the printing unions, either NATSOPA, (National Society of Operative Printer Assistants), or SOGAT, (Society of Graphical and Allied Trades) and get into the newspapers with the Daily Mirror or the Daily Express. I considered the options and realised that I was probably not cut out for such jobs as a tradesperson in construction or electronics and I certainly did not want to become a common or garden labourer. I would bide my time in whatever job that I took until I was old enough to realise my ambition. I would also have to wait until I was old enough to drive and then pass my driving test and then wait until I was twenty one tears of age before I could get my all groups licence which would enable me to drive large, heavy, commercial vehicles.

Some of the students in the same class as I stayed on to take their 'A' levels in their GCE's and others went on to higher education at various colleges to take their 'A' levels and some went on to University but my main concern was to get out there and start work to enable me to develop a certain independence; I had had enough of learning and now it was time for earning. Most of the friends that I hung around with left school at fifteen and were working and taking home, what to me, were large sums of money, albeit in dead end jobs and I wanted to equal their earning power.I finally left school in 1962 with only a handful of academic achievements and took a job as an apprentice in the trade of gold blocking and embossing; part of the printing trade and it would be another year, when I was made redundant from my printing job, before I actually moved into a transport based situation with British Rail at their Deansgate Parcels Depot in Manchester. But that is another story.

Lightning Source UK Ltd.
Milton Keynes UK
175728UK00001B/11/P